School of Dreams

EDWARD HUMES

School of Dreams

*Making the Grade at a
Top American High School*

HARCOURT, INC.

Orlando   Austin   New York   San Diego   Toronto   London www.HarcourtBooks.com

Library of Congress Cataloging-in-Publication Data
Humes, Edward.
School of dreams: making the grade at a top American high school/
Edward Humes.—1st ed.
p.   cm.
ISBN 0-15-100703-9
1. Gretchen Whitney High School (Cerritos, Calif.)
2. Public schools—United States—Case studies.   I. Title.
LD7501.C284H865 2003
373.794'93—dc21   2003005614

Text set in Minion
Designed by Linda Lockowitz

Printed in the United States of America

First edition
K   J   I   H   G   F   E   D   C   B   A

To Donna, Gaby, and Eben
for being endlessly patient
as I went back to high school

Contents

Author's Note

School of Dreams is based principally upon my observations at Whitney High School in Cerritos, California, during the 2001–2002 school year. I attended classes, struggled through some of the tests, spent time with the school counselors, taught a seminar in essay writing, found out (in the company of far-more-artistic seventh graders) about drawing on the right side of my brain, and learned, from the inside out, what a great public school looks and sounds and feels like.

Writing this sort of book requires the patience and forbearance of many people—in this case, school administrators, teachers, staff, and students, who agreed to a daily invasion of their domain. A writer could expect no more gracious welcome than the one I received after suggesting a book about California's top-ranked public school. Not only did the school's leaders say yes, they imposed no conditions. No subject was off-limits, no area of the school closed to me. I owe the faculty, staff, and students of Whitney High my heartfelt gratitude for this extraordinary hospitality, trust, and openness.

In particular, I wish to express special thanks to the following Whitney students, who went out of their way to help me understand their experiences and perspectives: Angela,

Nisreen, Cecilia, Anna, Christine, Dennis, Tony, Stella, Albert, Brian, Cher, Irene, Jennifer, Aisha, Ajay, Kosha, Nolan, Sharleen, David, and Mark. This list could be much longer; I extend a collective thank-you to all the students I came to know during my time at Whitney. I also owe a great deal to the teachers who endured having me in their classrooms on a daily basis: Rod Ziolkowski, Debra Price Agrums, Dave Bohannon, Ann Palmieri, JoAnne Charmack, and Susan Stinson (formerly Brannen).

Shirley Wold, one of the three grade-level advisors and a Whitney graduate, was an invaluable resource on the history of the school and its inner workings, unfailingly answering my innumerable questions and always leaving her door open. I must also acknowledge the help of her fellow counselors, Gary McHatton and Debra Logan, and their intern, Carey Lin; Coprincipal Patricia Hager; and secretary Kay Cottrell, who was there when Whitney opened and who can find out just about anything—especially if you ask her nicely.

Finally, I must thank Principal Thomas Brock, who opened the doors of his school to me without hesitation—and who kept them open during both good times and tough ones.

School of Dreams would not have been possible without the tremendous support of my agent and friend, Susan Ginsburg, my editor, Jane Isay, who is simply the best, and my wife, partner, and love, Donna Wares. I am blessed to be surrounded by brilliant women.

A NOTE ON NAMES AND METHODS

For reasons of privacy, students are referred to solely by first names throughout the book. In a few cases, names and identifying characteristics have been changed to protect the privacy of certain students; the descriptions of events involving them, however, have not been altered. An asterisk in the text denotes when pseudonyms are first introduced. Adults in the book are identified by their full names.

Descriptions of events and people at Whitney High School, including dialogue and interior thoughts, are based on my direct observation and reporting at the school, and on my interviews with the teachers, students, and staff.

STUDENT WRITING

A number of students gave permission for their original writing to be reproduced in *School of Dreams*, and they are credited here by their full names in the order that their work appears in the book:

Anna Choi, for the essay on her father

Christine Janet Hung, for her essay on SAT prep academies

Jane Park, for her essay on being Korean

Vivianna Huerta, for her essay on the supermarket line

Jeffrey Shum, for his essay, "The Chinese Parent"

Prologue

THE ESSAY

How honest should I be?

The question drifts in from the open doorway, a half whisper on the breeze. I look up to see Angela at the classroom's threshold, black hair straying over pale cheeks, eyes shadowed by circles as dark as the charcoal smudging her long fingers. Her usual shy smile is missing, the cumulative toll of all-nighters making her look frail and vulnerable, as if a sudden gust might send her skittering back into the school yard with the rest of the autumn leaves and spent potato chip bags. She waits there, haloed in honeyed morning glare, until she spies something in my face—utter confusion, probably— and she realizes I have no idea what she's talking about.

"I need to know how honest I should be on my *essay*," she explains. "I'm really afraid of screwing everything up. Is it possible to be too honest?"

Angela's concerns abruptly slip into focus with the magic word "essay," which is often enunciated around here as if accompanied by a noxious taste. Much of the Whitney High School senior class is in an obsessive panic over this late-autumn ritual—the final, procrastinated step in the college application process. More than finals, more than college boards, more than Advanced Placement exams or calculus Saturdays or even Mr. Bohannon's notorious history makeup tests for the attendance-impaired, many students at Whitney High fear and loathe the personal essay.

"Why don't you show me what you've written?" I ask Angela, playing it safe, meeting question with neutral question. "Then we can talk."

Her eyes widen at the mere suggestion. "Oh, no, I can't show it to you! I ripped it up as soon as I finished. It was *too* personal."

The personal essay shredded for being personal: This is the third time I've heard that same odd complaint since the start of the school year, when the principal first recruited me as a volunteer writing coach. The kids wasted little time letting me know how few other milestones in their college application marathon rival the stress induced by the abhorrent task of crafting a well-written (or at least passably readable) autobiographical page or two or three. Even some of the straight-A students at this top-ranked public high school confess they don't feel up to the task of hinging their future on 750 well-chosen words. They are supremely capable test takers in an era when standardized exams dictate everything from a child's educational future to a school district's future budget, but such tests are all about reading, not writing. Constructing logical beginnings, middles, and ends is no longer a schoolhouse priority (which may be why Harvard University, among others, requires all undergrads to take a course in expository writing). Yet college admissions offices continue to up the essay ante with portentous guidelines, such as this typical advisory from UCLA, a favorite Whitney destination: "Your personal statement is the best tool you have to show us the individual gifts you have to offer...a two-page opportunity for us to see the *real you*." So much rides on these essays—or so Angela and her peers seem to think—that the large, blank sections of their college applications have become a focal point for all the angst, insecurity, and pressure that have been pumped into college admissions since their parents' generation ambled through a much more relaxed version of the process.

Tom Brock, Whitney's congenitally upbeat psychologist-turned-principal, somehow failed to mention the minefield nature of all this when he signed me up. "They'll love having you," he assured. "Have some fun with it." When I parroted this notion to the kids, suggesting they look at their essays as a chance to relax and have fun with otherwise extremely formal applications, they stared at me as if I were insane. "Why don't you just ask us to take off our shoes and have fun walking on broken glass?" one young man finally replied. It would have been funnier if he were smiling when he said it.

Essay anxiety seems particularly intense at top academic settings such as Whitney, where the kids rank among the nation's highest achievers (familiar refrain: *My life will be over if I don't get into Harvard/Yale/MIT*) and where ultra-ambitious parents harbor the highest of expectations (*How will we face our friends and family if you don't get into Harvard/Yale/MIT?*). The school's college counselor runs an information-gathering network the CIA would envy, keeping everyone primed with up-to-the-minute admissions-office intelligence on how to construct (on paper, at least) the ideal applicant. Such knowledge is intended to help ease the pressure, but this year it's having the opposite effect, as the most recent ivory tower intell makes toast of some long-held assumptions. Foremost among these is the mantra that the Ivy League and other top schools covet something called the *well-rounded student*; the revelation that this is no longer the case has reduced to jelly all the basketball-playing, band-marching, church-volunteering, soup-kitchen-staffing, math-tutoring students like Angela with their inch-thick résumés and overscheduled lives. These are the kids who spent years amassing bone-crushing hours of extracurricular activities in order to appear triumphantly well-rounded in their personal essays, only to learn the same colleges that demanded all this have suddenly realized they had created an exercise in joyless résumé padding. Now the counselor is telling everyone that the ideal applicant is supposed to pursue a *great passion*—one deeply loved activity, two at the most, mastered with dedication and verve, with some room left over for having a life. The sense of betrayal at this turnabout is painful to behold in kids whose march to college began, in some cases, with after-school academies when they were still in kindergarten. "I gave up having a life because that's what they wanted us to do," a student in my workshop agonizes, as he tries to select one of his many passionless pursuits as a new great passion. "Now they say, never mind?"

A second buzzword at the top of the college counselor's intell list is *challenges:* Many admissions offices have let it be known they now welcome essays less about triumphs and more about difficulties students have faced in life (other than the exhausting rigors of appearing well-rounded). In a post–affirmative action age, this is one way colleges can still advantage the disadvantaged. But how, Angela wants to know, do you walk the line between a tale of challenges and a plea for pity? "Or is that what they want," she demands. "A pity party?"

A few of her friends have reached deep in grappling with this one: Budding filmmaker Sharleen writes of having a serial abandoner for a father, a man who time and again raised and crushed his daughter's hopes for a reunited family, ultimately forcing her to find comfort in a soaring imagination. "Now I could be imprisoned in an empty, pure white room and enjoy it," she writes. "A lot can happen in that room."

Cecilia writes gorgeously of her nervousness about volunteering to teach an arts and crafts class at a nursing home, where the determination of an arthritic old man named J. T. helped put her own artistic struggles into perspective: "I walked behind him and slipped my fingers through the large loopholes of the scissors to guide him through the lines of the pattern, and he rewarded me with a smile that turned his lips up and crinkled the crow's-feet around his rheumy brown eyes."

But those glimpses of life and heart seem to be the exceptions. Most of the kids come to my workshop desperately veering between numbing cliché—"I love to face challenges in life. That's what makes life interesting!"—and foolhardy confessional: "I started stealing things, but I got careless....I knew once those handcuffs were on me that I was done."

Angela has struggled as much as anyone. She shared her first draft with me a few weeks earlier, a sad little recollection of all the times she had to wait until after five o'clock for a ride home from school, left to doodle comic strips while sitting on the carpeted hallway floors outside locked classrooms. When she was old enough to drive, she made a point of offering rides to younger students who were similarly stranded by busy working parents, and much of the essay is spent telling one of their stories instead of her own. She called the piece, "Rescue Me," yet the urgency of the title was belied in the essay. Writing in a dispassionate, clinical voice, as if her life were a lab experiment, Angela revealed few of her own thoughts, feelings, or motivations. Reading it, you would never know the writer plays violin, piano, and drums superbly, or that the art teacher considers her one of the most gifted students at Whitney, or that she makes many of her own clothes, or that she had spent the summer in an impoverished Mexican village, teaching in Spanish and staging plays for the children. She spends hours of her own time

hanging student artwork around the school building, showing off the accomplishments of others. An American teenager with immigrant parents, an artist in a school of scientists
and mathematicians, Angela lives a kind of daily culture war,
keeping up by studying long into the night, then maniacally
painting until dawn. Yet in this essay she had reduced herself
to a whiny teenager whose only assets are a grudge and a set
of car keys. I suggested she start anew, that she needed to put
more Angela into Angela's essay, which momentarily seemed
to surprise and please her, though a short time later she
frowned and said, "Be careful what you wish for."

Now this girl who rarely raises her voice above soft is beside herself, the words flying and breathless: "The application
I was working on last night says to write about any factors
that could have made my grades inconsistent. That's what
really got me: I just didn't know where to start or where to
stop. You said I should have more of myself and my life in
these things. But I don't know how to tell them about my
brother and the gang that was after him to join, and all the
anger he's got, how he lashes out sometimes.... I don't know
what I should say about my parents, how they won't let me
study art. How whenever I ride in the car with my dad I just
pretend to fall asleep, so we don't have to talk. How they insist I go to Stanford or UCLA, even though I don't want to go
to either. I took one look at the UCLA campus and I said to
myself, *I do not want to be here!*"

She finally stops to inhale and her shoulders sag. She has
offered more about herself in thirty seconds than most
people in the school have heard her say in six years. "My parents don't even know I'm applying to this college," she con-
fesses, voice low now, as if they might suddenly appear and
overhear. "I really like it, but they don't consider it prestigious
enough. What will they do if I get in? What will I do? I tried
to write all this down, but I couldn't possibly fit it in the space

they give you on the application. Even if I could, I don't want to write something that would hurt my family. But I want the college to understand me. I ended up getting so mad I just tore it up."

Angela pauses again. She shifts her gaze, which had been fixed on the sun-dappled concrete school yard outside, and looks me in the eye. "So I need some help. Because I need to know: How honest should I be?"

COFFEE BREAK

A few hours later, a little before two in the afternoon, the Whitney High School pep squad performs one of its most familiar routines: Eight girls in white-and-gold cheerleading sweaters and skirts are bellying up to the coffee bar at Starbucks.

They are the very picture of wholesome teenage Americana, but for the triple grande lattes and towering mocha Frappuccinos they grab and guzzle as they race back to cheer practice. For kids whose waking hours can start before six A.M. and end somewhere around two or three the *next* morning—virtually all of that time devoted to schoolwork—the high-octane coffee drinks are no luxury. The only way through the day, they say, is to ride a caffeinated wave.

And they're not the only Whitney students craving a coffee buzz. This Starbucks in an open-air mall three blocks south of the school grounds has become a virtual campus annex. It's a teen meeting place, study hall, and new-age cafeteria rolled into one, where kids as young as twelve, some of whom have to stand on tiptoe to see over the tall counter, swill powerful espresso-based drinks the way previous coffee-phobic generations once pounded down Yoo-Hoos. Coffee hasn't just become *cool* in the past decade or so; for many high schoolers, it's now a staple.

Kosha, the irrepressible pep squad captain, provides a perfect example, a girl who entered Whitney in the seventh grade and who gave her life over to its rigors for the next six years. She is a model student, a born leader, funny, attractive, talented, charmingly sarcastic—the sort of classroom presence good teachers love, not because she's particularly agreeable, but because she's just the opposite: She challenges them constantly. (Her pithy encounters with former-savings-and-loan-executive-turned-would-be-education-guru Neil Bush, the forty-third president's brother, have become the stuff of Whitney legend following his visits to the school.) But like many of her fellow students, Kosha maintains a level of activity and time commitments—and accepts a level of stress and exhaustion in her life—that would have been unthinkable for previous generations, and that even today might stagger the heartiest corporate CEO. There are times when this rail-thin young woman with the dancer's erect bearing slips into her seat in class and simply cannot stay awake.

Fatigue is a way of life with the maximum course load she has taken in her senior year: five Advanced Placement classes, the equivalent of a year's worth of college crammed into four-fifths of a high school year. With AP classes in economics, English literature, Spanish, physics, and a second year of advanced calculus on her schedule, a more challenging course of study is simply not possible at any American high school, public or private. The byword here is *challenge*. The weighting schemes American colleges use to rate applicants vary and are often quite secretive, as with the Ivy League's infamous Academic Index, but there is one universal: Extra points are always awarded to those students who take on the most challenging courses of study at their high schools. AP classes are rewarded over honors, honors over college-prep, college-prep over general—the result being a kind of academic arms race among top high schools to see who can offer the most AP courses, which in turn compels kids to take on ever-greater workloads to keep up with collegiate expectations. At the end of the year, after a series of grueling national exams, Kosha's five AP courses (assuming she scores at least a four on each, out of a possible five) can allow her to shave a whole year off her college experience, a potential baccalaureate in three years. And with her sights set on Yale, the University of Pennsylvania, or Stanford next year—two Ivy Leagues and their similarly competitive West Coast rival—she could save not just time, but more than $30,000 in annual tuition and costs.

A course load like that would be enough to keep anyone busy. But to grasp Kosha's typical day, add to those five hours of college-level classes two hours a day of cheer practice; one hour daily as a history teaching assistant; a senior position in student government; prom-planning duties; participation in the Model United Nations program; an after-school and weekend tutoring job at an academic-preparatory academy; the crafting of college applications, essays, and interviews; and her very active competition in California's Junior Miss contest (she already won the local Cerritos Junior Miss title). With four hours of homework, course-related reading, and various class projects still ahead, Kosha gets home around six, has a light vegetarian meal and a short nap, then stays up late to get it all done.

Such is the life of today's top high school students. Kosha seems to relish it, projecting the aura of a kid whose life is hyperbusy but still in balance. Not all of her friends pull it off quite as well, they say, and even Kosha concedes there is little or no time left for dating, movies, shopping, or any of the other staples of teenage life—just the occasional coffee outing with her similarly burdened pep squad compatriots. Even her vacations are given over to school: She spent last summer rising at six in the morning to go to economics camp. And her schedule is not unique at Whitney, where the entire student body is college bound.

Small wonder, then, that the local Starbucks is such a draw for Whitney students. This is where kids with (and sometimes without) outside passes get a midday pick-me-up. This is where they rendezvous after school for group projects or study sessions. This is where they land just before eleven in the evening, when the coffee shop is about to close and the only obstacle to finishing that English project or cramming for that calc final is the overpowering urge to sleep. And this is also where a certain former student can be found hanging nearby some nights, peddling more powerful and illicit stimulants to a very small clientele, part of an alarming new trend: substance abuse not to get high, but to get by—an academic analog to the blight of performance-enhancing drugs in varsity athletics. Whitney has always considered itself immune to this sort of thing, but a nasty wake-up call is on its way this semester. A few of the kids at Starbucks see it coming, but no one is talking. Not yet.

And so all the awesome achievements of today's high-powered, college-bound high school students—with the equally awesome stress and strain many of them accept as the price of success—are on display daily not just in Whitney High School classrooms, but here, in a shopping-mall coffee shop, where savvy marketing, sweet flavored drinks, and heavy eyelids find a synergy any Madison Avenue executive would envy. Anyone who spends time at Whitney can see it delivers everything we could ask of a public school: hard work, dedication, academic excellence, a sense of mission all too lacking in other schools, a love of learning, a commitment to civic involvement, a safe haven, and last—but not least in this era of accountability and school budgets linked to performance—test scores to die for. But also on display are the unintended consequences of building the public high school of our dreams: the creation of a new generation of high-achieving, highly pressured young people who fall into despair not from failing a course, but from getting a B; who may tackle subjects and extracurricular activities not out of love and interest, but because of how they will look on their college applications; who sometimes feel that their lives will be over if they do not get into one of the top schools in the country; who may be tempted to cheat or take stimulants in order to keep up with impossible schedules and expectations; and who retake their grueling SATs, even after scoring in the 1500s (putting them in the top 99 percent of students). Why? Because an extra ten or twenty points might make the difference between receiving in the mail the thick Welcome-to-Yale-University envelope crammed with orientation materials or the horrifyingly thin Dear-Applicant-we-regret-to-inform-you envelope with just one piece of paper inside. The kids of Whitney did not give up sizable parts of the childhood most others take for granted in order to get the thin envelope.

Thick and thin, that's what it all comes down to in the end, Kosha observes morosely: Six years of insanely hard work boils down to peering inside your mailbox and shuddering or celebrating at the size of an envelope, knowing the outcome before you even open the missive in your quivering hands. This is an event Kosha and 163 of her fellow seniors are anticipating with delicious, horrible fear this year, the culmination of six long, wonderful, grueling years. Forget Generation X. Kosha belongs to Generation Stressed.

"Around here," a senior named Tony says with a mirthless laugh while waiting in line behind the pep squad girls, "four is the magic number. We all want 4.0 grade point averages. We all get by on four hours sleep. And it can take four big lattes just to get us through the day."

THE ESSAY II

"God, I hate this time of year," Rod Ziolkowski moans from his desk, a hefty stack of papers fanned out in front of him, soaking up his afternoon and threatening to spill into his evening and the weekend beyond.

His wife shoots him a sympathetic smile as she heads for the door. "You say that every year," she says gently. "But here you are." Then she slips out into the summery November of Southern California, leaving him to his least favorite task, the teacher's version of the dreaded personal essay: the college recommendation letter.

Ziolkowski has received a total of thirty-nine requests for letters this year. He never says no, yet after fifteen years of teaching, these letters have not gotten any quicker or easier for him—the one-page missives still take him about two hours each. He has been working on them for weeks, and now the deadline is looming, with an ample pile still left to write. As tempting as it might be, he will not just dash them off or use a fill-in-the-blanks template, even though teachers' salaries don't cover this sort of thing. It's one of those obligations to your students' futures you just accept, a privilege and a torment, and if the day comes when he no longer feels willing to put in the effort, Ziolkowski figures it'll be time to find another line of work. In the meantime, his gimpy back is killing him, crackling like a wet log in the fireplace from hours of bending over a table covered with reams of the kids' questionnaires, papers, and personal statements. He's searching for that distinctive something in each that can help him make one recommendation letter stand out from the next, looking for ways to quantify what makes a kid special, boiled down to four hundred words. Sometimes he finds what he's looking for in the students' own essays...

Way down upon a swanny river...far, far away.

Prior to this occasion, I had never sung in public. Ever since childhood, my father's favorite tune had been "Swanny River." He constantly asked me to play this chipper song on the piano so he could sing along; he had such an amazing voice. Despite the fact that I never practiced and always stumbled to find G-sharp, he insisted I was the finest piano player in the world, that he never heard anyone play as well as I, a talented virtuoso who tickled the ivories effortlessly. My father always pleaded with me to sing along with him, but I refused to do so. I was a dastardly coward incapable of doing anything as outrageous as singing among others. I was the youngest of three girls and rarely seized the opportunity to be outspoken. But one enlightening day, I discovered my voice; thanks to my father, I realized I had a voice.

My father passed away at 7:49 A.M. on Saturday, July 29, 2000, three months prior to his sixtieth birthday....

Ziolkowski teaches physics and a digital filmmaking class at Whitney High School. Teaching is his third career— "So far," he occasionally adds, particularly around recommendation-writing time. He worked previously as a Standard Oil executive and a stage and television actor (a younger version of the six-foot-six blond can still be spotted now and then on late-night TV ads for Del Taco). He is in his second year at Whitney, having spent most of his teaching career at a rival school, but he has quickly become one of the kids' favorites, which is why his briefcase came home bulging with recommendation requests not only from the hard-core science types, but from the science-phobes as well. When he's on a roll, they crowd around him as if sitting at a campfire listening to ghost stories, except he's riffing on the mysteries of light or gravity. There's almost always a hodgepodge group of kids hanging out in his lab, building robots or writing computer programs or trying to figure out why their force-and-distance equations for the water-balloon catapult Ziolkowski built from Home Depot scraps keep coming up thirty meters short. (The kids loved that one: Seven teams had to calculate how far their balloons would theoretically travel, draw a chalk target for Ziolkowski to stand in, then fire their water missiles across the school yard. An A went to any group accurate enough to soak their physics teacher.)

Ziolkowski writes three basic kinds of recommendation letters for his students, who are promised nothing more and nothing less than the best *honest* letter the physics teacher can write. The first type is the most straightforward, written for the kids who excel at physics, the ones who always have their hands up in class with the right answers. You tell the colleges how brilliant they are, how they'll excel at future scientific studies, and you're done. Easier still are the second sort of letters, for the kids who struggle with physics but who never quit trying, who fight and scratch for their passing grades— the ones who always have their hands up with the right *questions*. For them, you write how they'll excel at anything they put their minds to, because they never give up. These are the students Ziolkowski gives up his lunches and after-school hours to work with just about every day, and he pores over their essays now with particular care, looking for the memorable details that will bring them into focus for the admissions officers who have to wade through thousands of these things. He needs them to understand that the grades for such students only tell part of their story, and perhaps not the most important part.

When I arrived at La Palma Intercommunity Hospital on Friday afternoon at 2:34 P.M., my mother ordered me to stop sobbing because she would not allow my subjecting Daddy to pathetic blubbering. I quickly tamed myself and entered the room where he lay with tubes inserted up his nose; how deafening silence

could be. *Daddy, I'm here. Honey number three is here.* He
was practically comatose and did not seem to understand me,
but I knew the same Tae Chul Choi still existed somewhere
within that cancer-ridden body. In order to revive his spirits, I
began singing "Singin' in the Rain," the theme of our favorite
musical. We had both seen this masterpiece together for the
first time one month earlier. Although he rarely watched
American films, he adored Gene Kelly, Donald O'Connor, and
Debbie Reynolds's fantastic abilities to sing and dance. I had
desperately tried to remain tranquil and calm, but my voice
continued to undulate on account of excessive weeping. *I'm
singin' in the rain... what a glorious feeling, I'm happy again...*
Struggling, he managed to slightly open his eyes and crack a
smile from the left corner of his mouth. He knew it was me.

At my father's funeral, the pastor asked my sisters and me
whether or not we wished to say anything before our gracious
guests. I had been incredibly reluctant to do so, but among
those present, I knew my father would have yearned to hear
our voices the most. We delivered our messages in birth order;
my body trembled as I fought to maintain a handkerchief in
my left hand. At last, I stood before everyone—my father's
colleagues, his friends, his brothers and sister, strangers, and
my mother, who had suddenly become a widow at age fifty-
four. I looked straight into my mother's eyes and paused.
*Way down upon a swanny river... far, far away... I love you,
Daddy.* My tears did not permit me to sing anything besides
those nine words. I sang. I finally sang for my father. And I
knew he heard me....

The letters that Ziolkowski struggles with most are of a
third sort, the most numerous in his pile and the most excruciating to write. These are for the students who do well on
tests, who always do all their homework, who are never tardy
or difficult—but who also never speak in class unless called
upon or who rarely distinguish themselves, for good or for ill.
"How do I write a decent letter for them?" he complains.

"What do I say? They get As on their tests and they have nice smiles? Then what?"

Sometimes he teases out a theme from the questionnaires he makes the kids fill out, but even then he can come up short. The problem, as he sees it, is that good students are less inclined to take risks than in the past. The rise of standardized testing as the dominant force in classrooms, curriculums, and college admissions creates a powerful incentive for playing it safe. Kids who would love to take an advanced biology course do not go with their interests if they're good at math and have a better chance of scoring an A in his physics class, even if the subject bores them. Why risk getting a B or C in bio if it could hurt your chances of getting into the Ivy League? The same sort of incentives drive Spanish-speaking students to take Spanish as a foreign language, an easy A, even though the class bores them to tears and they'd much rather expand their horizons by learning French or Japanese. Ziolkowski believes this attitude grows more pervasive all the time, which may be one reason why so many bright kids at Whitney just sit through his class without ever raising their hands: Why put yourself out there and risk being wrong? They see no mileage in it.

Ziolkowski has waded through a series of files in this third category this evening—good kids, nice kids, smart kids—but no matter how hard he tries, the resulting letters all seem to sound the same. Dispirited and weary, he finally reaches the last folder in the stack. He sees it's Anna's. And he has to smile. Anna is the school mascot, who entertains assemblies and rallies with giant Mickey Mouse gloves and her own funny and sharp choreography—a sweet, bright movie buff who dreams of a career writing reviews for the *Times*. Anna struggled last year with his class so much that Ziolkowski suggested, as gently as possible, that she transfer out of honors physics and into the less-demanding college-prep version of his course. Instead of being crushed, she accepted his assurance that he considered her neither stupid nor slow. "Different people get it at different times," he said simply. "And you will get it." Anna soon proved him correct: She flourished in the new setting (with regular lunch and after-school sessions to help her through the rough spots) and she pronounced Ziolkowski's her favorite class. He ended up giving her the school's annual physics award, having no hesitation in singling out her achievements over those of the more naturally scientifically inclined.

He knew that Anna's junior year had few such bright spots, that she was uncharacteristically quiet and withdrawn when not throwing herself into her mascot performances. They had talked a bit about the death of her father, but this was more commiseration than conversation, for he had recently lost his dad, too. He had not seen her essay before this moment in his office, a single reading lamp lighting the darkened room, his wife beside him doing some work of her own.

Honestly, I know absolutely nothing about life. I had viewed countless episodes of the "Oprah Winfrey Show," the "Rosie O'Donnell Show," and the Barbara Walters special that showcased cancer victims. *Cancer? That is completely irrelevant to my life,* I once thought. There was a time when I actually believed I had the world in the palm of my hand; when I thought I was entitled to life on earth every single day. In reality, the world owes me absolutely nothing. After all, who am I to demand values I am not obligated to possess? I must admit that I have inquired myself regarding selfish matters: *Who will watch Dodger games with me and root for Mark Grudzielanek? Who will I wave my high school diploma at at graduation? Who will walk me down the aisle when I get married? Who will forbid me from sleeping with my socks on?* I know I have been petty to ask such questions, but at least I have asked them; I have asked them with my very own voice. Thanks to my father, I have a voice.

Ziolkowski tries to keep the tears that fill his eyes from spilling over as he finishes Anna's two typed pages, but he does not succeed. His wife notices his wet face and, alarmed, asks what's wrong. He just hands her Anna's essay and says, "Read this," and pretty soon she is crying, too, and they both are reminded why Ziolkowski spends so much time on these letters every year. Then he starts writing, his weariness replaced by a determination to come up with the best damn letter he can, a really, really terrific letter, so that Anna can go to whatever school she wants, whether or not her suddenly fatherless family can afford it.

PART I

Four is the Magic Number: Four Hours Sleep, Four Caffè Lattes, 4.0

It is the mind that makes the body rich.

—WILLIAM SHAKESPEARE,
The Taming of the Shrew

1

"We have great kids here, wonderful students. The best. I love teaching here." The drama teacher hurls the obligatory praise over her shoulder like a trail of bread crumbs as she leads the fresh arrivals on a quick tour of their new school. Then she gets to the inevitable *but,* her voice a stage whisper now, forcing the six new teachers hurrying after her to crane forward. "But there are two things you really, really have to remember about this place...."

Jodi Improta heads Whitney High School's drama department with good reason: She knows how to set up a line. "First, these kids are messy," she tells them. She bobs her blond head at a Coke bottle and some crumpled papers scattered on the ground outside the library, courtesy of the kids who stopped by earlier for textbook pickup. "They never pick up their trash. Unless you ride them."

The new teachers chuckle and relax a bit. Their tour guide's conspirational tone had left them worried there for a minute. But litterbugs? Even the greenest educator can handle that. Improta picks up the refuse, pitches it into a trash can, then pushes through a set of double doors into the old square warehouse of a school building. She pauses in her brisk stroll just long enough to introduce a barrage of passing faculty members in the hallway and to point out the alcove holding the all-important staff copy machines and laminator. The newbies nod blankly, trying to absorb it all. Improta has them lulled now. No one sees the punch line coming.

"Now, here's the second thing you gotta remember," she resumes cheerfully. "Some of our kids cheat. Big time."

Six heads snap to attention at this, a frieze of knitted brows and pursed lips. One of the new teachers laughs nervously. Trash on the asphalt is one thing, but this bald statement about cheating brings them up short.

This is, after all, Gretchen Whitney High School she's talking about, the top-ranked public high school in California, one of the best (and best-kept secrets) in the nation—prep-school quality at public-school prices. In an era when public education is derided daily by pundits and presidents as hopelessly broken, blamed for every social ill from a dearth of youthful patriotism to an abundance of youthful pregnancies, Whitney High is an unabashed success. It is a public school that *works,* without any special funding, charters, vouchers, union concessions, or private enterprise takeovers—none of the most-touted cures for what supposedly ails public education. There are no uniforms, no scripted lesson plans, no zero-tolerance policies. As such, Whitney is no one's political cause or poster child, and if its principal is treated like a celebrity abroad, he stands anonymous in the checkout line at the local supermarket; his school is not only off the national radar screen, it is a virtual unknown in its own state and even in neighboring Los Angeles, where other schools get all the press. Yet test scores at Whitney rival those at the nation's most elite private and public academies,[1] the best colleges in the country court and woo the seniors like starstruck autograph seekers, few years go by without someone (or two or three) scoring a perfect SAT. People don't just move from other cities to this geographically unfashionable L.A. suburb so they can send their kids to Whitney. They move from other *countries* to attend an American *public* high school. And come graduation night, Whitney doesn't have just one or two vale-dictorians. Most years a dozen or more 4.0s line up to shake the Whitney principal's hand.

"Don't be so surprised," the drama teacher cautions. "Our kids are so smart, they find ways to get around the rules. Ways you've never imagined." She goes on to describe an elaborate method several students worked out for beaming test answers to one another's PalmPilots.

It is almost too much to bear. First the six new teachers had to weather that interminable high school ritual, the welcome-back faculty meeting, with its meandering agenda, weak coffee, and insider references only initiates could follow. Later they were introduced to their classrooms, some to be shared with veteran teachers (who had already staked out most of the drawers, shelves, and prime wall space), others in varying states of cleanliness and repair (one new science teacher had to excavate a quarter century's accumulation of old papers; a Dumpster was thoughtfully provided). Then they sat through an inspirational video by a *National Geographic* photographer whose funereally paced pronounce-ments on "everyday creativity" sounded suspiciously like the old "Deep Thoughts, by Jack Handy," parody of *Saturday Night Live* fame ("There's always more than one right answer! Don't be afraid to make mistakes!").

And, finally, there is this ten-minute tour, the only orien-tation these new teachers will get before the students arrive in two days, a brief jaunt through the school's less-than-impressive physical plant. Like most newcomers, they gape at the aged carpets, walls, furniture, and double-decker rows of lockers in the halls, all colored in a rainbow of oranges, mus-tards, yellows, browns, and harvest golds—a palette tradition-ally reserved for certain 1970s-era suburban kitchens, but repeated extravagantly here in classroom after classroom. For those used to it, the extraordinary ugliness is a point of pride, testament to the fact that Whitney manages to be the top-ranked high school in all of California despite receiving less money per pupil than any other school in its district. But these are new teachers, unaware of such subtle charms. They're looking less prideful than shell-shocked.

Improta takes pity on them. She simply meant to inform, not to horrify, when she dished a little on cheating—better to be prepared than blindsided, she figures. "They're really good kids here," she promises. "This is a great place to teach. But they're under such pressure—from their parents, from us, from the colleges. Maybe it's partly our fault, but some of them feel compelled to cheat. So you really have to watch them, that's all."

And then they arrive back at the administration office suite, the tour ending where it began, next to the orange-and-yellow counter piled high with doughnut-shop goodies for the staff, with stacks of first-day student information packets ready for stapling, and with the principal, Dr. Thomas Brock, who for no particular reason at all is standing atop the counter, surveying his domain with a broad smile on his bearded face. "Welcome to Whitney High School," Improta remembers to say before heading off to prep her room.

2

The crush begins ten minutes before first period. The flow of cars into Whitney High's parking lot shifts from a trickle to an impatient line of silver and white SUVs, minivans, and the occasional pickup truck. The front-runners dive-bomb the limited curb space, the rest back up onto Shoemaker Avenue, a chorus line of blinking amber turn signals and snarled traffic half a block long. Young faces peer from tinted windows at the square single-story building that will claim six years of their lives, some looking eager, some anxious, some resigned, some just sleepy. The first day of school always arrives too soon, even at Whitney.

Aisha, student ambassador, heart set on Harvard, thinking: I can't wait. This year's going to be a blast.

The knotted tangle of cars is a frequent source of neighborhood aggravation, occasional fender benders, and periodic, if inconclusive, study by traffic-safety engineers. There's not much they can do: Built in 1975, Whitney came of age in an era when fewer students had their own cars, when the campus was surrounded by eighteen acres of mostly nothing, and the city of Cerritos still nurtured vestiges of its cow-town past. Now most of the older kids drive themselves (you can tell their cars from the teachers'; the student models are mostly newer and nicer) and the school is flanked by walled housing developments that have doubled in value in recent years (in no small part because of Whitney's proximity). The only cows are those painted on the sides of city buses in deference to the community's dairy-center origins. The once-quiet street fronting the school is today a busy arterial feeder to a shopping and entertainment center to the south, the nearby concrete chasm of the Riverside Freeway, and an unusually presentable industrial park a few blocks north. Cerritos is suburban in name only—it is mostly indistinguishable from the urban sprawl of Greater Los Angeles.

David, the computer savant with the slipping grades, thinking: I can't keep staying out all night. Or I'm never going to get through this year.

Once the older kids park (the seniors get the close-in spots—for a student body association fee) and the seventh graders lean in for (or away from) parental kisses good-bye, they all pour through beige wrought-iron gates lumpy with years of paint. The new students look tentative and very small, eyeing the squat brown walls before them, wondering what to expect on this first day of school, the summer heat of Southern California already swathing them beneath a pallid, eggshell sky. They stare gape-mouthed as a headphone-sporting junior, wearing a black leather jacket despite the warm weather, doggedly tells everyone within earshot his name has been changed to Nalon (his first name spelled backward) and, given his well-known penchant for the eccentric, some of the older kids half believe him. Returning students meander in small groups, friends separated since June exchanging greetings, eyeing one another's spiky haircuts and back-to-school clothes and shirt-pocket MP3 players. Backpacks are jammed heavy and full, and every other kid seems to have a Coke, a tall Starbucks cup, or the latest in cell phone technology in hand, though state law supposedly bans the ubiquitous devices from school grounds. Even at this early hour, kids are checking voice mail, making quick calls, or text-messaging friends elsewhere on campus: *Wr R U?... CU L8R?* They communicate in this way effortlessly, an e-language that seems almost their birthright even as it has become the bane of English teachers, who find no reason to *LOL* as this computer shorthand creeps into homework and school papers with increasing frequency, even among the high achievers of Whitney.

Nisreen, the seventh grader with the extra dose of personality whose mother teaches math at Whitney, thinking: I hate math, I hate math, I hate math. Why does my first class have to be math?

Every ethnicity, race, and national origin recorded by the U.S. Census appears to be represented among these students peering at their class schedules and filtering into classrooms, with Asian American faces the most numerous by far. A California State University study in the 1980s pronounced the surrounding community of Cerritos the most ethnically diverse in North America, and Whitney has been a major force in the transformation of a Dutch-Portuguese enclave into one of the few majority Asian cities in America. Thousands of Korean and Chinese immigrants have chosen Cerritos over other communities in the United States because of Whitney's reputation. Several real estate agencies in town have focused their businesses—and made their fortunes—courting future immigrants by placing advertisements in South Korean newspapers listing homes for sale in Cerritos. Whitney and its achievements are always prominently mentioned in the ads, the lure of the number one public school making an otherwise ordinary, landlocked slice of suburbia irresistible to foreign house hunters. Few people in the Greater Los Angeles area, much less the rest of the United States, are familiar with the excellent school known as Whitney High. But when the principal attended a conference in Seoul not long ago, someone on a bus spotted the name tag he still absentmindedly sported that identified him by school. "You're the principal of Whitney?" he was asked. Before he could respond, bus riders were lining up for autographs.

The sort of demographic makeover Whitney helped bring to Cerritos can easily cause rifts in a community—the divide between ethnic Koreans and African Americans in Los Angeles has been especially wide, as evidenced by the targeting of Korean businesses during the racially charged 1992 Los Angeles riots (sparked by the acquittal of policemen charged with brutalizing errant motorist Rodney King). Yet Whitney has remained largely immune to such strife. At many urban high schools, particularly in and around polyglot Los Angeles, the student body can appear as stratified as a canyon wall, divided into separate layers by race and ethnicity in the school yard, at lunch, in the hallways, and even in classrooms, a self-segregation that turns many campuses into mini-Balkans. Such stark divisions are not in view at Whitney, however, as the many varied ethnic groups converge with a seemingly easy harmony. Friendships (nonromantic ones, at least) often appear culture- and color-blind, and ethnic clubs—Chinese, Korean, Indian—welcome and even recruit kids from other backgrounds. (Club Kaibigan, the Filipino heritage club, is well-known in the area for training Asian, white, and black students alike in the elaborate folk dances of the Philippines, then staging performances at the local arts center.)

Angela the gifted painter, whose parents believe art as a profession is one step above begging in the streets, thinking: How can I apply to art schools without lying to my mom and dad?

There are other hierarchies in play, of course, the sort that have been woven into the fabric of high school campuses as long as there have been such places. They are shifting and overlapping but plain to see: the popular kids and the outsiders, the wanna-bes and the iconoclasts, the scrabblers and the slackers, the joiners, the silent majority, the dressers (but few jocks; the financially strapped Whitney didn't even have a gym for most of its existence, with P.E. once relegated to an open field that doubled as the site for commencement). And, as in any grouping of humans, regardless of their age, there are the leaders—academic, social, political—whose word always seems to carry a bit more weight, who invariably seem to be at the center of any gathering, as if the pull of gravity tilted in their direction: the kids who set the tone.

Charles, the popular upperclassman, thinking: My heart is pounding so bad, why won't it stop, what's going to happen, why did I take that tab of speed last night? Can I get through the year doing that shit? Can I get through without it? Can anyone look at me and tell?*

At five minutes to the hour, the school yard empties, the students find their classrooms, and then clatter and scrape into seventies-era plastic chairs with the attached mini-desktops made of simulated wood. This is the first class of the first day, and so the sparring begins immediately. Students focus on the practical—How hard and how often will the tests be? Are they multiple choice or essay? The teachers, meanwhile, run through the points they care most about, a litany of introductory remarks that alternately inspire, bore, and surprise their charges.

Each teacher's opening salvos are similar in content, yet unique in emphasis, and the kids plumb the words and tone like tea leaves, hoping to discern where foibles and priorities lie, matching reality against reputation, searching for hints of what the year will hold, even as the teachers are sizing them up in the same way. An eleventh-grade English teacher warns everyone to shut off their cell phones in class: "If it rings, it's mine. I've got a drawerful." The civics teacher assures her seniors they can bring snacks to class notwithstanding school rules to the contrary—so long as they share the chocolate ones with her. The seventh-grade pre-algebra teacher greets the newcomers with a quiz. ("Don't worry, it won't count on your grade," she promises the stricken twelve- and thirteen-year-olds. "I just want to see where you are.") At the same time, the eighth-grade social studies teacher—who holds the Whitney record for imposing detentions—passes out copies of her strict code of conduct, then has her students sign an anti-cheating pledge. The message is just the opposite a few classrooms away, where the tenth-grade English teacher is unconcerned about cheating, gives the same test to all his classes (rather than changing quiz questions every period to discourage sharing, as do other teachers here), and hasn't given a detention in twenty years. Meanwhile, the new marine bio teacher also makes classroom dishonesty an issue, alienating his already aggrieved students (*He's assigning* Moby-Dick *as a science text!?*) by parroting the cheating admonition from his faculty orientation tour, then promising ominously, "I'll be watching you."

"I love the first day of school," exults the new English teacher, Ann Palmieri, surprising her students because she sounds as if she means it, despite being greeted with groans from the sleepy seniors in her college-level Advanced Placement literature class. She has provoked the grumbling with her class syllabus, which is twice as heavy as her predecessor's, featuring large doses of Shakespeare, Chaucer, Brontë, Conrad, Dante, and assorted other authors from the traditional literary canon. Half the class threatens on the spot to drop the course; with their already overloaded schedules, these students can't handle any more piling on, they say. Many had been counting on a less-than-overwhelming workload for this class, leaving them extra time for the grueling work of calculus and physics. But they appear chastened when Palmieri tells them she is merely relying on the same syllabus she used at her last assignment, a barrio high school in the desert community of San Bernardino, a campus beset by gangs, drugs, and poverty and not well known for the sort of academic excellence taken for granted at Whitney. "Are you saying you're not up to the same level of work?" she asks mildly, one new teacher who is definitely not going to be intimidated by the top-scoring school in California or its students. "Well then, just turn in your syllabi before you leave. I'll use them for the next class. No sense in killing more trees than I have to." The grumbling hasn't stopped by the end of the period ("Make sure you're up to chapter eight in *Wuthering Heights*," she says with pleasant sadism to a new chorus of moans and whines), but not a single syllabus is handed back in.

A few classrooms over, Rod Ziolkowski writes his name on the blackboard, including a phonetic version—*zell-cow-skee*—although he suggests the juniors and seniors in his honors physics class just call him Mr. Z. Then, in the whirlwind space of five minutes: He explains how the next two months will be spent learning to describe objects in motion ("You'll gather data. Lots of data."). He wows the kids by having them do some complicated paper folding that results not in the physics experiment he led them to expect, but in 3-D tabletop name tags so he can figure out who's who. He shows the kids how to use his drawerful of cheap stopwatches properly ("No banging them as hard as possible on desktops like the seventh graders, please!"). And then he admonishes the girls not to defer to the boys if their stopwatch readings don't match up after timing an experiment, his voice alternating between a reasonably good approximation of an Arnold Schwarzenegger bellow and a timid mouse whisper to make his point. Finally, he winds up with a warning.

"Everyone has things that drive them crazy. For me, it's tardies. Everyone is late sometimes. There are legitimate reasons. It'll happen to you. It'll happen to me. But it's the kids who come walking in like this, carrying their McDonald's and their Starbucks, that really get me." As he speaks, Mr. Z steps into the aisle between the two rows of black-slate lab tables and transforms himself into the class dork, doing a kind of ambling, keep-on-truckin' stroll, his head on a swivel. He makes eating and drinking motions as he's walking, sipping a phantom latte, brushing invisible McMuffin crumbs from his shirt. The former actor in him knows how to work his gangly frame to maximum effect, and the geeky walk is hilarious—the kids break up. Then the funny gait and grin disappear and his mouth is a thin, uncompromising line—an expression that says, *You want to see me look at you like this as seldom as possible.* "They can make three stops on the way here for food and coffee, but they can't get to my class on time," he says in that almost whisper some teachers use to make sure everyone listens. "I can't help but take that as a sign of disrespect."

A few moments later Mr. Z says, "Come on, let's go collect some data," and he's almost through the door at the front of the room leading to the school yard before the kids realize they're supposed to grab those stopwatches and follow him.

On the other side of the building, Dave Bohannon, a Whitney history teacher revered and feared by students here for twenty years, has a very different approach. He is not there to entertain and cajole, but to lay down the rules for his classroom, which he says are enforced without mercy and based "on the shocking notion that kids who come to school learn more than kids who don't." Bohannon, with his iron-gray hair and quick, acerbic wit, is known principally for three things: disdaining school bureaucracy, paperwork, administrators, and computers (he claims to have never used one, though most students consider this urban legend); promoting intense and controversial discussions of history and politics in his classes; and giving brutally difficult makeup tests for kids whose absences coincide with exam days. Strategically timed "working absences" are something of a long-standing tradition among Whitney students seeking breathing room in their schedules; the tradition dies quickly in Bohannon's class.

"Don't worry, I'm not that scary," he assures one nervous student, as his teaching assistant, twelfth-grader Kosha, snorts in pointed disbelief. The history teacher ignores her and continues, "I'm not scary at all. This class is a democracy. Everyone of voting age has a vote." It takes a moment for the import of these cheery words to sink in: Everyone else in the class is sixteen or seventeen years old. "See," whispers the nervous girl. "He *is* scary."

In the art studio, the largest classroom at Whitney, with scarred wooden tables big enough to seat sixteen kids each, Debra Price Agrums is making her introductions to this year's Beginning 2-D Art class. This consists mainly of disabusing her new students of the notion that art is play. "You are going to work hard in here. And there will be tests, regularly. I think you'll have a quiz next week, as a matter of fact. And you won't just be learning to draw. You'll be learning art theory and, later, art history. And that test is TOUGH. Let me tell you."

The class is mostly seventh graders, with a smattering of older kids who put off art until graduation now looms, and they slouch as low as possible on their stools, whispering disparagingly at this bit of bad news. *Is everything at Whitney hard,* the new kids want to know, *even art?* Agrums has a small smile on her face; she's seen this reaction for the last twenty-four years, her whole teaching career. "As for talking in class, we're going to be using a technique called drawing on the right side of your brain, which is the part of your brain that you must tap into to draw well. But it is the nonverbal side of your brain. So you must be quiet. You have to remain silent for twenty minutes at a time before you can even *start* to draw."

More moans—"Now we can't even talk in *art* class," they're saying.

"It will be hard for some of you, but I will help you," Agrums promises, that mischievous smile still tugging slightly at the corners of her mouth. "When I see you're in a group of friends who just can't stop, I'll separate you."

On cue, the chatter stops.

Agrums is a diminutive bundle of energy and wild brown hair who has been at Whitney nearly as long as there has been a Whitney—she *is* the art department. It took her eleven years to get the school to buy a set of art textbooks, which she doles out like ingots of gold and which, though now thirteen years old, are still looking pretty good considering the hordes of students who have handled them over the years. She knows there will never be any more money for new ones—art is just not a top priority at Whitney, or in most other public schools, for that matter—and so she terrorizes her students into carrying them like glass. The school budget for art supplies is so paltry it barely covers a fifth of the materials she needs to properly teach the drawing, painting, ceramics, and crafts courses she has meticulously assembled, which is why she spends around eight thousand dollars of her own money each year on supplies. This also explains why she gets tyrannical with talkers and tardies and kids who don't take art seriously: She wants a good return on her investment.

But just when the kids are beginning to wish they could be somewhere—anywhere—else, Agrums pulls out two pencil drawings, both of them of a boy's face and head. The first is ludicrously bad, misshapen, out of proportion, the eyes buglike. This effort at capturing the human form would have to be improved tenfold just to look good enough to be called cartoonish. The other work is a beautifully crafted and shaded portrait, almost photographic in its attention to detail, right down to the individual hairs in each of the boy's eyebrows and the conchlike curl of the outer ear. The kids are suitably amused and impressed, perceiving that Agrums is offering them a typical teacherly object lesson: a bad student's and a good student's work, probably a tardy talker without a clue versus an attentive right-brain star. Agrums is wearing her tiny smile again. She points at the second, gorgeous picture.

"How many of you would like to learn to draw like this?"

Some hands rise limply, but most of the kids appear dubious. They are quite certain that, even if they behave, their work will always look more like tardy talker's misshapen boy than superstar's work of art. And, besides, they're almost all here at Whitney for the academics, not the arts: Few see a connection between the two, and many figure their parents would go ballistic if they ever got *too* interested in studying art, a constant battle for the art teacher. There have been some ugly parent-teacher meetings over the years, even a few shouting matches. The parent-led Whitney Foundation has made generous donations of money and equipment to the school, particularly for computers and the science department, but the arts are usually overlooked. And so the kids are less than hopeful when looking at the two sketches. One seventh grader mutters, "I'll never draw like that."

Agrums looks at him. "That's just what the boy who drew this said," she answers, holding up the superstar picture. Then she taps the misshapen portrait. "Right after he drew this."

The kids are astonished, as the art teacher knew they would be. They always are. "The same person did both?" someone asks.

Agrums nods. "Before and after, one in the first week of the semester and one in the last. I promise you, all of you will amaze yourselves here. You are going to blow yourselves away, because I am going to teach you how to draw like you never thought you could. Now, who's here to learn how to draw?"

This time, all of the hands go up.

Every so often—which is to say, every month—the local SAT prep academies send in full- or half-page ads and inserts to my school newspaper, hawking their services with one time-honored advertising strategy: the score testimonial. Airbrushed portraits of smiling students proudly crown astronomically high SAT scores, sometimes complete with sweet, generic quotes about the wonders Academy X can work on your math and verbal skills.

I don't know if the proudly emblazoned "1400 Guarantee" and "1500 Guarantee" slogans are completely watertight, but every time I stuff the neon SAT ads between the inky folds of each newspaper, I find myself buying—if only for a second—into the new American Dream: the high SAT score. Even as SAT I lessens in importance, even as 1600s occur so frequently they don't surprise anyone anymore, the cachet of those fatal digits still remains untarnished. In lieu of villas on the French Riviera or stables of shiny Mercedes-Benzes and Rolls-Royces, students these days show off their brand-new SAT scores with all the awestruck pride of freshly minted millionaires.

And why not? In a world where the hard, cold numbers still count for something, the "right" score means at least a chance at the jackpot.

On October 14, I found myself in a classroom at the ridiculous hour of eight o'clock, staring out the window at the blue Saturday sky, listening to the noises of traffic from the nearby freeway—and realizing, with a little bit of wonder, that the world really doesn't stop for the College Board. People are born, people die, wars are fought, peace is made, economies boom, governments rise and fall—and they all pay no heed to the performance of a given group of number-two pencil-wielding students on a three-and-a-half-hour test.

And yet—as we raised our pencils and began filling in the green information forms—something inside me flipped.

I'd devoted fifteen weeks from June to October roaming the hallowed hall (yes, it's singular) of one of the SAT academies that Cerritos grows like Idaho grows potatoes. Like many others, I'd succumbed to the appealing promise of one of the glitzy SAT ads in my school newspaper (backed up by the recommendations of friends), and signed up for the glamorously named "1500 Gold" course.

I won't go into the ordeals imposed on us by this academy, or the strange SAT tips, rituals, and strategies that have been passed around like folklore, with many embellishments among students for years—that would take up more room than this paper has.

Suffice it to say that I learned more about the SAT than I ever wanted to know, in the company of a group of similarly motivated students who were, like me, angling for a piece of the elusive dream. Some were incoming seniors, gearing themselves up for a last chance at boosting their scores before the relentless meat grinder of the college application process gunned its engines. Others, like me, were incoming juniors, hoping to get a good head start on the hellish maze of tests and grades looming ahead. (There were even one or two crazy future sophomores present... but I won't go into that either.)

To hear all of us talk, you'd think the SAT was the be-all and end-all of one's life: the sole watershed of one's youthful existence, the turning point that could make or break one's future. Never mind that students get three of these turning points before—horrors!—the College Board decides to start averaging the scores; the mantra was, depending on your goals and practice test scores, a number anywhere from 1300 to 1600. And as we slaved away at quantitative comparison problems and ground out analogies, as we suffered unspeakable cramps in our hands and cut up thousands of flash cards, no one ever let us forget the goal of those numbers—our potential tickets to the great lottery of life.

But there were fun times too: making fun of the College Board test makers, laughing at absurd reading passages, sneaking french fries and onion rings during five-minute breaks, sharing weird stories and college rumors, playing unsuccessful games of Pictionary with vocabulary words, praying in a circle around a late-night feast of Domino's pizza (a week before the test).

And sometimes—in between all the fuss about making the right grade, about getting the right letter choice—there was really actually something to be learned: Japanese gender roles, college-life factoids, Greek logic problems, radio astronomy, probability, the anatomy of a mystery novel.

Things that don't stop for one test.

Sitting in the path of an impossibly warm sunbeam, I picked up my (lucky green) pencil, took a deep breath, and waited for the proctor's signal to start the test. He was obviously almost as uncomfortable and restless as we were, but in an admirably patient voice, he intoned the magical word: "Begin."

I opened the booklet to the first page and locked eyes with the first math problem. My hand was shaking slightly—nerves, excitement, or both—because, despite all the other vastly more important things in life, this little test was what it would all boil down to... for the next few hours, at least. The long stretch of prep time, of hard training, of morale boosting, was all over: now it was time to fight.

And win.

—Christine, Whitney senior

3

The first time Shirley Dycks set foot inside Whitney High School she was barely eleven years old, fresh from the sixth grade, and not at all certain high school was the right sort of place for this tiny, shy daughter of Dutch immigrants, a kid with knobby knees, a shock of strawberry blond hair, and a collection of stuffed animals still occupying a place of honor in her bedroom closet. High school was *scary:* The twelfth-grade girls looked like grown women, for god's sake. The guys had to shave, or at least some of them did. Knowing in the abstract there would be really big kids at this school was one thing, but actually seeing them in person and realizing you were going to have to avoid being trampled by them in the hallway—well, Shirley realized, that was another thing entirely.

Still, nothing was decided, not yet, not on this first visit. Both Shirley and the school had yet to commit, were still checking each other out. They sat her down outside the principal's office at a huge round table of simulated wood-grain Formica atop an uncertain collection of spindly metal legs, then handed her a sheaf of legal-size papers: the Whitney admissions test. This was the test that would decide if she had the stuff to become a Whitney student in the fall, or if she would go to the regular middle school she had always planned to attend, where she would know most of the kids and never have to worry about dodging Bigfoot between classes.

When she first heard about the Whitney test, Shirley had decided reflexively against taking it. She'd stick with her friends and her neighborhood middle school, even though its reputation was not all that great. Her parents left the decision up to her, although they favored Whitney—not so much for the academics, but because they figured it would be the safest possible environment for her. Shirley's older sister, however, was against her going to the "nerd" school. Big sister's opposition had a predictable effect—it made Whitney seem more enticing to Shirley, not less.

There was a certain appeal to applying in order to see if you would win out over other students, Shirley thought. It might be fun. And taking the test didn't mean she *had* to go to some snooty high school that actually selected its students, rather than just taking everyone in the neighborhood like any other public school. Then Shirley heard from several friends that they planned to take the test, too. "All right," she said finally. "I'll do it. Just to see."

The three-hour Whitney entrance exam, she decided, was hard but doable, thought-provoking, and occasionally weird. She almost laughed out loud at one question: Who performed "The Yellow Submarine"? The exam tested her knowledge and understanding of math, science, literature, history, civics, grammar, culture, and current events, and it required a lengthy writing sample as well. She wasn't sure why, but she liked the test, felt invigorated by it and more positively disposed toward Whitney by the time she put down her pencil and left. Maybe this wasn't such a scary place, after all. Much later, in comparing that test with others she had to take in her school career, she would realize the eclectic exam had been crafted by

Whitney's teachers not simply to sort out smart kids who knew algebra—an off-the-shelf aptitude test would have sufficed for that—but to try to identify inquisitive, independent thinkers with the potential and desire to learn and a willingness to try something new and different.

Shirley did well enough on the test to be invited to enroll. The letter of congratulations arrived in the mail with the same heft and gravity of a college admissions letter, which didn't hurt when it came time to close the deal. It was actually pretty cool, she admitted to her sister. Very grown up. By that time, Shirley had become attached to the idea of switching schools only once, moving from primary grades to high school and then staying put, rather than the dual uprooting to middle and then high school everyone else endured. Why go through the pain of being the newest and youngest twice when you could take care of it all in one shot? When she heard that several good friends from her current school had done well on the exam and decided to switch, too, that cinched it. She became one of the youngest members of the incoming seventh-grade class, a decision she never once regretted as she became an unabashed Whitney fan and booster.

Whitney, Shirley decided soon after arriving, was a blast. Even the intense workload didn't seem to faze her or her friends; coming directly from sixth grade, they had no point of comparison. That was the great innovation Whitney's founders hit on, setting it apart from every other public high school in the state at the time: get them young and malleable, before adolescence kicks in; keep the school small, so that no one could slip through the cracks; and set the expectations high ("You're all going to college...Period!" Shirley remembers being told early on).

And so the kids thought the push for universal college attendance, taking almost all honors and AP courses, slogging through several hours of homework every night, and coming to school an hour early twice a week to sip hot chocolate and

discuss Dostoyevsky was just the way high school was supposed to be. To Shirley, there was nothing unusual about
Whitney's extraordinary interdisciplinary core classes, which
combined literature, social studies, grammar, and world history into one two-hour class. *Roots* became a text not only
for exploring a great American novel, but a sourcebook for
studying the politics of slavery, a primer on grammar and the
use of colloquialism and dialects in literature, and a means
to survey the history and exploitation of the African continent. She didn't realize at the time that budget crunches had
limited the number of teachers and textbooks available to
Whitney, and that the core approach used a relative handful
of teachers to do it all (and all at once) as a cost-containment
strategy first, an educational innovation second. It was the
same when the school's shoestring budget made varsity sports
teams impossible—with no gym, there was no place for home
games, anyway. The principal instead passed out bus tokens
to the students and sent them to the Pioneer Bowl for ten
frames of physical education, followed by some rigorous sessions at a nearby racquetball court. The kids added to the
physical education offerings by building a skateboard ramp.
P.E. at Whitney, for all its lack of facilities, became the envy of
all the other local schools.

"We didn't know any better," Shirley says now. "That was
the only high school we ever knew. We thought it was cool.
We didn't know just how different it was."

Shirley liked most of the teachers as well: They were young,
excited, interesting. Gin Pooler, the stern science teacher who
insisted on teaching etiquette and manners as part of the
health education curriculum, became like a second mother
to Shirley, and an informal counselor to many of the kids
at Whitney. Sure, a few of the teachers seemed a bit odd or
stressed out—one left abruptly, said to have suffered a nervous breakdown as the school grew increasingly rigorous and
competitive. There was the scary English teacher with the

gigantic red fingernails they all called the Mistress, who was actually quite nice once you could take your eyes off the talons. And there was the unpleasant male teacher who became notorious for looking down girls' blouses and always seating the short-skirted cheerleaders, Shirley among them, in the front row. (*"Yu-uck,"* she'd hiss to her friends, stretching the word out to two syllables loud enough to be heard, though the teacher never seemed deterred.)

Even so, Shirley found something unique at Whitney in its intimacy and unexpected sense of family. Part of it was the fact that her seventh-grade class barely numbered a hundred. But another, less definable factor lay in how the kids never seemed to rush to the exits at the end of the day. They liked to hang out, sitting in the hallways, talking with teachers, doing extra work. There were outings with teachers, trips, dinners, tutoring sessions. When one beloved teacher got married, the kids showed up en masse at her house for a painting party. Shirley became a cheerleader, a yearbook staffer, a founding member of the Whitney softball team, a science and math honors student. Whitney offered more than academic focus; it offered a chance for kids like Shirley who would have been on the social periphery of a larger, comprehensive high school to be in the thick of things—to become leaders.

"We never really understood what a unique thing we were building," she says now. "Or what a fragile thing it could be if we don't treasure what we have here. We're different, which means, in the world of education, we're seen as a threat. And someone's always gunning for us. There's always someone who wants to shut us down."

Today Shirley is sitting and chatting with students at the same round table with the same rickety legs outside the same principal's office where she took the Whitney admissions test. Twenty-five years have passed.

Now she is known as Mrs. Wold, though her marriage to a guitarist is recent enough for many of the older students to persist in calling her Ms. Dycks. She has been a biology teacher here for ten years, still blond, but no longer so small or so shy. In a school that has become since her graduation more traditional and less innovative, adapting to the times and the college admissions race by focusing relentlessly on the bottom line of test scores and Ivy League acceptance ratios, Wold seems to have become a surrogate conscience and scold for her alma mater. As a member of the academic magnet school's first crop of seventh graders, she considers herself a trailblazer who helped build a school no one was sure would survive the seventies, much less prosper through the turn of the century. Now she seems intent on making sure Whitney keeps some of its original heart, from her always-open door, to the one-dollar bills she collects from the principal each time he teases someone with a trademark one-liner, to the large teddy bear named Thomas that perpetually rides in the backseat of her Honda. The bear honors Thomas Lim, a sweet senior, a 4.0 student and basketball center, killed in a car crash in 1996 (followed two years later by his brother Sam, killed in a hit-and-run).

This year marks a new phase in Shirley's relationship with Whitney: The former student has just become a counselor, one of three new "grade-level advisors" assembled during a crisis reorganization over the summer after a previous plan to create six new deans fell through at the last minute in the face of union opposition. She has the tenth and eleventh graders this year, but she will follow those same kids through graduation as the counselors rotate through the grades.

The new duties have given Wold enough work to fill the days of three people: She still teaches Advanced Placement biology (a "zero period" class that starts an hour earlier than most classes), even as she counsels, dispenses discipline, provides college guidance, and is in charge of administering at

Whitney standardized tests used to track the academic proficiency of every school—and every school kid—in California. But her most important job, as she sees it, is the least defined: helping kids navigate the increasingly charged and stressful process of surviving and thriving at Whitney High School.

It is a task she and the rest of the faculty now see as crucial, though when she attended Whitney a quarter century ago, launching such a mission would never have occurred to anyone. The high-stakes accountability tests didn't exist as they do now. If you were a typical college-bound public school student, you took the SAT—once. Few outside of private prep schools took test-prep courses in advance. The prototypical Whitney parent—like certain parents across the country at comparable schools, such as Boston Latin or Bronx Science or Stuyvesant High School in Manhattan, the type who hire preschool counselors and college-application consultants and who wear their children's GPAs like badges of honor—didn't exist then, at least not in appreciable number. "We had pressures then, too, of course—but it seemed more us driving ourselves," Shirley muses. "Now it seems like the students feel like they're being driven from outside."

Driven students make for driven counselors, it seems: On the first day of school, Shirley Wold is, hands down, the busiest person on campus. The big round table is covered with papers as she wades through computerized rosters, trying to find places for all the incoming seventh graders who have flooded the school at the last minute, each with their own requests for certain courses and electives. Teacher assignments have to be juggled, class sizes balanced, conflicts resolved. This is a routine task dealt with months earlier at other schools, but at Whitney, the process has become an annual nightmare of delays and deluge, linked to the whims of a statewide testing bureaucracy that has assumed command of the Whitney admissions process. "It really sucks," Wold mutters, her desk already buried in forms, Post-its, and phone slips from angry parents. "The tests results were late. Again. It just isn't fair."

A typical neighborhood school has no such problems; it takes students from, obviously, its neighborhood, all comers welcome. Open-enrollment schools accept anyone in their school district and sometimes beyond; tests have nothing to do with admissions there, either. But Whitney's enrollment process, like that of other academic-prep and magnet schools around the country, employs admissions standards based on achievement and potential. Wold laments the demise ten years earlier of Whitney's original method of measuring those key but elusive qualities—its quirky teacher-authored test and interview process, which, at least as Wold sees it, worked like a charm. But there were complaints of favoritism, of ethnic bias, and of elitism from educators at other area schools who wanted to shutter Whitney despite its stellar academic record ("Or *because* of it," gibes Wold). The school district sought to placate the critics and to set a more objective standard for admissions, so it compromised by removing control over admissions from the Whitney staff. District officials handled the testing and admissions decisions for a time, but after several bungled and problematic years, they decided to rely on California's battery of statewide standardized reading and math tests administered every spring to all students in order to determine who is eligible to attend Whitney.

The results of these STAR (Standardized Testing and Reporting) tests—which are also used to rank every school in the state—are either anticipated or dreaded at each campus, for they determine whether a school is improving or not (improvement, rather than excellence, being the main arbiter of awards, extra funding, and how much or how little scrutiny a school receives from Sacramento). But the timing of the arrival of the test scores is irrelevant to the daily operation of most schools. Only at Whitney are they essential, and only at Whitney is their perennial lateness a cause for hair-ripping frustration. Nothing can be done about the incoming seventh graders without these test results: The school and the kids and their anxious parents remain in the dark until nearly the last minute about just who they are and where they'll be come September. The test results first were promised to Wold in July, the beginning of August at the latest, but those dates passed without a word, and there was nothing anyone could do about it. In mid-August, a little more than two weeks before the start of school, the results finally arrived with a thump and the madness began. Wold came in every day for the rest of the month, joined by her two fellow counselors, as they rushed to belatedly notify the seventh graders eligible to attend, then dove into the arduous process of cobbling together new schedules for the kids and teachers.

Of course, such delays are only one reason the state's standardized testing program is so despised by many teachers. Even if the scores showed up on time, this annual spring ritual would be hated, as many teachers view these tests as destructive interruptions that absorb nearly a month of school time with little to show for the effort. They are part of a state-by-state, nationwide attempt to measure students' progress while holding failing schools accountable—a universally lauded goal. But these off-the-shelf, commercially developed tests can fail to match up with the curriculum being taught in the state's classrooms, which is why standardized tests sometimes feel like an interruption to lessons rather than an addition. Still, they are essential because a school's reputation and funding are pegged to the tests; at Whitney, high test scores are the basis for the school's top ranking in the state. So even as they are privately derided by faculty and students here, the tests are publicly celebrated as evidence of the school's quality—an irony not lost on Wold or Whitney's perceptive students.

The late arrival of the test scores only rubs salt in the wound, as it makes juggling course requirements, electives, and scheduling for the new students a race against time, one that, as usual, the school has lost. A passel of seventh graders with blank spaces on their rosters, courses they didn't want, and schedules that put them in two places at the same time are lined up outside Wold's and the other counselors' rooms, waiting for help and wondering if they made a terrible mistake by coming to Whitney.

Wold has her work cut out for her. As school starts, all her colleagues have to do is focus on getting their classes up and running. Wold has to do that, too. But she also has to gear up a series of classroom presentations with the school's college guidance counselor for juniors and seniors on navigating the university application process. She has to deal with twenty or so students on academic probation because of poor grades from the year before. She has to figure out the arcane discipline process she inherited that somehow saddled a hundred kids with last year's unserved detentions. Her predecessor, the previous vice principal, can't be of much help, as she now has her hands full running the music department, a move prompted by the unexpected departure of a band teacher prosecuted for allegedly having an affair with a student. The domino effect of that personnel shift has made Wold's job infinitely more difficult. She can't find anything.

First, though, she has to get through this mess of mangled seventh-grade schedules and an onslaught of calls from parents complaining that their children should be put into more advanced math or language classes, and from other parents expressing outrage that their son or daughter has not been offered a slot at Whitney. Today's Whitney parents often start preparing their children for the Whitney entrance exam in kindergarten. Others who moved here with expectations of a Whitney education will not take no for an answer. "What can I do to get my son in?" one caller keeps asking, even after

Wold explains that the test results are the final arbiter—no appeals allowed—and that they are handled by the district and the state, not the school. "There's always a way," the caller insists. "Just tell me how much to put on the check."

She escapes the caller and waves in a student, a junior, who she has to put on a special behavioral contract because of his many cuts and other rule breaking, most of it nonserious, except in the aggregate. "You'd be gone already back in the old days," she tells him.

Outside at the big round table, a group of kids working as office assistants this period overhear and one of them asks, "How has it changed? How does Whitney today compare with nineteen... nineteen... nineteen what?"

"Nineteen seventy-seven. That's the year I started," Shirley says, ignoring the my-god-you're-ancient looks on the faces of kids who were all born after she had graduated, kids for whom Vietnam and Watergate and Nixon and Iran-Contra are not formative experiences but merely dry entries in a history text. She sighs. "You don't really want to know. It just breaks my heart."

They press her, though, and she tells them that Whitney today, in every measurable way, is a better school than it has ever been—higher test scores, kids getting into great colleges, kids going on to fabulous careers and high-paying jobs. Everyone is so incredibly smart here, and doing such high-level work. But... She falls silent, thinking. But something has been lost along the way. The core classes are gone, in favor of standard Advanced Placement and honors courses, which are easier for colleges to understand—though they are no different than the courses taught at a thousand other high schools. The skateboard ramp and bowling trips are long gone, too—lawsuit and liability nightmares in this litigious age. And outings and painting parties and slumber parties and socializing with teachers? In this age of concern about sexual harassment and molestation? Out of the question. The school district has just commissioned a video explaining to staff members why they would be fired for even suggesting such conduct. And the parents have such high expectations. The kids are under the gun so much, they are so fearful of getting a less-than-perfect grade or of not getting into every college on their application list. She cannot say any of this to the kids, of course, but they are waiting for an answer, and so she gives them one.

"I guess I felt like back then we worked hard because we wanted to be here. We *liked* being here. And I think most kids on most days still like being here. But now it seems like too many of our students are motivated by pressure these days. And by fear."

She half expects, and hopes, the kids sitting at the big round table will disagree with this assessment. But they don't. She looks at them and sees they are nodding.

Another call comes in a short time later, an anxious woman speaking in a thick accent. "How can I get my daughter into Whitney?"

"Well, what school is she in now?"

"She's in sixth grade here, where we live," the caller says. "In India."

"It's just that kind of day," Wold says after hanging up.

She waves the next kid in and tilts back her coffee cup for a sip, but the cup is empty. "Things will be back to normal by next week."

It seems a reasonable prediction at the time, despite the hectic pace. It's a sunny Thursday, with a short first week of school ahead. Shirley Wold is at heart an optimist, and why shouldn't she be, just four days before September 11, 2001.

4

Monday morning: JoAnne Charmack's fourth-period Advanced Placement civics class meets right after the ten-minute morning snack break, which means most of the seniors come in toting their ideas of wake-up food (a vision apparently shared by the school's cafeteria where they buy the stuff): candy bars, chips, Cokes, cookies, doughnuts, rock-hard bagels with a silver packet of generic cream cheese, bear claws, and Flamin' Hot Cheetos "Big Grabs" (the winner in the unhealthful snack food category, with 35 grams of fat, 560 calories, and ten orange fingers per jumbo bag). Anna, in her white-and-gold cheerleader-mascot uniform, defies the trend with a peeled orange, which she attacks with a pair of chopsticks, surgically removing the meat with deft and delicate tweezings. Her fine motor skills provoke an expression of awe from the teacher. "That's really remarkable, Anna: I've never seen anyone eat an orange quite like you."

She blushes a bit at the compliment and smiles her Anna smile, which in full bloom involves her mouth, eyes, nose, shoulders, hands, and a flick of her short brown hair. "I just don't like to get my hands sticky," she says between miniature bites. She would happily eat Cheetos the same way, pulling them from the bag with chopsticks one by one without cheesing her fingers. "But I'm trying to watch my diet."

Charmack nods and looks over the classroom of twenty-four seniors. She wonders, as she does every September, just how she will engage kids whose focus has narrowed almost obsessively to two main goals: getting into college, followed by survival to graduation day. Though the kids recognize the advantages to starting Whitney in the seventh grade, six years still seems like an impossibly long stretch to serve by the time senior year rolls around, and getting them fired up about anything on the homestretch can be a challenge. *Senioritis,* the kids call it, a national epidemic from which Whitney has no immunity. The symptoms—lack of enthusiasm, lack of participation, obsessive complaining about homework—can be especially acute in Charmack's classroom. Civics has a reputation for being a relatively easy AP course, so the seniors flock here to boost their college résumés, only to find its nuances do not come so easily to kids whose experience of American politics begins and ends with Bill Clinton and Monica Lewinsky. They were toddlers when Ronald Reagan left office; Richard Nixon is a picture in the history book and Jimmy Carter is that old guy who builds houses for poor people and shows up for elections in places like Ecuador. So far, they have seen no war, no real national crises, no economic upheavals, no duck-and-cover drills, no fallout shelters in school basements, no space race or arms race or domino effects. They have never doubted America's place in the world, nor their own, and so they come to Charmack's class with an innocence that is as unique among recent generations as it is fragile.

As she stands silently at the front of the room—the universal teacher signal for *Be Quiet and Listen*—half the class remains oblivious. Several of the kids are talking among themselves, others are focused on their food, a few are trying to sell candy to classmates to raise money for the yearbook or the marching band (sometimes it seems the school runs on candy). Kim, with her flaming yellow stockings and army surplus ammo box/lunch pail, is reclining, eyes closed, on a vinyl beach chair, which she folds up at the end of each period and hauls from class to class. Charmack is surprised the first time Kim does this but says nothing. It is safe to say most public high schools would react negatively to a student who brought her own beach furniture to class, lest every classmate follow suit, inviting chaos. But here, Tom Brock, the principal since 1998, sets a different tone: *If she's doing her work and not disrupting the class, I don't care if she stands on her head.* He knows Whitney's problem is not too much iconoclasm; if anything, the problem is too much conformity and convention. There are no tattoos or green dye jobs or tongue piercings in sight at Whitney; Kim's eclectic wardrobe and rebellious chaise longue is about as wild as it gets, genially tolerated by her fellow students, though never coveted. As for the teachers, many of whom fondly remember Whitney's less-regimented origins, they accept Kim's gesture at individuality almost gratefully. The only problem Charmack can foresee is the tendency for the seventeen-year-old to doze as she lies back, as she has now. The illusion of sixties-style rebelliousness is rudely shattered by Kim's comments when Charmack gently awakens her. "Sorry, I got up too early this morning to trade stocks online. You wouldn't believe what Cisco Systems was trading for! The dot-com bust is just one big investment opportunity!"

"Okay, class," Charmack says, deciding it's time to grab everyone's attention. "Show me your money."

Her students fall silent and look at her blankly. "Go ahead, dig out some money. Don't worry. I'm not going to take it. Just look at it."

The students dutifully fish out coins and bills. Charmack is duly impressed by the quantity of fives and tens that pop out of purses and pockets, rather than the measly quarters and one-dollar bills her high school peers would likely have produced. "What do you see all over the money?"

"In God We Trust," Anna says between bites of orange.

"In God We Trust," Charmack repeats. She is a thin, fifty-something woman with an unflappable demeanor, a daughter in college, a new position as the school union rep, and a talent for clog dancing, which she has displayed more than once in the annual "Faculty Follies" talent show. She was a teacher at Whitney when Shirley Wold was still a student. "Our money talks about God, the Pledge of Allegiance talks about God. What do you know about the separation of church and state?"

The students are still fiddling with their money. No one answers. "Now, come on, I know you all had U.S. history last year, because it's required." She waits, but they still aren't biting. "Okay, as you know, we have no official religion in our country. The Constitution is quite clear on this. So how do you explain our money and our pledge?"

Silence. The tooth-pulling session continues as Charmack doggedly goes over ground she knows they know, though they stubbornly remain quiet. No matter. Charmack understands the ebb and flow of senioritis, which, she knows, is far milder at Whitney than at many other public high schools, where senior year all too often can become a wasteland.[2] Senioritis at Whitney is mostly a matter of attitude. The kids still do the work, and lots of it, although they will try every trick in the book to talk their way out of it if they can, complaining loud and long all the while. So Charmack tells herself to be patient: Sooner or later, someone will be unable to hold his or her tongue any longer, and the dam will break.

She again breaks the silence. "The Framers were not godless men, but it would be difficult to call them Christian as we define the word today. They believed in a Supreme Being, they sought divine blessing and inspiration, they believed in setting good examples for America through personal behavior. They saw themselves as good men, acting selflessly for the nation, divinely inspired, with the divine being the source of goodness. But they took part in no organized worship and were adamant that there be no national religion or support for any particular religion."

What Charmack hopes is that the kids will escape for a moment the bonds of contemporary thinking—the narcissistic, twenty-first-century, politically correct filter many teenagers (and modern high school textbooks) apply to history, literature, and culture—a filter that might well detect a contradiction between the First Amendment and a government that expresses reverence for God with its money. In this room peopled by young Buddhists, Muslims, Christians, Hindus, Jews, and assorted others—some quite sensitive about perceived slights to their faiths—it can be hard to grasp how the Framers might find no such contradiction in invoking God while building a wall between church and state.

Charmack knows this is a controversial subject, one that has launched many a heated discussion to jump-start her class, but not today—there are still no stirrings in the room. "Okay, let's talk about something else: political power. What is power?"

Kim looks up from her lounge chair, suddenly engaged. "Power is the ability to manipulate beliefs," she offers.

"No," Tony, president of the school's award-winning Space Set club and the class archconservative, counters. "Power is money."

"Is there a difference between power and authority?" Charmack wants to know. "Does President Bush have either or both?"

Dennis speaks up now. He's a gifted pianist whose parents want him to pursue a more "practical" career. "He has power. But authority—after that 2000 election—authority, he has none."

"Constitutionally, he has authority, doesn't he?" Charmack asks. "He holds the office. You can have authority but little power?"

Now the class is getting interested. "He stole the election!" shouts Stella, the yearbook business manager and easily the most boisterous student in the room, if not the school. "He shouldn't have authority or power!"

"You'd rather have Al Gore?" sneers Tony.

Stella stops and thinks about it a moment, then deadpans, "No, I'd rather have Brad Pitt."

"Yeah, yeah, Brad Pitt for president," Anna agrees, backed by a chorus of several other girls.

"Let's look at your homes," Charmack says. "Who has power in your houses?"

Now the chorus says, *"My parents"*; but Charmack asks them to be more specific. Half say Mom, half say Dad, has the last word. Anna has fallen silent, her smile gone. "I ask my dad for money," one girl explains. "I ask my mom for *permission.*"

"Power is them getting us to do what they want," Stella says.

The discussion continues now, alive and vibrant, more voices joining in as the connection is forged between the power of parents and the power of politicians, each of them able to influence events and discern the needs of those they govern.

"It's easy to see how parents know what their kids want and need. But how do politicians know what the people need or want? How do they know what Stella wants? Beside Brad Pitt for president, of course."

The answer to these questions will resonate long after this class ends. Yes, there are elections and polls and you can call your congressman and give him an earful, but what Charmack and her students end up talking about most are the *expectations* Americans have of their country and their leaders:

a common culture through which America's hopes, wishes, and concerns are expressed. We expect to enjoy personal freedoms that are envied the world over, but we also expect to be secure, to be safe in our homes, safe from violence, safe from war, the kids point out. They speak of expecting financial security, for our country and for ourselves—of a good job awaiting them after college, a shot at success.

"And we expect justice, fairness, our day in court," Charmack adds. "We all expect the American Dream.... You've heard of Horatio Alger?"

Seeing the blank looks, she exclaims, "No?! Never heard of rags to riches? Well, he wrote stories that have to do with the idea that you can start out poor in America and better yourself. With a strong work ethic, you can have success. These are the expectations many of your parents came to America with."

The kids are nodding now. Most of their parents are immigrants from Taiwan, Hong Kong, South Korea, the Philippines, India, Pakistan, Mexico, and other countries offering far less freedom and privilege and far fewer expectations. Many of their parents *are* Horatio Alger, and many have taught their children that liberty, safety, opportunity, and justice were not so easy to come by in their homelands. Whitney has forged a unique blend of cultures, where the dominant element has constantly shifted over the years, from Dutch to Portuguese to Filipino to Japanese to Chinese to Korean. Few of these students have ever worried about their expectations for the good life, for their piece of the American Dream. Their formative years took place in a time of unalloyed peace, prosperity, and economic good times, in a school remarkably free of intolerance among disparate and, in some cases, historically hostile, cultures.

This discussion in AP civics seems all the more poignant and even prescient the next morning, when four airliners are transformed into weapons of mass destruction, and the life-long expectations of these students seem, for the moment at least, lost in the rubble and those awful images of devastation being beamed into every classroom at Whitney High. Kids who never harbored a minute of doubt about America's in-vulnerability and the shape of their future arrived at school the next day to find a very different world awaiting them.

5

Aisha stands outside the principal's office in tears, waiting for Tom Brock to look up and notice her waiting there, shoulders shaking. He escorts her in, offers her some green tea, and sits her down.

"I feel under attack," she blurts.

Brock's solicitousness turns to alarm. Aisha is one of the kindest students he knows at Whitney, a serious young woman who gets along with just about everyone; she's the senior Brock most often tags as head "ambassador" to shepherd visiting VIPs around campus. But Aisha's father is an immigrant from Pakistan who married his American college sweetheart, Aisha's skin is dark, and she has made Islam her religion. And yesterday, a group of Islamic extremists killed thousands of Americans. At least one Whitney student lost a relative, and Dave Bohannon, the history teacher, who was visiting New York, hadn't been heard from immediately. Everyone is on edge. "Has somebody hurt you?" Brock asks, leaning forward in his chair.

Aisha nods, then shakes her head, then nods again.

"Here? Someone at this school?" He's alarmed now.

"No, no, no. Not here. Online."

Brock closes his eyes a moment, relaxing a bit. "Did it involve a student here?" he asks. He sits back in his chair when Aisha again assures him no. "Well, tell me what happened, and what I can do to help."

Aisha nods. She begins with the obvious, how she had been left reeling by the terrorist attacks that leveled the World Trade Center and damaged the Pentagon. Later, she found it extremely difficult to return to business as usual as the hours passed, to go back to calculus and civics and student council as if this were any other day. She had been surprised to see some kids had actually been engrossed in doing homework during the next period while the story was still unfolding on CNN on televisions in every classroom. "I know everyone reacts differently to a crisis...but I couldn't think about schoolwork."

She had arrived at school on the morning of September 11 just as the South Tower was struck, when it was still possible to watch the initially confused news reports and believe the devastation had been some kind of accident. Indeed, it was impossible to believe otherwise—until Aisha found herself gaping at the footage of a second jetliner augering into the Trade Center. Then the images of war played and replayed throughout the school for much of the morning, the teachers staring agog at the television news reports, just as transfixed as the students, perhaps more so, lesson plans forgotten. The spell was broken only when President George W. Bush appeared on screen and offered his painfully inarticulate initial remarks to the nation, evoking groans from gatherings of students with his awkward promise to "hunt down and find those folks," followed by his non sequitur vow, juxtaposed with images of the fallen Trade Center towers, that the attack "will not stand."

A short while later, most of the TVs were off and classes were back in session. Announcements of auditions for *Midsummer Night's Dream* filtered over the public-address system, along with reminders that admissions officers from Stanford and the University of Pennsylvania were to be in town that night and the next, eager to talk to prospective applicants, marketing their schools, handing out business cards. Kids ate their snacks as usual, the halls were their usual crowded chaos between periods. But the signs of something momentous were unmistakable: Brock was out in the parking lot with his walkie-talkie, reassuring parents who had driven to the school out of a vague sense of unease, materializing hours before classes were to end. "We must retaliate. Massive retaliation," one dad exclaimed through his car window, as if the principal were in a position to effect defense policy. "We must stand together."

"Let us all be of one voice," Brock responded, sounding more like a preacher than a principal. "We are grateful for each other here."

The father nodded absently, muttering as he drove off, "We must launch the bombers."

By early afternoon, the news had spread that Islamic terrorists led by Osama bin Laden were the prime suspects, sending a chill through the school. Aisha and the other Muslim students at Whitney were horrified. They already felt that many people viewed their religion with suspicion. People who look like them have been the stereotypical bad guys on TV and in films for years. This would only make matters worse.

"It's not us. Those are the bad people," one young girl in a white chador felt compelled to blurt out to her friends as the day and the headlines wore on. "That's not what we believe in." Her voice had a pleading quality to it. She was not responding to any particular comment. She just had to speak it aloud. Her friends nodded, but they didn't say anything.

When Aisha got home that night, she did what comes naturally: She got on the Internet, looking for information, combing news sites. But when she signed onto a forum at the

ABC News Web site, Aisha found herself unexpectedly immersed in angry and hate-filled messages deriding her ethnicity and religion. She signed off, shaken, feeling violated, only to learn a short time later that hateful and threatening e-mails had been sent to her mosque, forcing the place of worship to shut down. Over dinner, her father openly worried about the family's safety. For the first time in her young life, she felt fear in the man she most looked up to.

Aisha had tried to put on a brave face, but at school today, after talking to other kids who had seen angry glares and heard muttered slurs from strangers on the street, she could no longer cope. Everything seemed wrong at school, out of sync. Betty Zavala, the college counselor, was making the rounds of the senior English classes, giving out tips on what colleges want in their applicants, urging kids to follow their passions, speaking of "best-match" schools and the value of a firm handshake and the 3,300 colleges out there waiting to be explored. Aisha could barely listen. She found the whole thing positively surreal. When the entire fabric of the country seemed under attack, she could hardly stand being told, "You are the arbiter of your future. But your parents are paying the bills. Work together. Discover your passions!" Aisha finally had sought out Brock.

"I'm an American. I was born here. I love this country. I am just as angry and sad about what happened as anyone. But I'm afraid of a backlash. I'm afraid people don't understand my religion or will look at the color of my skin and see an enemy. Lots of people are afraid. And I think we should do something. Make some kind of statement condemning terrorism. But also telling everyone that Islam is not about violence. That it does not endorse hurting and killing of innocents, and that people should not be confused by media hype or take anger out on groups because of appearance or belief or national origin."

Aisha stops crying, a look of determination replacing the anguish. Brock sits silently a moment, studying her.

This is the same girl who had arrived home from school one afternoon last year, schoolbag slung over her shoulder, only to find her house padlocked, NO TRESPASSING signs boldly pasted to her door, barring her entrance. Her family home had been repossessed after a costly lawsuit against her parents' business ruined them financially. Their company had made fancy ribbon for girls' party dresses sold in high-end stores; a defective metal wire in a ribbon had cut a girl's leg that, untreated, had become infected and eventually had to be amputated. Aisha never knew the extent of her parents' legal woes until she came home to find everything gone. She had kept this from nearly everyone at school, partly out of pride and embarrassment, but also because she couldn't stand the notion of being pitied. Instead, she had thrown herself into her studies. Brock would have expected even his best students' performance to suffer under the circumstances, but Aisha ended up earning the highest grades that year she had ever gotten at Whitney.

It doesn't take long for the principal to decide exactly what he needs to do for Aisha. He has decided against offering vague words of comfort. He will not, as Aisha suggested, address the student body on issues of hate and vengeance. He decides, in essence, to do nothing. He has a better idea.

"I think *you* should do something about this, Aisha. You and any others who share your concerns. I'll help you any way I can, but I think you're the right person for the job."

By the time Aisha leaves the principal's office, she is pumped up about the idea of staging a rally for the school, feeling excited and eager and grateful for Brock's support. She will pull together like-minded students and help spread a different sort of message, one that would bring Americans together. "I'm going to get started right now," she promises.

It is only later, while Aisha walks to class, that she realizes she has been *Brocked,* a familiar sensation around campus for students and teachers alike. "No matter what your complaint or concern, Dr. Brock has this way of comforting you, of making you feel better, of boosting your confidence and enthusiasm," Aisha would later say with grudging admiration. "So you hardly notice, until you're out the door, that he hasn't given you jack. That he's put it all back on you. He's really good at that."

This sort of turnabout is classic Tom Brock, an approach that has at times endeared him to his students and faculty, and at other times left them sputtering. Sometimes both at once.

On the one hand, he treats students (and most teachers) as mature, thoughtful individuals capable of great things, not just great grades; let the kids run the show once in a while, he argues, and whether they succeed fabulously or fall on their faces, it's still all about learning, responsibility, high expectations, growing. Brock calls this building "a community of learners," a popular term these days in education circles, though elsewhere it often seems little more than lip service belied by the prevailing trends in public education, in which ever more intensively programmed methods, testing, and curricula are the norm. Brock sees his job as tilting against these trends, holding out Whitney as a model for other schools: smaller, leaner, stripped of bureaucracy, built on high expectations for its students, and imbued, most importantly and relentlessly, with a clear mission—something lacking in many schools. As a member of a team that visits schools nationwide for the federal Blue Ribbon Schools program, which annually names some of America's best and most improved schools, Brock has seen firsthand what a sense of mission—or its absence—can do for a school. For Whitney, that mission is high-level academic achievement and getting students into the nation's top one hundred colleges. But the model, he believes, could easily be employed elsewhere: at schools whose mission is focused on the sciences or the arts or business or teaching or any other trade or specialty in which a need is perceived and a focus makes sense, so long as students are offered increasing levels of responsibility as they grow and progress. Brock's vision of a model school that considers its students assets rather than charges, that offers them the chance to be responsible for more than just homework and tardiness, lured Rod Ziolkowski, for one, to Whitney—a school he once believed should be shut down.

On the other hand, the physics teacher soon discovered the downside of Brock's vision of principal as cheerleader-in-chief: Often charming, thoughtful, and supportive, Brock also could make for a maddeningly indecisive administrator, particularly when the issues at hand veer from the visionary and toward the nuts and bolts of running a school in an era of shrinking budgets and growing mandates. Some complain he is too often away from the office, spreading the gospel of Whitney as a model for improving schools in general, schmoozing with corporate donors, or traveling the country with the Blue Ribbon team. "He can't say no," Ziolkowski says, a shortcoming Brock doesn't admit, but doesn't exactly deny. "And sometimes a principal needs to be able to say no. Loudly and clearly." (This year, the school district has hired a coprincipal for Whitney for the first time ever, a successful no-nonsense administrator from nearby Huntington Beach, Patricia Hager, who *can* say no.)

Brock is nothing if not a study in contrasts: an administrator with little interest in administration, an official upholder of rules who has a healthy appetite for breaking them, an educational visionary and liberal thinker who delights in battling the teachers' union ("What do we even need the union for? It's not as if teachers are being abused like coal miners."). With his short, graying beard, thinning hair, and ubiquitous three-piece charcoal suits, the fifty-seven-year-old looks every inch the former psychologist. But the serious appearance belies a childlike demeanor that one moment seems deliberately calculated to be outrageous and the next seems simply the giddy expression of someone who has found his dream job and cares not a whit what people think of him. He continually tweaks people with mock racial stereotypes in this majority Asian school, playfully mispronouncing names. It's generally understood that this is Brock's antidote to political correctness, and though it can be a tonic at times, some faculty members are appalled by his sense of humor. Several blanched during a meeting when he answered his phone and then declined an invitation to happy hour by saying, "No thank you, I do all my drinking during school hours." Shirley Wold has been appointed (by Brock himself) as the principal's unofficial minder, and she sometimes flashes a large computer printout that reads, "Thomas!" whenever he goes too far in her estimation, at which point he must put a dollar in the coffee can Shirley maintains. The school year is barely started, yet the can seems to be filling quickly, its deterrent effect dubious at best. Brock brings extra dollar bills to work just so he can insert them with an impish flourish. He is, in short, a likable man who gives every indication of loving his school and his work. "Why wouldn't I? I'm principal of what we consider to be the best public college-preparatory school in America. What more could you ask for?"

Brock never set out to be a principal, much less principal of a school like Whitney. He went to Washington High School in South Central Los Angeles, a more or less typical comprehensive public high school forty years ago, though today his alma mater is reputed to be one of the more troubled schools in L.A., portrayed in the *Los Angeles Times* as a campus where students interrupt teachers to converse with one another across classrooms, crime and drugs are constant companions, and prostitutes are said to operate out of the students' bathrooms.

He attended California State University at Long Beach on a YMCA scholarship, then went to work for the Y organizing clubs and youth programs in six school districts, a popular form of outreach and character building in California public schools at the time. He set up peer-counseling groups and snow camps, worked on a massive mock legislature program, and started projects that sought to offer alternatives to street-gang life in the tough Lennox area in the noisome industrial area just east of Los Angeles International Airport. From there he was recruited to help set up counseling services at the Lennox Middle School, which was an unusual assignment for two reasons: he had no prior experience as a school faculty member, and he had no school counseling credentials (although he did later obtain one). What he had was a young and idealistic principal newly installed at Lennox who believed in his school's importance, in his kids' potential, and in Brock's abilities—and who showed it by heaping responsibility on his new protégé. It was a formative experience that clearly stuck.

"Everything I know about education, I learned at Lennox," Brock says now, sounding surprisingly wistful over his old barrio school. "Where else could a twenty-five-year-old snot nose set up an entire counseling program in a school where there had been none?"

He had his work cut out for him: Lennox was about as far from the Whitney of today as could be imagined, the sort of dangerous, hope-impoverished urban setting where, each year Brock was there, at least one of his students would find a dead body somewhere. A substantial number of teachers had all but given up, if they had ever cared at all. Many of the kids could barely read, a problem exacerbated by the unexpected influx of sixty non-English-speaking Cuban refugee children in the early seventies. The middle school was small, troubled, and understaffed even before the refugees arrived just after the school year began, and once they were there, Brock had to do a bit of everything just to hold things together: counsel, teach, administrate. When the teachers' union complained that Brock lacked proper credentials, the principal fired back and said, "Fine, we won't call him counselor. His title will be *friend at large.*"

This sort of creative skirting of the rules to accomplish a greater good was greatly admired by Brock and has become a hallmark of his Whitney career, whether he's exploiting a loophole to allow all students to carry cell phones despite a state law banning them in schools, or outflanking union opposition to Whitney's use of popular teachers like Wold as counselors, or simply smiling and nodding when a student disdains regulation seating in favor of her own beach chair. At Lennox Brock relied on some unorthodox measures when he proposed running summer camps for sixth-grade graduates who were headed to middle school in September but who might be unprepared for seventh-grade rigors or fearful of their school-to-be's dreadful reputation. Brock wanted to bring in Lennox's best teachers, parents, student leaders, and the incoming middle schoolers, take them to some pleasant and wholesome surroundings in the mountains, and use the time to raise their comfort level, forge relationships, build confidence, and do some early tutoring. Naturally there was no money in the budget for any of this, so Brock began what was to become a second pattern in his career: scrounging up private-sector donations. In this case, the first Lennox summer camp relied upon $2,000 provided by the Beaver Shot and several other civic-minded strip-club owners in the seedy

airport area. Brock recruited the wife of a local Baptist minis-
ter for this fund-raising task; she not only successfully prodded adult businesses into ponying up contributions, but her
status provided a welcome inoculation against potential criticism of the source of the money. The camps generated such
teacher, student, and parental enthusiasm that the school district agreed to cover most of the costs in subsequent years as
the school gradually remade itself into a model campus.

After seven years at Lennox, Brock left for another district, taking on vice principal and principal gigs at several different schools, then finally leaving education altogether to
open a marriage and family counseling practice with the advanced degrees he had earned while working. Later he focused on setting up a hospital-based mental-health program
in the Cerritos area. He first became acquainted with Whitney High School around this time through a restaurant the
school ran as a vocational training program, which offered
some of the area's best (and best-priced) plate lunches while
training students in the culinary arts. He'd meet clients or
colleagues there for three-dollar steaks with all the trimmings.
His wife, Carol, later went to work as a school nurse in the
ABC Unified School District, which encompasses Whitney.
Their two daughters attended Whitney as well, making Brock
a familiar presence at the school.

In 1994, the principal at Whitney mentioned to him that
there was an opening for a visiting professor to teach one
elective class. Would he be interested in teaching psychology
one period a day?

"Sure," Brock responded. "If I can do it during lunch,
and if I can walk in and walk out of the class. No faculty
meetings. No extra duties. Just the class."

The principal told him no problem, and Whitney had its
first (and only) Advanced Placement psychology teacher. It
had been many years since Brock had run a classroom, but if
he was rusty, it didn't show: Word of mouth about the class

was so good that twice as many kids signed up the following year. Suddenly Brock found himself agreeing to teach two periods of psychology every morning. After two more years, he was teaching four, one period short of a full-time teaching position, though he had still not attended a single faculty meeting.

When the beloved principal then at Whitney, Mary Lou Walling, transferred to another high school in the district, the superintendent asked her to recommend a replacement. To everyone's surprise, particularly her nominee's, she suggested Tom Brock, who she believed had the credentials and the vision needed for the job. And, just like that, the job was his, first as interim principal, then permanently after a nationally advertised search. He closed down his practice and brought the desk and other furnishings he had used in his counseling office to Whitney later that month, where they've stayed for the past six years.

Shortly after arriving, Brock realized Whitney, with all its many positives, had two problems he needed to confront, echoing hurdles he had faced two decades earlier at Lennox Middle School: Whitney had a group of teachers that was at best uneven—some excellent, some adequate, and some who simply didn't belong in public education; and Whitney needed money—it was the poorest school in the district. All the extra federal and state spending on education, beyond the basic per pupil sum each district spends, goes in other directions: special education, remedial programs, athletic programs, outreach programs, incentive grants to poorly performing schools that have shown some improvement. Whitney qualified for none of it. "There's not a lot of money out there for overachieving middle-class kids," Brock says good-naturedly. "So we have to look elsewhere."

When Aisha came to him in tears, he had been in the process of dealing with each of those two issues, building cases against a couple of problematic teachers and forging partnerships with corporate donors, chief among them the computer chip company Intel, and the president's brother, Neil Bush, who had remade himself from a failed savings-and-loan executive to a self-styled education reformer. Now the 9/11 crisis had threatened to derail all of it.

Aisha and a committee of student volunteers are calling the event a "Unity Rally." In the space of two weeks, they have invited speakers from all major religions, garnered press coverage in the local newspaper and on television news broadcasts, and wired the gymnasium (the only facility on campus capable of holding the whole student body) for sound. All of this is accomplished without adult intervention. The keynote speaker is the best friend and college roommate of Todd Beamer, the passenger on United Flight 93 whose last utterance via cell phone—"Let's roll!"—was immortalized when the plane crashed after passengers swarmed the hijackers.

Attendance at the assembly, held over a long lunch hour, is voluntary, yet 98 percent of the student body unexpectedly crams into the gym. Each of the religious speakers talks about tolerance and the common bonds between religions, with the rabbi, the Buddhist, and the representative from the Los Angeles Islamic Center inspiring the most sustained applause. The students imposed a strict ban on proselytizing, prayer, and outright preaching (in deference to the Constitution, the multiplicity of beliefs at Whitney, and the one condition principal Brock laid down), a restriction only the evangelical Christian speaker fails to observe as he abruptly implores the gathering of Christians, Jews, Muslims, Hindus, Buddhists, and assorted others to accept Christ as their personal savior. Aisha looks like she is about to faint when he suddenly begins closing his eyes in prayer, forgetting he is not, for the moment, at the pulpit. "I went over the rules with them three times," she whispers to the student next to her, who just shrugs.

It is a small hitch in an otherwise well-reviewed event: At a meeting afterward, several teachers go out of their way to praise the students for their efforts, although others remain silent, having privately voiced their discomfort at the religious content and what they saw as the school's official abdication of responsibility for the affair. Once again, a Brock decision to invest the students with responsibility is both criticized and congratulated.

There are other mixed messages. Aisha's desire to emphasize unity and to stage a positive, inclusive sort of event had the opposite effect on her relationships with some students, who more or less stopped talking to her afterward amid a flurry of hurt feelings and wounded egos. A group of student leaders who initially joined Aisha in organizing the event had wanted a rally devoted more to decrying hate crimes, bigotry, and negative portrayals of Islam in the media. These kids were troubled and wounded by what they saw as Islam-bashing in the media, particularly by some endlessly publicized incitements from a bestselling, radical right blowhard who advocated in a column, "We should invade their countries, kill their leaders and convert them to Christianity." This group ended up feeling disappointed and outmaneuvered by Aisha, and at a follow-up meeting in Brock's office they expressed their disappointment in the tone of the rally and the absence of student speakers to make the points they considered most important. "If this were really about unity, instead of one person's *idea* of unity, then there should have been student voices at the rally, even if they caused dissension," the student president complains. The "one person" he clearly means—Aisha—looks like she has been kicked, but she bears the criticism in silence, her smile frozen. Brock facilitates the meeting, but, refusing to take sides, just listens.

Brock's neutrality could have stung further, but Aisha had already been braced by Shirley Wold in private when the same students reduced her to tears immediately after the rally, deflating the rush of pride she felt after the event. "Some people, all they want to do is tear things down," Aisha had complained bitterly. "They didn't want unity. They just want to play the victim."

Wold had reached over and shut her door, then pointed at the glass of water on her desk. "Aisha, look at that glass, and what do you see? You see it's half full. It's cliché, but it's true: Some people can only see that it's half empty. They can't see the positive. But you can. You always do."

If that wasn't enough to make her feel better, more support comes at the faculty meeting from an unexpected source. "I've never been prouder to be at Whitney," Toni Squires, the eighth- and ninth-grade history teacher, announces. "I can hardly believe students put this on. Embracing diversity is our country's great hope, and that's what we do here so well." Squires is widely considered to be the strictest teacher on campus—the kids say she gives more detentions than most of the other teachers combined—but on this day, Aisha wants to hug her.

Tom Brock just smiles and nods and sees it all as a learning experience that never would have happened if he had stood up and taken over when Aisha first came to him in tears. The results weren't perfect, but they came pretty close. And he figures—correctly—that Aisha, at least, will have no trouble finding a good topic for her college application essay now. If the admissions officers want someone who has taken on challenges in life, this girl now has plenty to talk about.

There's a saying in the Korean culture: "If you know five Koreans, you know them all." When I was young I didn't understand how that could be possible, but now I realize that Korean Americans have created a definition of their own, certain characteristics and habits that characterize them as "Koreans." And as much as I would like to be an "American," these characteristics have been branded on me through many generations of ancestors.

We are a race that is generally small in stature, and basically yearn to possess the abundant height of the Caucasian race. A 5'9" Korean woman will always be admired by friends and relatives for being tall and slender. Milk is our magic growing potion that makes our bones long and makes us grow. Every short Korean child is scolded by their mother at one time or another for not drinking enough milk. Unfortunately, though, many Koreans are lactose intolerant and thus take calcium supplements to compensate. Supposedly, riding a bike is supposed to help lengthen the legs. My dad, by order of my grandfather, has many a time tried to teach me to graduate from my training wheels, but he has had no success. I still can't ride a bike and hate milk with a vengeance.

Koreans, rich or not, tend to be quite extravagant. The key is, "One must look well off in front of others." When Korean men express their approval for each other's wealth they say, "You've grown," which is figurative language for, "My, you're living well." A rich Korean man will buy a cell phone for his son's tenth birthday and a new car for his twelfth. His wife will indulge herself by getting her hair professionally blow-dried twice a week at a salon and by buying clothes and jewelry. Korean people are not typically known to be very stringent on the fiscal level. I think, however, that my parents cannot identify with this definition; they are quite stingy.

Looking "inferior" is greatly dreaded by Koreans as a whole. We are a race with a lot of pride. This most appropriately applies to Korean women—they are simply fierce. They have this natural instinct and urge to show off and brag about their mediocre child. Listen to a conversation between two Korean mothers and you hear things like, "My daughter is taking this class...my daughter is just so busy with SATs...oh, by the way, my daughter is receiving this award." You can just smell the animosity in the air, even though on the surface it may appear that they are holding a normal conversation. Of course, if our success or assets help make our parents feel "bigger" we're happy to help, but sometimes they need to realize that it just puts more pressure on us. I heard about a Korean boy that was accepted to Rice University in Texas, but ended up going to UC Berkeley by his father's will. When asked why he didn't allow his son to attend the school of his choice, he answered honestly, "My colleagues in Korea have never heard of a Rice University. What would I say to them?" That's Korean.

In the Korean culture, a student is strictly a student. He or she is not expected to do chores around the house or run errands—their job is simply to study and get good grades. Very different from Caucasian, Americanized homes where usually the children take a big part in house chores, in addition to their studying. Likewise, a Korean student is not expected to pay any part of his/her college tuition. In many cases, their grandfather will pay half of it and their parents the other half. On the other hand, many Caucasian children would have to work between jobs in college to help pay for their tuition. Credit card debts are a big issue for college students. Many will still be working jobs to pay them off after college. But Korean parents, with a little scolding, will pay them off for you. Money comes quite easily into the hands of Korean children, perhaps because every holiday is reason enough for twenty bucks here and there from relatives—New Year's Day, Christmas Day, then there's birthday, for getting an award, and the list goes on.

Besides the pressure to be tall or a super whiz kid, being a Korean teenager is not too bad, once you're in touch with your Korean side. Living in Cerritos for almost thirteen years, I think I can tell a Korean when I see one, and as much as I would not like to be, I realize that I am just another one of those typical Korean kids.

—Jane, a Whitney senior

6

Browns, blacks, and dark reds streak the canvas—deep colors, abstract forms swimming into focus, painted in thick, angry strokes. Angela has been at it now for five hours nonstop, venting, her black-handled brush a blur. It is three in the morning, the house silent as a crypt, except for the hollow, sandy sound of sable on canvas, almost like breathing. School—her senior year—has barely started, but she is as stressed as if it were finals week. Only the painting helps, keeps her hands from trembling, the tears from flowing. She is already on her second canvas.

She steps back, squints at the easel. More red, Angela thinks. She squeezes a blob of acrylic paint the color of blood onto her palette and mixes in white, a touch of blue. Then she closes her eyes, a deep furrow etching her pale forehead beneath unruly strands of dark hair. She can still hear her mother's words, pricking old wounds: *"Don't you want to go to college? A good college?"*

The argument is always the same. Angela has heard it for years, knows it by heart: She is ruining her life. She is making bad choices, pursuing the wrong goals. Art should be a hobby, nothing more. Her parents' arguments have grown even more urgent in the wake of 9/11. This is the real world. War is on the horizon; America is no longer safe; the economy is tanking. This is the time for a practical career, not for throwing yourself into art. Did she want to be poor? Sell paintings on street corners and at swap meets like those idiots with the black velvet Elvises, begging for a living? You have to make something of your life. Be a doctor, a lawyer, an engineer. Something *respectable*. And don't even get me started on that boy you like so much. Stay away from him!

What Angela wanted to shout back, but didn't—couldn't—was what always runs through her mind at such times: *I'm so damn respectable, I make myself sick.*

The truth is, Angela has always been a good girl, studious, respectful, obedient. She doesn't cheat. She doesn't drink. She hates drugs. She doesn't even date, at least not in the way many of her friends would define it ("You know," Angela says uncomfortably, "I don't do any 'bad stuff'"). And, until the last year or so, she has always accepted, without question, without even a blink, everything her parents wanted for her future, enlisting dutifully in the long march toward college that began with the little girl who taught herself to read at age four.

When her family moved to the area so she would be eligible to attend Whitney, then switched her in second grade to private school, she never let on how much she hated the change. When she turned eight and they packed her off to after-school academies, she said fine. There were the twelve years of piano lessons, the ten years of violin (her favorite), the eight years of Chinese school—no complaints. She has studied with obsessive determination, four hours of homework most nights (even weekends), summers spent watching her friends head off to tan at the beach while she hunkered down under the fluorescent glare of SAT cram classes (fifteen hundred bucks a pop, sixty-point improvement guaranteed or your money back), or with a private SAT tutor or a private Chinese language instructor. Summer vacation has always been an oxymoron for Angela, filled morning to night with programmed learning, reading lists, math and science camp, volunteer work—but never art or sports or other nonacademic pursuits. What good were they? And when her mom and dad made Ivy League–caliber Stanford University her dream school early on, her first choice, because that's where a niece who became a physician went, she accepted that, too, although no one actually asked her what schools *she* might have dreamed about.

All the while, silent fears gnawed at Angela that she just might not be (or, worse, might not want to be) Stanford or Ivy League material. Even admitting this privately felt like sacrilege; speaking it to her parents was out of the question. But the evidence seemed clear, at least to her: She considered her solid Bs and occasional Cs to be mediocre grades, particularly by Whitney standards. She found no consolation in the fact that she could have been a top student at almost any other high school in the area; only at Whitney, where half the student body has been identified as "gifted" by their elementary schools and where the courses she chose were exceptionally tough, could she find herself stuck in the middle of the pack. Her parents said she wasn't trying hard enough and she rarely contradicted this conclusion. Every negative comment, every criticism, she took to heart, quietly brooding over them. She can still remember the offhand remark her ninth-grade history teacher made once when she got a B-minus on a test: *Do you ever want to go to college?* It had blindsided Angela, who had been fiercely debating to herself whether she should tell the teacher that several of the kids with the highest grades on the test had cheated right under her nose. Angela could have joined in the answer sharing but didn't, and she had decided to remain silent about the cheating when the teacher made her cutting comment. The teacher undoubtedly forgot it five minutes later. But four *years* later, Angela can close her eyes and hear it as if it were yesterday, still envision the purple outfit and matching boots the teacher wore, still seethe with the silent humiliation and anger at this notion that one test, one damn slip, could be so pivotal that her entire future could be affected. She knows this is ridiculous, yet on some heartsick level she believed it entirely, reinforced by her parents' all-too-similar refrain: "*Do you want to go to college? A good college?*" With each passing year at Whitney, as graduation and college applications drew inexorably closer, she had become increasingly withdrawn, keeping more and more to herself.

Then, in her sophomore year, Angela took her first art class. And the girl who had become awkward and reticent, feelings buried deep, found a voice she never knew she had. Faces leaped off her sketch pads. Enormous flowers unfolded ethereally. Portraits of her classmates were dead-on, capturing not just their features but their personalities, wry or sarcastic or arrogant or sad. Ms. Agrums had almost sent her away, the beginning art classes full by the time Angela mustered the courage to inquire. But something about this girl's brittle determination—and the crushed look on her face at being turned away—had persuaded the teacher to let her challenge the class, a sort of trial by fire that would allow her to move directly into more advanced instruction if she could show sufficient skill and raw talent. Angela stayed up all night doing a detailed pencil sketch of a tube of toothpaste, revealing every edge, squeeze, and wrinkle in the crumpled metal, then shyly presented it to Agrums. Her talent and potential were immediately apparent to the art teacher. Agrums had other students successfully challenge courses in the past, but Angela was the first to walk in with absolutely no art instruction and just blow her away. Angela's rapid progress astonished the teacher that year, as did her speed, as if her paintings and drawings had been waiting for years, fully formed, to spring out of her. Angela branched into crafts as well, painting and embroidering whimsical chairs out of thrift shop castoffs and selling the results for hundreds of dollars. Her friends lived to shop for clothes, but Angela preferred simple jeans or making her own skirts and blouses, saving her money for her own idea of shopping nirvana: a leisurely, basket-cramming visit to her favorite art store. Toward the end of Angela's junior year, Agrums began talking to her about applying to colleges with serious art programs— or possibly a dedicated art school. "You have the talent," the teacher would tell her. "It's what you love." In good moments, Angela would allow herself to believe she had found her place and her calling.

Except her parents would have none of it. They were upset with Angela, upset with the art teacher, upset that their careful plans, their scrimping and hoping, might be undone by some charcoal and a few tubes of paint. They were not mollified by the fact that Angela had brought all her grades up even as she developed her new interest in art (though this did prevent them from branding art classes a distraction that had to go). Agrums tried to talk to them, tried to get them excited about their daughter's abilities. "In just two years, she's become one of my two or three absolutely best students," the teacher exulted. "She could get into almost any art school." This did not help. The oddest thing was that Angela's father was an artist himself, a lithographer, but that ended up working against her. Lithography is a dying art, its stone and grease pencils falling into oblivion in the face of computer software that can simulate in minutes what it took him days to accomplish. His bitterness grew as the work grew scarce. "You are not going to make the same mistake," he told his daughter.

Things hit rock bottom when Angela announced she wanted a sewing machine for her crafts work. She had saved up for months, hoarding her earnings from the violin lessons she gave fifth and sixth graders, and had shopped around until she found just the model she wanted, a superquiet Swiss-made machine. She was quite proud that she had done this on her own. But her parents were beside themselves; the idea of a sewing machine tapped into age-old immigrant fears that hadn't even occurred to the American-born, Americanized Angela. Both of her parents had emigrated from Taiwan, and though they were college-educated professionals, they had grown up with others not nearly so lucky. The sewing machine summoned archetypal fears of sweatshops and garment districts, of old women's hands worn to scarred clubs by a thousand steel needles. "Why don't you just quit school and get it over with," her mother said in despair. "Become a seamstress!" The word *seamstress* had been spat like a curse. There would be no sewing machine.

And so here Angela is, already pulling an all-nighter in the first month of school, already being pulled in all directions. She has taken on a rigorous academic schedule to satisfy her parents—four Advanced Placement and honors classes—and she has vowed, this year for sure, to earn that elusive 4.0 grade point average. At the same time, she is the art teacher's assistant this year, spending more time than ever in the studio. And, quietly, she is compiling information on colleges other than Stanford and the backup schools on her parents' approved list, information on art schools in Chicago and Pasadena, a religious school on the East Coast, a private university in nearby Orange. Now she has a couple of months before those college applications have to go out, six or eight weeks in which to convince her parents to waiver from their eighteen-year-old dream and to accept hers in its place. She was anticipating and dreading the coming year. Now she feels like she's been plunged into boot camp.

"I'm worried about her," Debbie Agrums says the next morning, watching a pallid Angela hauling her canvases into the art room, stooped and tired. "I worry that she's feeling desperate, and I'm not sure what she'll do. I'm not sure she's okay."

Agrums remembers a former student, a young man with a gift for drawing, who had been offered admission to a prestigious art school, but whose parents insisted he enter a premed program instead. They had worked hard to achieve that goal for most of his life, and their vicarious ambitions could not be sidetracked. So he obliged them, but unhappily, doing a lackluster job at his studies, turning to alcohol and other substances for relief, then finally dropping out of school and never earning a degree. Then there was the boy whose family was involved in organized crime, who drove a Porsche to school and disappeared to Vegas each weekend, who only wanted to be free to study art, but who was compelled to prep for law school instead, the family's heir apparent. And just last year, another of Agrums's star students, Cecilia, who dreams of a career in anime, had a terrible fight with her parents about the direction of her studies, an argument brought to an abrupt end with her portfolio, a year's worth of work, being hurled into the street in a heap. It sat there for five hours, cars running over it, before Cecilia was permitted to pick it up. To her relief, there was little lasting damage—it was the symbolism that hurt. "I could stand your hair on end with some of the stories my kids share with me," Agrums says. Her eyes follow Angela. "This room is their sanctuary.... But only for an hour a day."

In English literature that same morning, Ms. Palmieri passes out a mock exam, a literary personality test that attempts to determine whether a person's attitudes are dominated by a romantic or a classical view of the world. It is supposed to be a fun little multiple-choice introduction to two radically different literary traditions and the mind-sets behind them, but the first question unintentionally cuts to the core of most any teenager's insecurities, hitting Angela as if it were written just for her: *"When things go wrong and you feel angry and confused, what do you customarily conclude?"* The typical romantic's answer would be *"(e) Damn the fates!"* But Angela, after sitting and staring for some time, checks the classical response: *"(a) It's probably my fault."*

7

Although most of the eleventh graders in honors U.S. history are noisily ignoring it, Channel One is blaring in the background, the terrorist attack and its aftermath dominating the twelve-minute canned newscast the school is obliged to play each morning during homeroom. Mr. Bohannon has asked his students to watch, or at least remain quiet while the program is on, but most seem to have forgotten this request—for the moment, at least.

Out of habit, he still calls the program "Whittle," after the founder and former owner of the service, Chris Whittle, who put free TVs, VCRs, satellite dishes, and plenty of commercials into 12,000 cash-and-technology-strapped schools nationwide in exchange for the promise that his program will be played in every classroom, every day. Today Channel One reaches an incredible 40 percent of American teenagers five days a week, a captive audience in a coveted demographic no other media property can come close to matching. (The name changed in 1994 when Whittle sold out to a company now called Primedia for a tidy $300 million, allowing him to focus his attention on Edison Schools, his ill-fated dream of mining private profits from stubbornly unprofitable public schools.)

Between soft-drink ads, promos for the new Harry Potter movie, and military recruiting spots (a buff rock climber scales a sheer mountain face, then morphs into a Marine in dress blues wielding a can-do attitude and a shiny saber), the twenty-something news anchor in the oversized football jersey is talking up the old World War II slogan, Loose Lips Sink Ships. The Bush administration, he says, is angry over news leaks about Osama bin Laden and the war on terrorism— which is rapidly transforming into the war on Afghanistan's Taliban—and the parallels with past conflicts and their security concerns are obvious. "How much information is too much?" the news anchor asks. Then the camera cuts from World War II footage to ABC News personality Sam Donaldson opining that all presidents *say* they want to stop leaks yet seldom ever do (and some, Donaldson confides, are the biggest leakers of all). He is followed by a "boy in the halls" interview with a high school student in Gardena, California, who thinks, "Some things should be kept secret." The few students in Mr. Bohannon's history class bothering to listen to the youth-oriented newscast seem to agree with the latter position: This is not the time to be insisting on press freedoms.

Others are preoccupied with more immediate concerns. Nolan is frantically penciling in the homework Bohannon will collect when homeroom period ends in five minutes and history lessons begin in earnest. Megan is making entries in her crammed day planner, in which events are booked months in advance. David and Mark sit in the last row, their heads tilted close together as they lean their chairs back against the wall, a precarious-looking shelf of books and other classroom props sagging a few inches above them, its underside riddled with small bits of graffiti invisible from other vantage points. The boys are anxiously reviewing last evening's activities, wondering what the consequences will be. David, in defiance of his mom's curfew, stayed out all night (though he showed up for class on time). Mom called the school and now David is holding a yellow slip of paper, handed out by Mr. Bohannon, his eyebrow raised, instructing him to report to Shirley Wold's office after this period. This is not good. Wold has always had a soft spot for David and most of Whitney's other "problem children," as she affectionately calls them, partly because she figures they're basically good kids who just need some extra help and can't get it elsewhere, partly because she can afford to: there are a lot less problem children per capita at Whitney than at most high schools. But there is a bottom line, Mark reminds him: David's already on academic probation and any further serious missteps could send him out of the school, where the one hard and fast rule is the need to maintain at least a C-plus average. David's ace in the hole has been his status as Whitney's computer wizard: he works with the tech-support department (which consists of one science teacher and David) in keeping the school's aging computers, printers, and eternally conflicting software afloat, as well as crafting the PowerPoint presentations on the principal's laptop for various high-level meetings and conferences. When a VIP like Neil Bush comes and needs a computerized projector setup, David's the guy who puts it together. Mark, one of several other Whitney students out late with David last night and holding a yellow slip this morning, is worried his friend's balancing act may be about to crash.

"You should lay low after last night," Mark says. "Just tell Wold you'll stop staying out all night."

David looks at him. They both know it's not that simple. "We'll see," he says.

Bohannon stands in front of his class and stares sternly at his inattentive juniors, thinking, *Things sure slip quickly when you're away for a few days.* He wishes more of the kids were listening to the news; if ever there were a time to pay attention, to learn the lessons of history repeated, this is it. He's just back from New York, his annual pilgrimage for a grass-court tennis tournament cut short by terrorism. His students and colleagues had been worried about him for a time. He was out of touch, like most of New York City, in the wake of the World Trade Center attack, and it took the better part of a day for him to get through and let everyone know he was all right. Now he's itching to get the kids invested in current events. That is his key to teaching history—engaging kids year after year by drawing parallels between their lives and concerns and the otherwise dry and distant events he must compel them to study. The shock of the attack has worn off already for most. They have no idea what may lie ahead. Bohannon, who served in the Army Reserves in the Vietnam War era and who is at once deeply patriotic and deeply skeptical about the pronouncements of government, decides it's time to remind them what's at stake.

"You boys," he says when the news program ends and the screen goes blank. "I'm sorry, *young men*. You young men need to pay more attention to this. Because if there is a war, and it certainly looks like one is coming, there may be a draft again. So you may be more involved in this than you realize, whether you want to be or not. Your future plans, your choices—everything you've taken for granted for so long—may change."

"Do you really think that's possible?" asks David, his sleepy-eyed, out-all-night posture suddenly straightening a few notches. "I mean, do you really think the American public would stand for that?"

"I think wars are caused by fat old men who make these decisions," Bohannon says, provoking the intended laughter. "We should let the fat old men fight it out and laugh at them. But that's not the way it works.... The information is just beginning to come in about what has happened and what's going to happen, but war certainly appears to be the direction we're headed. Of course, the information we have is all coming from the government. And you always have to decide how much of that information you can accept at face value. Because there is a long history of leaders who are—how shall we say it?—less than candid. Sometimes for the right reasons. Sometimes not."

This would have been almost too obvious a point to make for the kids he taught twenty years ago who, if anything, were too skeptical. Now the pendulum has swung the other way, and Bohannon worries his students these days are too ready to accept official pronouncements unquestioningly, or they're just too busy to give them much thought either way. But Bohannon's third-period honors class is different, one of the brighter spots on his schedule this year. Unlike the more rigidly programmed AP History, which is essentially prep for the very rigorous AP exam and is all he has taught for the last several years, honors U.S. history leaves much more room for discussions, side issues, and current events. So when the politically conservative Bohannon, who is wearing a white T-shirt today emblazoned with the image of a bald eagle chomping on the head of Osama bin Laden and captioned THE EAGLE'S FURIOUS, signals that it's okay to challenge the official line in this classroom, the kids are suddenly filled with questions. Will Middle Easterners be interned as the Japanese Americans were after Pearl Harbor (a burning question in a majority Asian school)? Will there be a depression if there are more attacks? Will we lose our privacy and personal freedoms as the pressure to gather intelligence grows? Will the war really last for years, as President Bush keeps vowing? "It really, really scares me," Jennifer says. "My uncle is in the National Guard, and his unit will be one of the first to go if it comes down to that."

These are all good questions, Bohannon says, clearly delighted. And then, in answer, he brings it back to what they're studying: the founding of the Republic and the war for independence, when, he tells them, many of these same questions, or ones very much like them, were first confronted in America. Why, he wants to know, were the Founders so adamant about placing the military under civilian control? He waits a beat, sees no hands, and answers his own question. "Because they didn't want the generals to decide when to go to war. Why? Because generals are trained to fight. The Founders knew, if America and its ideals were to work, that authority had to rest elsewhere. That war had to be a political decision, not a military one....Let me explain it this way. Power: We have it. But how do you use it? How much good does it do you? Let's say a kindergarten girl rushes in here and kicks..." He pauses, and his eyes find Ryan, with his dark hair dyed an unnatural blond. "She rushes in and she kicks Ryan and then laughs about it. What do you do? You grab her and yell stop—and she starts screaming. If you let her go, she knows she can get away with it. So what do you do? It's a silly example, but it makes the point: You have the power, but can you use it? And what are the consequences if you do? Who do you want to decide?"

A collective *ohhh* can be heard in the room, the small, telling example making viscerally clear to every kid in the room with a little brother or sister just how exasperating the choices facing this country might prove to be. "Yes, *ohhh*," Bohannon agrees. "Now we're going to find out the answers to those questions. And how they are going to affect us, you most of all. Some of the assumptions you've all made about the future may have to change."

This is Dave Bohannon's gift for teaching history: seamlessly spanning the centuries in a single question, encompassing bin Laden, Vietnam War disinformation, the American Revolution's philosophical underpinnings, and annoying kid sisters in the space of a few sentences. Though he is traditional, strict, at once physically imposing and curmudgeonly, he remains a perennial favorite of the students, who admire and respect him for many reasons, not the least of which is the fact that he has their number.

Small-time issues of discipline can be a nagging, niggling problem at Whitney. Talking out of turn, forgotten assignments, tardiness, and other assorted minor offenses are a regular part of the repertoire for kids who consider themselves both privileged and overburdened and who therefore feel they deserve some slack. There is none of the really awful, disruptive sort of behavior that plagues some public schools, just little things historically given a free pass at Whitney— except in Bohannon's classroom. "We grumble about it," says Jennifer, "but the truth is, it's nice to know you can't get away with the same ol' same ol' in here. It makes it so much easier. Keeps you focused. Kids know better than to try anything in here." And so their incessant habit of neglecting to bring textbooks to class (a classic way of burning five or ten minutes in the hallway) is dealt with in this way: Bohannon obligingly lets them use class time to go to their lockers to fetch the books, but when the miscreants return, they find a blank paper on their desktop and an assignment to write a 200-word essay on how much history their lockers were able to learn from the textbook, *American Pageant*. Kids who are tardy or absent on test days—the scholastic equivalent of blue flu—get to face brutally hard makeups. There are few two-time offenders here. Bohannon relishes telling his students that their lofty opinions of their own academic prowess may be a bit overblown, notwithstanding the school's top ranking in California; years ago, he taught fifth graders in a poor barrio school and gave them the same tough U.S. presidents test he gives to eleventh graders now. "My fifth graders did better," he tells them with a smile.

Bohannon tells his students he is aware that some Whitney parents tend to be ultracompetitive, and that this creates a whole set of potential problems. He has been called many times by parents who find reasons to object to any grade lower than an A and who will lobby, complain, and even threaten in an attempt to persuade him to raise a grade—to no avail, he says, unless there is a mathematical error of some sort. "Unfortunately, some of our younger teachers—and some in our administration—have buckled under to this sort of pressure. It's hard to say no. But it's worse to allow the system to be stripped of integrity....If I change someone's grade to one that is undeserved, it cheats everyone who earned their grades. Some teachers hand out As here like candy. An A should be worth something."

Bohannon assures his students he understands they face the same sort of parental pressure as teachers, and that this attitude, to do whatever it takes to get that A, can create the temptation to cheat. And so he makes it easy for them by making it clear from Day One that he is taking steps to foil cheating. He gives any paper, test, or homework an F whenever there is evidence of cheating, and he spells out these rules and his other classroom expectations in writing. "In years past, I never had rules of behavior. I would just say, Behave. And everyone knew what I was talking about. But thanks to lawsuits, certain administrators, pushy parents, I've now found it's better to write them down to protect myself. So here they are."

He makes them sign this contract on conduct in his classroom, and they're supposed to have their parents sign as well. "Which reminds me," he adds with trademark sarcasm, "when I get notes from home with two signatures, your parent's and yours, and it's in the same handwriting, at least do it in a different color ink....But you should be careful about that. If your parent comes in and complains about your grades, about my taking points off without explaining, I can just say, 'Oh yes. Here's the contract you signed.' Then they look at the paper they supposedly signed. And then I might as

well not be in the room anymore, because they are done at-
tacking me. And they are going after you." Kids usually smile
at this image: A large majority don't forge or cheat, Bohannon believes, but they still like to know they won't be put at a
disadvantage by those who do.

After class, some of the kids walk through the swarming
halls and discuss why everyone, even Megan, the student who
pronounced him scary on the first day of school, seems to
like Mr. Bohannon. "It's strange," Jennifer says, shaking her
long, beaded braids, "but you can relax in Mr. Bohannon's
class *because* he is so strict. You would think it would be the
opposite, because, you know, we're teenagers and we like to
get away with everything we can. But when kids know they
can't, then you just relax and learn. I think that's really why
everyone likes his class so much."

Bohannon's popularity with his students has not endeared
him to Whitney's principal. The two men have little in common and less to say to one another. Brock's and Bohannon's
mutual dislike, once hidden beneath a veneer of civility, is
now pretty much apparent to all, even the students, who
are famously oblivious to faculty relationships. Whenever
prompted by his students, the history teacher fondly lam-
bastes the school administration, never by name, though his
meaning is clear. At the other end of the school, Brock holds
leadership meetings several times a week with selected teachers, during which all major decisions at the school are mulled
over and made in a remarkably open and democratic fash-
ion; Bohannon is conspicuously absent from these pivotal
gatherings.

Brock considers Bohannon "old style," a teacher who
uses grades as a weapon to get compliance from kids, beating
them up with tough makeup tests, taking away points for

misbehavior, elevating grades to the most important aspect of his classes. Brock considers this a poor way to motivate learners, although his ideas on this point are sorely tested at Whitney, where many of the students will say nothing matters more to them—or their parents—than the grades. The principal concedes, however, that there is more to Bohannon than report card terrorism; how else to explain his immense popularity with the kids other than he is a gifted teacher, old-school approach or not.

Bohannon, on the other hand, who finds the virtues of clarity and sense of purpose in his traditional methods, considers Brock a shifty character whose finger is always in the wind. He has long clashed with the principal on union matters. Until he stepped down from the position this year while his wife recovered from cancer treatments, Bohannon was chief negotiator for the teachers' union in the ABC School District, where labor-management relations have until recently tended toward the ugly. Bohannon helped lead a teachers' strike in the early nineties; at one point he was quoted in a television interview harshly criticizing the district leadership's tactics (the words "fascist," "Nazi," and several other negative historical metaphors came up). He says he has been branded a troublemaker ever since, given punitive assignments over the years "for mouthing off," even though the union won a stunning victory in that strike, with parents rallying behind the teachers and voting in a new school board majority of union-backed candidates.

The difficult relationship between Bohannon and Brock reached its current nadir in spring of the last school year, when the history teacher abruptly pulled out of the plan to create six deans, one for each grade at Whitney, to act as combination teachers and advisors. This novel approach was intended to solve a long-standing problem at Whitney: overworked counselors who rarely saw or knew the kids because each of the two full-time advisors had five hundred students to counsel and spent no time in the classroom. Like the counselors at most public high schools, they didn't really know most of the students, having little opportunity to connect with them except during some sort of crisis. In the pressure cooker environment of Whitney, with stress and sleeplessness increasingly common, and where there is a strong cultural bias against admitting to being less than perfect, this old counseling model wasn't cutting it anymore. Replacing the counselors with classroom teachers who knew the kids well seemed so sensible that, once it was proposed, no one could understand why it hadn't been done years before. Each new dean would have only 170 or so students to supervise; even splitting their work hours evenly between teaching and counseling would leave each dean enough time for a substantive visit with each of these students at least once a month, and more as needed. "We want to go from crisis management to avoiding the crisis in the first place," Shirley Wold told the other teachers at the time, as the administration geared up to sell the plan to the staff.

Bohannon, no fan of change for change's sake, enthusiastically endorsed the idea as well—at first. He even agreed to join the committee that would select the deans and define their job, and one of the six new positions would have been his for the asking, no matter the principal's personal feelings. Brock knew that having his prickly but influential history teacher's support for the program could help make it fly with the union and many faculty members, who would have to fill in gaps created when six full-time teachers became half-timers with demanding counseling duties the rest of the day. These gaps were likely to be substantial in a school with only forty-one full-time faculty members, and where many of the teachers had been at Whitney for a decade (or two), and were not known to be overly receptive to sweeping changes at a school they helped build. In the fractured political landscape of a modern public high school, the difference between success and failure for anything new can rest on a few key alliances; Brock needed Bohannon. To their credit, the two men shelved their antipathy for one another in the interest of a plan each believed could benefit the kids.

But the cooperation abruptly ended when a conflict arose with the union leadership, which complained about being left in the dark about the plan, a concern that seemed more about process than the actual merits, although the roadblock was just as real. The plan required a number of labor concessions due to the mix of management and teaching duties the deans would have to assume. And the implications were far greater than the fate of six teachers at the smallest high school in the district. If it worked well, other schools in the district might go the same route. A meeting between Brock and union leaders to try to patch things up flopped, and letters soon appeared in all the teachers' mail slots announcing the union's formal opposition to the plan as a violation of their contract with the district. Brock and Bohannon blamed one another for the breakdown in communications and the history teacher quit the committee. The six-deans plan died.

Brock had made it clear that he would forge ahead no matter what, even if it meant scaling back the plan. He found that there was precedent in the district that allowed principals to appoint teachers to special administrative duties when needed, to be paid for out of administrative funds controlled by the principals, and that the union had no say in the matter so long as the teachers involved were agreeable to the change in duties. Brock had enough money and staff to finagle three counselor positions in this way, only half the number originally planned, which meant two grade levels and 340 or so students per counselor. Still, this would be a vast improvement over the current, impossibly huge counselor workload. It also meant few if any teaching duties for the new counselors (only Shirley Wold insisted she could do both at the outset). Brock had found a way around the union's objections, but the revolutionary plan had been reduced greatly, leaving soured relationships in its wake.

It surprised no one, then, when tensions between Bohannon and Brock only worsened over the principal's other new initiative: courting technology companies in order to build a "school for the twenty-first century." Bohannon was more than indifferent to technology. His refusal to use a computer was a source of endless amusement to his students, but his attitude—shared by many others on the staff—also created a barrier to introducing new technological innovations at the school. Bohannon felt, not unreasonably, that textbooks, teacher salaries, and ensuring that all the basic needs of the school were met should take precedence over introducing new gadgets with unproven value. It takes years to build a solid lesson plan and curriculum, to sort out what works at the head of a classroom and what doesn't. Introducing multimedia presentations, software-based materials, and other technologies requires an enormous amount of rethinking, reshaping, and redesigning how a teacher teaches—dozens, if not hundreds, of hours of it. And teachers do this sort of prep work pretty much on their own time, unpaid. So the incentive for a successful teacher to scrap twenty years of accumulated teaching strategy and methods is not always obvious.

But Brock, who promises no new technology will ever be forced down any teacher's throat, nevertheless eagerly seeks partnerships with technology companies and has a grand plan for building "smart" classrooms in his boxy, seventies-era school. He tries to exploit a natural synergy: Whitney is a public school and, therefore, needs pretty much everything when it comes to tech; and companies with new educational technology and software are always eager to showcase their products in one of the nation's top schools, where the chances of success (as measured by kids earning high grades) are great with pretty much any product. When Brock met Neil Bush at a conference and invited him to visit Whitney, the marriage seemed perfect. Bush's Texas-based Ignite! Inc. had what appeared to be exciting interactive software that engaged middle school kids in the study of history by adapting to each student's particular learning style and using the natural appeal of computer gaming to keep kids' attention from wavering.

When the president's little brother came to Whitney last year for the typical VIP tour—planned and conducted, as usual, by the students—it included a visit to Bohannon's history class, where the students had an unusual welcome prepared for him. Kosha and several other students had researched Bush's misadventures in the savings and loan industry, where mismanagement of his Silverado Savings and Loan cost the taxpayers a $1.3 billion bailout, led to a $50,000 fine leveled against Bush (but paid with the help of Bush family and Republican fund-raising), and caused Bush to be banned for life from the banking industry. He disappeared from the public eye for many years only to resurface with Ignite!, inspired, he says, by his own and his son's difficult experiences in school. Now, in the midst of a discussion of banking abuses, failures, and economic depressions in previous centuries, the students decided to make a connection to more current events—the savings and loan debacle of the 1980s. Bush fled Bohannon's room so fast, the students later recalled, he was almost running. Brock was embarrassed at the lack of respect shown his guest, but Bohannon stood by his students. The subject was relevant to the class discussion, he said. "If you can't stand the heat," he added, "don't come in here. No one else seems to want to ask this question, but I think it's a valid one: Are we going to do business with this man?"

The answer for Brock was decidedly yes. Bush and Brock agreed that Whitney would test out the new history program in one eighth-grade class this year. The teacher who volunteered to use the program, Jenny Shellhamer, along with the head of the social sciences department, JoAnne Charmack, and Brock had been scheduled to leave in a few weeks for the Bush family compound in Kennebunkport for a celebration and training session when the terrorist attack occurred and the plans were canceled. Now Neil Bush and a technical crew from Ignite! have arrived at Whitney instead to get the program rolling, with newly assigned Secret Service agents in tow to protect the first brother.

Bush takes another tour of the school and stages a demo of his software, although it is still not fully up in Shellhamer's class, and it has been plagued by bugs and frequent crashes. "I hope he has better success in the educational software field than he did in the savings and loan business," Bohannon observes dryly, as the entourage passes by in the hall. The tour carefully avoids pausing anywhere near honors history.

Which is more important, learning or the grade? Wow...hard question. As much as I would love to act the scholar and say, "The learning, DEFINITELY!" I'll be truthful and say probably the grade. Although learning is something that is definitely important and will eventually help you as you move along in life, you can't GET anywhere in life nowadays without the grade. Albert Einstein would have been hard put to find a job nowadays with his Cs and Fs on his report card; the people with "talent" are those that get the higher-than-godly-possible GPAs. Someone could be as smart and talented as oh...say... well, a really smart and talented person (argh...brain failure right there...) and without a diplomat stating that he has a Ph.D., a master's degree, he won't ever make a living out of much other than flipping hamburgers or maybe making his own company and being gainfully self-employed. Unfortunately, for the latter, you must have capital and we don't hear much about rich happy geniuses without high school diplomas anymore....

I hope to learn a lot. I try to make sure that I do in addition to taking the test. But I guess if it came down to it, I'd rather accept an A in an easy class rather than fail a hard one and learn a great deal from it....Something like that is like a brand on your transcript; it won't go away no matter how well you

do in your other classes or how much you know as a result....
People do insist on staring at your report card and filing you
away as a serial number in a cabinet. The report card doesn't
tell you how hard it was to get there, how much sweat and
effort you shoved into your essays or arithmetic to get the
grade, it just shows the final result, which is basically all anyone
cares about nowadays....

This kind of thinking will probably not slack off in college,
more than likely it will get more intensive.... Everyone wants to
be the best, but they have to and would climb over a stack of
textbooks and corpses to do so. There just isn't enough work to
go around now; I've heard how hard it is to get a job...and
because it's so difficult, people stop caring about other people
and just start trying to take care of themselves. Berkeley
engineers, great example: My mom told me when she studied
there, when she was sick, people wouldn't tell her the
assignment because they were afraid she'd get ahead of them.
When there were reference books that they needed to study,
the first people there grabbed 'em and never returned them;
rather, they paid the rather hefty fine instead. My first reaction
is, DUDE, THIS IS CUTTHROAT, but I realize now that college is
only a microcosm of life in the future.... What will it be like
when you actually have to step out on your own with a
knapsack over your back and your own two feet to move you?

...So yes, sad to say, I'll take the grade over learning. What
choice do you have?

—Cecilia, senior, writing on the value
of grades and learning

8

"I am just finishing the most hectic day of my academic career," Irene says. She sounds exhausted. Her head is down on folded arms, lying atop the cool, black slate top of her lab table in Mr. Ziolkowski's physics class. Sixth period is about to begin: just one more to go. "Seems like an eternity," Irene says, voice muffled by her forearm.

Last night she was doing homework, but nothing was coming. She was running on empty. It was still early, nine o'clock or so, but she was so tired. I'll just put my head down for a bit, she thought. Just a ten-minute nap, a quick refresher. Like I always do.

"Next thing I know," she tells her lab partners in physics, "I open my eyes and the clock says 6:30. I had done none of my homework. I had calc. I had physics. I had an essay due." So she did her English essay on *Hamlet* in Ms. Palmieri's class, and handed it in at the end of the period. She did her calculus homework in history (God knows what was being discussed in there; she'll have to look over somebody's notes later on). Now she sits up and waves her physics homework, a limp, blue-lined flag covered with dense, surprisingly neat rows of equations calculating the speed and acceleration of a variety of hypothetical moving and falling objects. "I did this last period. I got it all done. Somehow." She puts her head back down and closes her eyes. The circles beneath them make her face look bruised.

"That's life at Whitney," Albert, one of her lab partners, offers. "That's why our hair turns white." He and several classmates then begin a spirited discussion of which seniors at Whitney have the most white hairs sprouting. Irene listens but doesn't say anything; she has been checking her own head for stray grays recently and has been relieved to find none. "So far," she confides.

If you ask if her time at Whitney has been worth the effort, she will reflexively say yes, that for all the hard work and struggles, she can't imagine replacing her time here, the sense of achievement and of family she enjoys here, with life at a "real" high school. (This is one way in which many students and teachers define the difference between Whitney and other high schools: one is *real*, the other is not, although this can be either a negative or a positive distinction, depending on the context.) If there is a bit of rote to Irene's response, it's not out of lack of sincerity. "It's just that I have to keep telling myself," she says. "Sometimes you let yourself think, if I was at some other school, I could be near the top of my class and work a lot less. But then I come to my senses." Yet there's no missing the slightly wistful quality. Irene is a good student but nowhere near the top of her class at Whitney.

When class comes to order and Mr. Z makes the rounds, using a red rubber stamp to mark completed homework, he sees the weariness on Irene's face and starts to ask her what's wrong, then keeps moving. She is one of the kids he worries about in this mixed class of juniors and seniors. She's smart, she's nice, but sometimes he worries that she's "checked out," her senior year at Whitney leaving her spent and let down— and mystified about what to do about it. "She's really going to have to raise her game," he says later, shaking his head. "She's capable of so much more."

Irene is in many ways a typical Whitney student: bright, reserved, well-mannered, conflicted. Her parents are South Korean immigrants, while she was born in the United States, and the usual cultural conflicts are in play between the traditional values her parents brought with them and her own American teen sensibilities. She seems to feel something is missing but can't put her finger on just what it is, and a flurry of activities—soccer, student government, being in charge of the school marquee (posting WELCOME, NEIL BUSH and GIRLS VOLLEYBALL TONIGHT messages with a giant pole)—only leaves her feeling frazzled. She is well liked in the school, witty and kind, but like a majority of her seventeen- and eighteen-year-old classmates, she has never had a boyfriend or been on a real date, and she seems deeply embarrassed by the mere mention of it. "Oh, no, no, no—no boyfriends," she says, shaking her head. "I'm not ready for that. And my parents *definitely* are not ready." There are several young men enamored of her at the school, but they have never let her know how they feel except in the most oblique and veiled ways, which is also typical at Whitney. It is traditional here for guys to profess their admiration for Whitney girls in the final week before graduation, when they are all about to go off to different colleges and it's way too late for anyone to do anything about it. The social scene is refreshingly retro here. Angst over relationships that don't exist greatly outweighs the more typical high school preoccupation with relationships that *do* exist, and this arrangement seems conducive to learning: Pining for a romantic relationship is invariably less distracting at school than actually having one. Young people actually talk about morality and their personal conduct in the same breath at Whitney, where being "a good kid"—or at least maintaining that appearance—seems to be the norm. At "real" American high schools, it is not unusual to see girls and boys kissing on campus while students walk by their lip-locked friends and barely notice. At Whitney, such a sight is all but unheard of, and would make for a jaw-dropping spectacle if it did occur. It is not exactly cool to be unattached here, but it carries little stigma; open displays of affection, however, are considered decidedly *un*cool.

Irene's struggles with her course load this year are mirrored by her conflicts over what will happen next: Should she choose a college to pursue an interest in biology? In pre-med? In journalism? Her interest will determine her college choices, assuming she gets in everywhere she has applied—which may be an unrealistic assumption (she's going for the very top schools without the very top grades). She penned a first attempt at a college application essay in which she portrayed herself in a flip sort of way as a super girl who took on all three careers at once—a leaden piece of writing she soon discarded in favor of a more personal and telling story in which her wit and writing skills shone. She wrote about her lucky pants, which she had worn on many a triumphant occasion (aced exams, passed driver's test, soccer wins, a student election victory) and that she therefore absolutely had to wear to take her SAT II tests (the subject-specific tests that supplement the general math and verbal exams of the SAT I). Unfortunately, all that constant wear had left her pocket full of holes, and when she sat down to take the all-important college entrance exams, her pencil lead refills and erasers were gone. She cast frantically around for some sort of writing implement, getting only shrugs and shakes of heads from the proctor and her fellow students, until someone finally took pity on her and passed over an extra lead core for her mechanical pencil. But no eraser. She sat there a moment, paralyzed at the thought of having to bubble in hundreds of answers without the ability to erase a single one. Then inspiration struck: She reached into her mouth and removed one of the two little rubber bands from her braces. She wrapped it around the end of her pencil, then tried to erase a mark. It worked—crisis solved, just as the timer started and the kids cracked open their SAT workbooks. "How incredibly ironic that a quarter-of-an-inch rubber band, a harness of torment for the mouth, proved to be a jewel in a time of despair.... Unfortunately, my braces are coming off in a week or two: will I manage to survive college?"

Irene came up with a small story that tells a great deal about her and her resourceful personality, much more than her grandiose first effort. It was one of the best essays that came out of Whitney that fall: entertaining, original, and charmingly self-deprecating, yet she managed to mention several of her accomplishments and pursuits without ever sounding boastful. She topped it off by photocopying her essay with one of the small circular bands hanging in the upper margin.

The essay highlighted a cleverness and sparkle in Irene that has been all too difficult to spot of late, which is why Ziolkowski is worried about her. Like so many of her friends, Irene has become fixated on her grades, on accumulating the sort of transcript she needs for college; the curiosity and sense of discovery and joy she once felt for learning have been all but extinguished, even as she has put together a report card most high school students in the nation would love to have.

Ziolkowski knows Irene is not unique: One of the conundrums facing Whitney's teachers and administrators lies in balancing genuine learning and experience of academic subjects with the sometimes conflicting need to shine in objective measures of a school's success—test scores, AP offerings, GPAs. Mr. Z is deeply involved with the school modernization program Brock is championing, the introduction of new technology and computers in the classroom, which the physics teacher welcomes—to a point. He worries that the technology is no panacea for the isolating nature of being at Whitney and that it could even make matters worse while doing little to resolve the grades-versus-learning conflict he sees growing in the classroom day by day.

This conflict has been on his mind since before the school year began, when he spent the last days before classes helping a young science teacher he recruited clean out her new classroom. The long-delayed emptying of Room 24 was something of a watershed for Whitney, marking the end of an era and the final departure of a beloved personality with a most unsentimental, sedan-sized trash bin parked at the classroom door. With Mr. Z's help, the bin rapidly filled with a papery tide of manila folders, old lesson plans, dog-eared workbooks, teacher guides, newspaper clippings, chipped microscope slides, stubs of pencils, dried-out pens, bits of chalk and crayon, an Easter basket—the stuff of twenty-five years of teaching, priceless to its owner, useless to her successor, reduced to landfill. Ziolkowski found himself staring at the eclectic collection of old papers, posters, and magazines, some of it used daily for decades, bits and pieces of it untouched for nearly as long, wondering how the school would compensate for this loss as he heaved armful after armful of Gin Pooler's life into the old green Dumpster.

Pooler—that's how all her students referred to her, last name only, a measure not of disrespect but of awe—had died seven months earlier, a little more than midway through the last school year. In all the months since, no one had found the heart to dismantle her domain or to wade through her cabinets, drawers, and closets. "No one here wanted to say good-bye," Ziolkowski told Nita Song, the new teacher who had inherited Pooler's room and who was understandably shocked at the immensity of the cleanup task confronting her. "It'll be okay. We'll get it done."

Everyone had known about the cancer diagnosis and treatments for five years, and Pooler's decline in the last few months had been obvious to all. Yet her death seemed to take the school by surprise. None of the kids and few on the faculty truly believed she could be vulnerable to anything. She had been a fixture at Whitney since the school opened, the one teacher about whom all the students invariably warned their kid sisters or brothers, the instructor who intimidated them, the teacher they loved, one of a handful they remembered years later. Ziolkowski would hear them standing around the lockers outside his physics lab: *Wait till you get Pooler, she'll eat you alive,* the older kids would tell the underclassmen gleefully. *Wait till you see her slides,* they'd say cryptically. *Just wait, man, you'll never want to eat cauliflower again.* Three of the teachers at Whitney had been her students; they told the same stories, too. Even Dave Bohannon deferred to her; when she asked him to do something, he could never say no.

Pooler was all angles and straight lines, nearly six feet tall, with an erect, brusque, almost military bearing that matched her no-nonsense, unedited classroom demeanor. "That's a poor excuse for an excuse," she once snapped at a student who claimed she couldn't take a test because her pen wouldn't work. Pooler grabbed the pen the girl was twiddling, struck a match in the middle of class with a severity that made kids three rows away flinch, heated the ballpoint, then returned the restored writing implement to the gaping student. When Pooler said, "Now, get to work," every head in the classroom simultaneously whipped downward in concentration, excuses vanishing from their brains, at least for the next fifty-five minutes. Pooler was at once unique and a throwback to another age: She doggedly included a section on etiquette and table manners in her curriculum, insisting the kids desperately needed to learn how to act, and she forced them to tend roses she had planted on the sparse concrete campus, arguing they needed to grow something besides grade point averages. Only Pooler could have gotten away with the collection of medical slides she had assembled for health education, conveying to generations of underclassmen the perils of unprotected sex with a host of ghastly images, including an unfortunate growth that resembled the now-legendary cauliflower. Only Pooler would leave in the middle of the school day to hunt down a frequently tardy and absent student who she correctly guessed was at home in bed sleeping, not sick. She shook him awake, terrorized him, then ordered him to get to school, teacher and truancy cop rolled into one. The learning Pooler's students remember best seems to have less to do with science and more to do with living, which may be why so many of them, against all odds, connected with her, why kids who rarely got dirt under their nails and never cut their own lawns would happily (or at least busily) weed and water Pooler's garden. She was so old-fashioned she was cool, they'd say; it was Pooler they often sought for advice or comfort, sometimes years after leaving her classroom behind. When one eleventh grader was killing himself to graduate ahead of time so he could enter college a year early, it was his old eighth-grade science teacher, alone among the boy's friends and other instructors, who said, "What's your hurry?" No one else had questioned the drive to achieve so much so soon, or the wisdom behind it, until Pooler simply asked, "What will it get you? So you can graduate a year early and start working for the rest of your life a year early?" No one else had framed the essentials so simply for him before. He decided to slow down and graduate with his classmates. "She changed my life," he says, an epitaph any teacher might envy. "Pooler was one of a kind."

As Ziolkowski threw a pile of old files into the trash bin, one flopped open haphazardly, labeled in red: "Manners." Inside were lessons on proper restaurant behavior, what to do when you spot a hair in food served at a friend's house, the basic rules of introduction (use *hello,* not *hi,* in formal introductions, and never *yo* or *how ya doin?*). The accompanying etiquette quiz had three essay prompts, two multiple choices, and a series of true-false statements: *Your bread and butter plate is always on your right side. It's all right to talk with food in your mouth if it's only a small amount. You should never help with the dishes, you're a guest and guests don't work.* Pooler's handwriting, bold strokes with red felt-tip, provided the answer key.

No one expects that her young replacement in Room 24 would or could fill the void Pooler has left at Whitney. And while he prizes his own ability to forge connections with his students, Ziolkowski's not the sort to work the physics of place settings and etiquette into his lesson plans (he once left a partially dissected owl pellet he was using in class on his dining-room table—all summer). But he sensed during that day of cleanup that there was something more fundamental at stake in this changing of the guard, something the school could not afford to chuck in the trash along with the old files: this insistence of Pooler's that there are things of value, unforgettable things, that must be taught whether they fit into the official curriculum or not. Pooler believed in the importance of a kind of learning that could not be measured by SATs or GPAs or the ever-growing legion of standardized tests mandated by state and federal governments, tests that have everything to do with satisfying bureaucracies but which, at best, quantify only a piece of what ought to go on in a classroom. We may have lost Pooler, Ziolkowski found himself musing, but we shouldn't lose the big idea she embraced, the reason her students remember her so well: the simple notion that good grades and good learning are not necessarily the same thing. And that the learning should take precedence. This is what Ziolkowski figures kids like Irene need to remember, to believe.

Of course, that is easier said than done in an education system in which test scores are the sole arbiter of a school's reputation—and budget—or at a school like Whitney, where anything less than an A could throw a kid into depression or send hyperambitious parents charging to the principal's office to demand an explanation (and a better grade). So many of them harbor the constant dread that just one slip, just one bad semester, might cut short the dream journey to Stanford or Princeton or MIT. It could be particularly tough in a class like physics, where the Twilight Zone mysteries of gravity, light, and time might endlessly enthrall Ziolkowski, but capture the imagination of only a handful of students each year. The rest, for the most part, simply wrestle with the graphs and equations until they score the grade they need, then move on—competent, but uninspired, learning little that stays with them over time.

So he has been mulling over a question: Could he take a page from the Pooler book and change that grades-versus-learning equation, at least for a little while? He had been jolted recently by something a friend said to him about her own college experience: She once had a professor who introduced himself to his new class by announcing, "There is room for only one teacher in this classroom. And that is me." He was supposed to be quite brilliant, but Ziolkowski's friend immediately dropped the course. The story struck a chord: To Ziolkowski's way of thinking, a guy like that shouldn't even *be* in education. There had to be room for many teachers in a classroom; everyone should be in a position to contribute knowledge and insight if they so chose, rather than just receiving it from on high. Because if kids could teach something, really teach it, it meant they had to *know* it.

So, with that in mind, he has been trying to devise a project, some sort of experiment or research problem or independent study, that will allow his class to learn physics and also teach each other—and their physics teacher—something new. Not just about the equations and mechanics of physics, but about scientific curiosity, independence of spirit, and self-reliance. He still had to work out the details, but he figures on spending a whole quarter on it, a project he envisions as less about learning science and more about learning to be a scien*tist*, less quantifiable, perhaps, but more meaningful, something that would serve his students well in college and in later life. He wants it to be something that will *stick*. And yeah, something that will let them pass the test and get a good grade, too. Ziolkowski, like Pooler before him, is a realist, and he knows you've got to feed the beast even while you're bending the rules. *Especially* when you're bending the rules.

It could be something they'll remember for the rest of their lives, Ziolkowski figures. Or it could be a disaster they'll try hard to forget. As smart as they are, he knows, most Whitney students prefer structure and predictability. They'll say, *Mr. Z, tell us what chapter to read, give us the lecture, and we'll ace the test.* And they will. Just about every time. They are test-taking machines. But Ziolkowski has in mind a new sort of challenge, something unpredictable, independent, outside the box, where the usual test-taking strategies and all-night cram sessions won't cut it. He knows some of the students— some of his best, probably—might fight him on this, balking at the newness, the long days or weeks it might take when they are used to cramming at the last minute, and the uncertainty that is anathema to kids who have their eyes on the bottom line of grade point averages and the admission standards of the Ivy League. *We're doing great with the status quo,* they'll say. *Why change things?* But for kids who have lost their way just a bit, for kids like Irene, and for those who have struggled all year, it could be a turning point. Whatever the outcome, Mr. Z is not the sort who can do the same thing in the classroom year in and year out. Every year is different. Cleaning out Pooler's room only helped crystallize for him just how much might be at stake: The school has a vacuum this year it has never had before. Ziolkowski was going to do his part to help fill it.

"Next quarter," he tells his class, "we're going to do something completely different. You are going to teach me. And it's going to be totally cool."

In art class, Nizzy is pining, as only a freshly minted thirteen-year-old can pine. Shyly, in the minutes before Ms. Agrums calls her class to order, she shows off a poem about a boy she has eyed since second grade ("Five years of hell!" she moans), who has remained stubbornly oblivious to her affections (he's still twelve, after all, with the smooth face and soprano voice of a choirboy and an attention span more suited to Game Boy than the *Dating Game*). The phrase, "I love you," appears eighteen times on the poem's single, double-spaced page. "Do you think it's too mushy?" she asks without a trace of irony, as she sets to work on the latest class project—creating a collage-covered portfolio to hold the year's work.

Nisreen is Irene's opposite number at Whitney: the charming seventh-grade motormouth with heart doodles on her notebooks, still figuring out how to cope with six very different teachers instead of the customary one at elementary school. If Irene's considerable achievements over the years, along with her occasional mental and physical exhaustion, exemplify the benefits and costs of spending six years at a premium academic-prep school, Nisreen's foundering start here reveals the culture shock that can send many incoming preadolescents reeling in their first year of six.

For Nisreen, the running tally of grades as her first report card approaches tells the story: a C in math, a B in science, don't know about English yet, a D in social studies. This is not the sort of performance expected from the middle daughter of a Whitney math and physics teacher. Her status is made all the tougher by an older sister doing well in her junior year and a sixth-grade brother with straight As, champing at the bit for his turn at Whitney. Her history teacher has taken to reporting her poor performance to Nisreen's mom during daily visits in the faculty lounge; the seventh-grade math teacher has repeatedly mentioned poor attitude and inattention in pre-algebra.

"Oh, that drives me crazy. Nobody else has to put up with their mom knowing every little detail, every day. She's always here—I can never get away from her," Nizzy moans dramatically, though she is the sort of person who smiles even when she's complaining, making it hard to know how upset she really is. "'Course, there's an upside: When I forget my lunch money, I can always borrow a buck or two from her."

So far, Nizzy's only clear shot at an A on her first Whitney report card, besides gym, is in the sanctuary of Ms. Agrums's room. "Thank god for art," she says with a shrug. "But I'll do all right. Seventh graders are expected to flounder here, except for the geniuses. And that ain't me."

If floundering isn't exactly expected here, it is not all that unusual for seventh graders to find the transition difficult. Whitney has long tried to make life easier on its smallest members by offering student-tutors to all who need them and by pairing up older student mentors with incoming seventh graders, although this practice, once universal, now seems more sporadic.

The world inside and out of school has changed since Shirley Wold entered Whitney. The academic demands have never been greater, with new testing, new graduation requirements, and new, more advanced subjects confronting the incoming kids. The preference is for seventh graders to begin first-year algebra right away, leaving time for six full years of higher math, including at least one year, if not two, of calculus for a majority of Whitney students. Shunting new students into pre-algebra burns a whole year and throws this equation off, decreasing the number of kids who have room on their schedule for calculus or other advanced math. But the catch-up time is unavoidable for many students, particularly from some of the more troubled elementary schools in the ABC District.

At the same time the scholastic demands have grown, the incoming classes also seem to be more sophisticated about life's realities—and more exposed to them—than past generations. Some of the seniors are openly envious of the social skills of the underclassmen, who as a group seem far less shy and retiring than their elders. Older brothers are getting advice from younger siblings on how to meet girls; Nisreen, for one, has no trouble talking to the older kids and holding her own in Art I, which is one of the few classes at Whitney with a mix of all grades in the same room at the same time.

There's a downside to this precociousness, however: Several of Nizzy's twelve-year-old girlfriends are already sneaking beers and smoking marijuana, and these worrisome pursuits accelerated—alarmingly so, Nisreen feels—once they arrived at Whitney and found like-minded older kids to hang with after school. At least one of her friends is sexually active now; Nisreen and most other kids in her circle disapprove, although they would never reveal the kid's identity to any adult unless they perceived some imminent physical danger. Nisreen, while flighty in some ways, is sensible where it counts, not a follower of the pack and certainly not anyone's doormat. "Oh, gross," is her take on a certain Whitney junior who kept hitting on some of the taller seventh-grade girls until an observant counselor told him to back off. Nisreen feels little pressure at Whitney to join her minority of friends who drink or experiment with drugs. If anything, the peer pressure goes the other way, to *steer clear* of sex, drugs, and alcohol. "Most of my friends think like I do: That it's just stupid to get into all that. Like I already don't have enough in my life to deal with? Soccer, piano, volleyball, homework, my parents, more homework. Jeez, I barely have time to go online, much less get into all that other stuff."

Nisreen turns to the painstaking task of gluing colored tissue paper in an elaborate, repetitive pattern on two large sheets of heavy-duty cardboard. Today the class is deeply into a weeklong project of constructing portfolios for their work, using the layers of tissue and clear-drying white glue to create a lacquered, stained-glass effect. The color scheme has to demonstrate the set of design elements and color principles the class just learned, and they will be graded not only on artistic merit and craftsmanship, but on their understanding of the principles Agrums has taught them with the same detailed notes and rigorous explanation of theories that the kids are getting in science class. After teasing the kids with the drawing-on-the-right-side-of-the-brain demonstration on the first day, Agrums has spent the entire beginning of the year not on drawing, but on color theory and the basic elements of design. The kids are champing at the bit, but she insists on bringing them along slowly, building skills and knowledge. Art the Agrums way begins with *unlearning* a number of things the kids thought they knew, but which will get in the way of drawing well—most notably the ingrained habit of drawing what you expect and remember rather than what you actually see (the heart of the left-versus-right-brain theory).

The results of the portfolio exercise are quite gorgeous; most of the kids from past classes end up keeping theirs for years. Nisreen, of course, provides a running commentary on love and life while she works—"My mom was freaking over the summer, because all my friends got their Whitney admissions letters and none came for me, and I was worried I wouldn't get in; Jeez, that would have been a disaster, we already fight enough about other stuff…"—until Agrums shushes her in her best stern-teacher voice. "Do I have to separate you, Nisreen? Or are you going to STAY QUIET?"

"Sorry, sorry, sorry," she says with a silver-braces smile. "I'm zipping it."

Debbie Agrums hates talking in class, but she gets a kick out of Nisreen, partly because the seventh grader is passionate about art, partly because her talkativeness is a bit of a relief—most of the seventh graders are stubbornly monosyllabic when they're not whispering to one another. (Dr. Brock has a story about one of Agrums's students she finds particularly amusing: The principal asked the thirteen-year-old boy what he thought of Aisha's Unity Rally. The kid thought a moment, then said tonelessly, "It was emotional." When he tells the story, Brock does a startlingly good imitation of a sullen teenager's sullen mumble. "Is that good?" he asked the student. The kid thought about it for a good five beats, then said, "I dunno. But it was emotional. I guess that's okay.")

"I love my little seventh graders," Agrums says. "The hormones haven't kicked in yet; they haven't gotten crazy and surly like the eighth graders. They actually want to learn."

This year's Art I class shows particular promise and talent, Agrums thinks, from the three boys affectionately nicknamed the "lunkheads" for their likably clueless behavior around girls (and pretty much everyone else), to her older juniors and seniors, who have discovered belatedly the importance of balancing hard-core academics with an invigorating dose of fine arts. This sudden discovery happens every September for some, but more so this year, as the University of California has made at least one year of art or music a requirement rather than an option for its future applicants.

Next year, the state of California is making art study a graduation prerequisite as well, for the first time ever, which is likely to make her classroom a very crowded place. "About time, too," Agrums tells her class. "Art should be part of every well-rounded education."

Her classroom is a bustling sanctuary, busy even during lunch periods, when she lets whoever wants to work, eat, or hang out linger until the next class begins. "It's a safe place for them," she says. "These kids, for a lot of them, it's all academics. They need some hang-around time. That's why they stay here, or in the halls, after school. Ironic, isn't it. If they're home, they have to study. They stay at school to get some time off."

The reputation of Whitney rests with its academics, but Agrums's unheralded, one-woman art program, where kids produce college-level (and sometimes professional-caliber) work, is one of its unexpected gems. Her students come to her mostly unschooled in any sort of artistic technique, but they leave her room painting, drawing, sculpting, and weaving with impressive sophistication. Her room is a chaotic hodgepodge of works in progress and finished pieces accumulated over the years and purchased at the annual art show and fund-raiser she and her advanced students stage during Whitney's Open House (where Agrums is her own best customer, spending hundreds of dollars to snap up her favorite student pieces).

Whitney's remarkable art program exists not out of some grand design, but because Agrums was already here when Whitney evolved into an academic magnet school from its vocational/alternative school origins. It continued because she is passionate about using art to bring balance into the lives of kids who might otherwise be consumed by academic drudgery. Just as crucially, it exists because Agrums pays to make it exist, having worked out the finances long ago with her husband, who also teaches and who doesn't object (too strenuously) when she pumps a substantial percentage of her salary into keeping the kiln and the paints and the potter's wheels and the handpresses going. When the teachers went on districtwide strike a decade ago and the administrators and nonunion substitutes took over running the school, she couldn't stay out. Though she supported the union's position, she just couldn't bear the idea of anyone disturbing her equipment or ruining her carefully collected sets of brushes and watercolors and expensive pastels. Without her watchful presence, things would disappear, they would be broken, and that would be the end of everything she had built. Who knew what might happen to the kids' work, months of accumulated effort? Agrums's priorities could not be swayed by a contract dispute; if she abided by contract terms on overtime and personal expenses, Whitney would have nothing like its current art program. She apologized to her colleagues, but she just had to cross the picket line. She still worries some of them never quite forgave her. She's kept to herself ever since, rarely lunching with the other teachers. She badly misses her old friend Gin Pooler; the science teacher had convinced Agrums, like a lot of others at the school, to come with her back to Cal State to get their master's degrees a few years back. Agrums might not have done it without that urging.

The art teacher occupies a peculiar place in the academic school, she knows, one that is not always appreciated. She has nearly, though not entirely, given up trying to convince dubious parents of their children's ability to pursue art as a course of study; she has had difficult meetings with several of her current stars' parents. She cried when Cecilia told her about her portfolio being hurled into traffic, and her maternal instincts suggested she ask for a meeting and try to work things out. The look of terror on her pupil's face at the suggestion, as well as prior experiences with being shouted at by other parents who brook no distractions from pure academics, told her that such a meeting would be a mistake.

She now contents herself with creating a refuge for talented students who may never get a chance to pursue their artistic longings after high school and so deserve as good a program as she can offer. After more than two decades of teaching, Agrums still bounces around her classroom with enthusiasm, oohing and ahhing over kids' pieces, the long drive to her home in semirural Yorba Linda (birthplace of Richard Nixon) flashing by in a happy blur when one of her students does something great. "Or, even if it wasn't so great," she says, "but just something that was great for them—that's such a high for me."

She remembers Ron,* a student of hers a few years back, a James Dean clone, she calls him. He was wild, undisciplined, a constant behavior problem. When he was old enough to drive, he would hop in his car with a few friends and drive to Las Vegas for the weekend, playing blackjack and craps, trying to come up with mathematical models to boost their chances of winning. They'd arrive back just in time for school on Monday, often with thousands in their pockets.

Over the course of the school year, Agrums grew close enough to Ron for him to share his secret, the reason he could get away with such hijinks: his father was a powerful chieftain in one of the Triads—Chinese Mafias. Ron wanted to go to art school, but he knew it would never be allowed. She still has some of his pencil drawings, delicate, beautifully shaded. Her collection of student artwork, dating back to the seventies, is like a photo album to her, each piece with its own story. She wonders what became of Ron.

She worries about the pressures her students endure, good kids who try their best, who are, by and large, well behaved and anxious to learn. They confide in her inside the closed world of the art room, encouraged by an atmosphere that feels separate from the hectic pace of the rest of the school, a room where an hour can glide by effortlessly and, unlike virtually every other class, the kids actually wish the period wouldn't end. Some of the stories kids share with her horrify Agrums: two students have confided that they were beaten for failing tests. Another shamefaced and confused kid said a parent told him it was okay to cheat if he earned an A, because his future was at stake. Just don't get caught, he was warned.

"How do you counter that?" Agrums says. "To his credit, this kid had the character to say, no, I'm not going to do that. That's so cool. I'd like to think this school and the values we teach here had something to do with that."

Agrums likes to put on a tough facade with the kids in order to maintain discipline, but few really seem to buy it. They behave in her class for the most part because they like her, not because they fear her. And when that doesn't work, it drives Agrums crazy: Even after all the years of teaching, she is still stricken when a student doesn't like her class, which in her mind is the same as not liking her. She frets and obsesses over it, wondering if she said something wrong or hurtful without realizing it, or if the kid needs some help and isn't getting it. Like Linda.*

Linda is the ringleader of a coterie of giggling seventh-grade girls, rolling her eyes at the teacher's every remark and not-so-quietly jeering Agrums since the first day of class. The art teacher has repeatedly reprimanded her, which only seems to make things worse.

"What's up with Linda?" Agrums asks another girl after class.

"I don't know," the girl answers. "She says you pick on her."

"Well, yeah, I need to get her attention somehow."

The girl looks at her teacher, who isn't much taller than most seventh graders, and you can see the emotions playing out on her young face as she debates whether she should share the peculiar wisdom of the preteen girl, which on the nature of interpersonal relationships among seventh graders is encyclopedic in its depth and breadth. She likes Agrums, and she is no fan of Linda's, and that decides it for her. "You should know she's poisoning the other girls in class about you, about what a bi— I mean, about how rotten you are. And they'll go along with it because she's not very nice to her friends, either, and they figure better you than them."

The art teacher is stunned. Linda skillfully managed to create a situation in which she could both misbehave and simultaneously gain sympathy from the friends she routinely mistreats. Whatever Agrums does from here—whether she lets her get away with it, or reprimands her—Linda wins. If Linda would just use those smarts for art, where she has demonstrated raw talent and considerable finesse, she'd be an A student, Agrums glumly observes after her informant departs.

A few days later, Agrums gives the class a quiz on the principles of color theory ("Which color scheme is analogous?" Nisreen hisses in a panic as she hastily crams for the test in the two minutes left before it begins). Agrums spots Linda cheating during the test, sneaking a peek at her notes, then hastily scribbling her answers.

The art teacher asks Linda to stay after class and then confronts her. Linda responds, "I didn't cheat," then sits in stony silence, shaking her head, eyes downcast, avoiding Agrums's stare as the teacher says, "I know what I saw." Linda just keeps shaking her head, eyes fixed on the tabletop.

It's not really about the cheating—Agrums will fail Linda on the quiz, but that will have a negligible effect on the girl's grade...in isolation, at least. It's what will happen tomorrow and the next week and the week after that one that the teacher worries about.

"I know you don't like me, and that's okay—you don't have to," Agrums says, standing over Linda, arms crossed.

"For you to be this nasty at this young an age, you must have had something bad in your life happen to you. You've got a hard shell, but I think maybe you're really sweet inside all that toughness. You couldn't draw so beautifully otherwise."

The girl, her expression hardening, looks away. The room is uncharacteristically quiet, the only other sound coming from the opposite corner of the room, the chalky soft whisper of pastels as Angela works on an abstract piece, oblivious to all around her. When Linda says nothing, Agrums prepares to walk away, until she sees a silent tear trickle down the girl's face.

She is reminded of another student, Raymond,* whom she can barely speak to these days. He is graduating this year, his sights set on a prestigious college, a goal he is about to reach despite (or, rather, because of) a reputation for cheating and a smirking arrogance—and parents who always seemed to excuse his behavior and bail him out of trouble. The boy is talented, but he never studied for tests, and rarely handed his work in on time, if he handed it in at all.

Early in his career at Whitney, Raymond had worn out his welcome in the art room, but this year, he swore he had reformed. Agrums reluctantly accepted him in an advanced class after several other teachers urged her to give him another chance, and after she extracted from him numerous promises of good behavior.

Whitney's reputation for having mostly well-behaved kids, with few of the hard-core behavioral problems many other high schools face, is well deserved—but it has led to a lackadaisical and easily manipulated discipline system when there is misbehavior. Agrums once assumed star students with their eyes on prestigious universities would be afraid to misbehave with so much to lose, but she learned the hard way that that is not always the case. After a short honeymoon, Raymond reverted to form, ignoring repeated warnings about incomplete work, failing to complete assignments on time, then lying about it and claiming, among other things, that it had been Agrums's screwup, not his.

When she threatened to give him a failing grade for the course, Raymond's father called to complain, and Agrums finally saw where the child's attitude originated. The father's goal was not to find the truth about his child's performance—he showed little interest in ample evidence that this incident was only one of many. Agrums concluded from his bluster and arrogant manner that he merely wanted to bully her and anyone else he could into raising his son's grade. There were threats of formal complaints, of going to the school district, of lawsuits over the potential damage to Raymond's future prospects. In the end, Agrums let the boy turn in the assignments late—they were excellent—and then she graded them down for lateness. He received a C he did not deserve. And another chance to smirk.

Agrums does not want to turn around in six years and see that same smirk on Linda's face.

"Please look at me," the art teacher says gently. "Look at me."

Slowly, Linda's brown eyes meet Agrums's.

"It is just a hard shell, isn't it? I hit the nail on the head, didn't I?" Agrums says. "Somewhere, somehow, you've had a hard time."

More tears fall, still silently. The eyes go back down, but then Linda nods, two little bobs of her head that barely disturb her shining black bangs.

Agrums stares at her a moment. "Okay," she says quietly. "Maybe we can start over fresh tomorrow. I'll see you then."

Linda looks suspicious—the lecture on cheating she expected to get never arrived—and so she gets up without a word and leaves, clutching her books to her chest. A sleeve shoots up and discreetly wipes away the tears before Linda is out the door. Agrums hears a burst of girlish laughter from outside—Linda's friends. She isn't positive, but she thinks Linda's laugh is not among them.

"It's a start. Maybe. We'll see."

Across the room, Angela looks up from her pastels, her hands a red mess. "Did you say something, Ms. Agrums?"

The art teacher just smiles and shakes her head, then walks over to gaze at Angela's work, lavishing her with praise.

9

Comp time is approaching—the weeklong period of exams that marks the end of each quarter at Whitney High. Everything tends to pile up in the two weeks before the testing begins: work, meetings, college application deadlines, good news, bad news, problems. Lots of problems.

The epicenter seems to be Shirley Wold's desk, a mass of Post-it notes, pink and blue referral slips, transcripts, and files. She has been meeting nonstop with her problem children and their parents, trying to set things right before it's too late, salving the insecurities of valedictorians who live in terror of a mere B, and bolstering the flagging confidence of probationary students who would trade limbs for that same B. Wold's computer is barely visible beneath piles of papers, which is perhaps a good thing, because the debris muffles the sounds that keep emanating from the machine: Thanks to some of her favorite hacker students, the computer has stopped issuing the relaxing sounds of flowing water she chose at the beginning of the school year and instead makes random, crude comments and yelps in the voice of indolent cartoon character Homer Simpson. Without warnings, he may shout *"D'oh!"* or *"Can computers do that?"* She keeps meaning to have them change it back, but so far she hasn't gotten around to it.

One day in late October, she sits down in the faculty lounge with the other science teachers for their department meeting and sighs. "I met with John's* parents," she says.

Nita Song, the new science teacher in Gin Pooler's old room, laughs uneasily. She had referred the ninth-grade student to Wold after his parents called to complain about their son's poor progress report, an advance warning mailed to some parents to let them know that their child's upcoming report card might not be satisfactory in at least some areas. "Unsats," these forms are called, and some of the kids are highly skilled at intercepting them, screening the mail before mom or dad. When Wold doesn't hear from a student's parent after an unsat goes out, she always makes a follow-up phone call to make sure the news got through. John's arrived unscathed, with predictable results: His mother called the next day, beside herself. He was a smart kid, but had been defiant in class, refusing to complete assignments, and his grades had suffered. He just wouldn't listen to Song, and his parents seemed to gravitate between despair and denial that there was a problem. "So what happened?" the science teacher asks.

Wold shakes her head. "It was interesting. The mom asked, 'Do you think he needs professional help?' I said, 'No, he needs to do his homework.'"

The small group of science teachers laughs as they sit in their booth inside the lounge (formerly Whitney's training-ground student restaurant, still resplendent in brushed Toast-master chrome and orange vinyl). Students who pass their tests but skip classes and blow off homework, still expecting to get passing or even high grades in their courses, have often gotten away with such behavior at Whitney. They were smart enough and good enough to pull it off or had parents who'd write phony sick notes or teachers who withered under a bar-rage of pleas and phone calls. No more, Wold says, at least in John's case. "He's a smart kid, but he's lazy; he won't do the homework. Well, we have to hold his feet to the fire. Mom promised to help, too, once I convinced her he didn't need a shrink."

The new grade-level counseling program has been a success, judging by the flow of students into all three counselors' of-fices. Wold seems especially busy. Taciturn teenagers who had never before visited a school counselor now hole up in her office each day. They come to her when they're upset, when they're angry, when they're worried about something—knowing she will listen, that she'll lean over and shut the door for a quiet moment in a notoriously small and unpri-vate school, that she'll try to help regardless of her workload, not judging them when possible, reaming them out when deserved.

Don* comes by later in the day, not with a problem, but to celebrate. He got an A on his latest chemistry test. "I just wanted to let you know," he tells Wold with a smile. This is huge, as far as Wold is concerned. Two years ago, Don had been ready to leave Whitney. He had been misbehaving, re-bellious in class, refusing to do his work. But as Wold had gotten to know him and learned his tragic history, things slowly changed.

A few years back, Don's father died of cancer. Then his mother became deathly ill and returned to her native Philip-pines, leaving him with elderly grandparents, stern, tradi-tional, with whom he had a very rocky relationship. He assumed the role of the man of the family, with a younger brother and sister to watch out for. He was only in seventh grade. Don was terrified, overburdened by the responsibility he felt, angry at everyone—and his schoolwork suffered. But after he opened up to Wold and her fellow counselor, Debra Logan, they talked to his other teachers, who then made a concerted effort to support and mother him, to get him extra help when his grades bottomed out, to give him someone to talk to when he needed that. Now things have turned around for him at last. "You're having a great year," she tells him as he heads back to class.

Wold's role model in this is her late mentor and close friend, Gin Pooler, who helped her as a painfully shy under-classman so many years earlier, then again when she came to Whitney as a young teacher. Wold remembers what Pooler did a few years back for a student whose parents drove him so hard he had no time for friends, no way to relate to any kids outside the world of studying and academics, no time for fun. He would be a shoo-in for HYP (the holy trio, Harvard, Yale, or Princeton), yet he was miserable. So Pooler assigned him to watch television. He had to channel-surf the most popular shows of the time among teenagers—*Melrose Place, Beverly Hills 90210*, a handful of other absolutely worthless melodramas and comedies. Just so he'd have something to talk about with the other kids. Just so he could relax. His parents thought he was working on some kind of project cooked up by his health sciences teacher, which he was. "Your project is to get a life," Pooler told him. Wold loved that.

Such pressures have only grown in recent years as Whitney has been pulled in different and opposing directions by the college admissions arms race, budget cuts after years of plenty, and national education policies and programs that focus on the failures of public education rather than its successes. The school Wold grew up with is long gone. When she entered Whitney, it was still struggling to survive; the teachers and students still had to prove themselves and their approach. Now the school is the gem of its school district and the star of the state, and Whitney kids see themselves, with some justification, as academic Goliaths, having been at the top of the heap so long that many of them have come to take it for granted. There is a constant search for scores and qualities that will impress HYP, and a habitual comparing of test results, not only among students but also among their parents. This year, when two Whitney students scored perfect 1600s on their SATs, one of them—known best at Whitney for his affability and athletic skills—asked the school to refrain from identifying him. His parents overruled his modesty, however, with an advertisement in a community newspaper, congratulating their son for all to see.

The increasing dominance of Advanced Placement classes as the preferred course of study for upperclassmen at Whitney and other college-prep schools epitomizes these sorts of tensions. They have become the gold standard for those who aspire to enter the most elite colleges. AP courses revolve around their climactic tests, given each May by the Educational Testing Service, which also oversees the SAT, which makes them an all-or-nothing proposition.[3] Score high, get college credit. Bomb out, and you have—from many students' point of view—wasted a whole year. Because in AP, it's not necessarily about the learning, it's about the test. The results at Whitney, on paper at least, are impressive—high scores, extra college credit, phenomenal schoolwide passing rates (100 percent of Whitney kids who took AP exams in 2001 in advanced calculus, chemistry, computer science, economics, and physics passed the tests, versus national passage rates in those same courses of 79, 58, 61, 63, and 72 percent respectively). Passage rates in every other AP course offered at Whitney, while not quite 100 percent, exceed the national average as well, sometimes by large margins (97 percent of Wold's most recent crop of biology students passed, versus a national average of 59 percent).

Even so, for many the joy—and, more importantly, the ability to retain and continue to use what they memorize for the test—can be sucked from the AP experience: Kids are learning to pass a test on French or biology or civics, but their interest in the subject may go no further, or may even be extinguished, by the rigors of AP, especially in recent years, as the number of such classes that competitive colleges have come to expect on students' transcripts has gone from one or two to four or six. There are students at Whitney with ten or more. Tony's reaction after taking an AP test at Whitney is fairly common: "Now I'll never have to speak French again." It wasn't about learning the language and taking that knowledge with you for life, he explains: "It was about memorizing enough to do well on the test, then putting it behind you. I just took it to increase my chances of getting into a great college." This is not what Shirley Wold, or any other caring teacher, wants to hear.[4]

Some high schools have grown so concerned about the dark side of APs that they are limiting their offerings. At least one prestigious college-prep school, the private Fieldston School in New York, did away with them completely, offering only in-depth honors courses rather than the survey courses typical of AP. Officials at Fieldston report no measurable impact on college admissions for their graduates, but so far, few schools have taken such a drastic course. Whitney students and parents would probably stage a revolt if any such change were attempted here, Wold says. And many teachers, Rod Ziolkowski among them, are strong proponents of AP courses as sound educational tools—when taught well, and not taken four and five at a time. The students rave about the understanding and mastery of their subject after a course with Whitney's advanced calculus teacher, Steve Murray. "You have to really know physics or chemistry or calculus to do well in those tests—you can't fake it," Mr. Z says. "Yes, you teach to the test, but unlike a lot of the tests our kids have to take, the AP tests are really good ones, and they're based on a course of study designed by experts in the field."

So AP classes and exams are here to stay at Whitney, and students are likely to continue loading up on them, not just in their senior year, but as juniors and sophomores—yet another area in which Whitney students are dealing with stress beyond their grade level. Wold's junior advisees are already beginning to panic a full year before their college applications are due, worried that many of their friends know what their major course of study in college will be, while they still have no idea. Wold and the other counselors have been going around the school, speaking to classrooms of juniors about college choices and the application process, trying to give them a long head start to ease the stress of the whole process, but the effort seems to be stimulating more anxiety. Now she has sixteen-year-olds coming in certain they're abnormal because they don't know what they want to do with the rest of their life. They want everything to be set, well-defined. Uncertainty is an unwelcome sensation in their highly programmed academic careers.

"There's nothing abnormal about that," Wold tells Nellie,* a particularly nervous junior who has no idea what she wants to do with her life. "You don't need to decide that now. Lots of kids don't decide until they've been in college a year or two. Actually, that used to be the norm for many, many students."

"But so many of my friends already have decided," the distraught girl says.

"Believe me, kids who seem to know already only know because someone *told* them," Wold says. "You know how... *certain* about things some of our parents can be. Be grateful you have the chance to make your own choices. Take stock of what you truly enjoy. That takes time. And you have plenty of time."

But the truth is, Wold knows, many kids don't have the time: They must decide on their majors before they are ready. Admissions to the top campuses of the University of California—Los Angeles and Berkeley—are so competitive that kids are constantly checking to see which majors are the least popular and therefore give them an edge in admissions. Pursuing "impacted" majors—the really popular ones, like engineering or film—makes getting in that much harder, which is why more than one Whitney student has considered horticulture as a major, though their interest in the field is nil. Of course, much of this stress is of the students'—and their parents'—own making. There are 3,300 colleges and universities in this country, many that are unique in their offerings or have individual programs that are as good as or better than those at the big-name schools. Fewer than one hundred of these schools have truly competitive admissions; at the rest, most Whitney students would be virtually assured of getting in. But a majority of the students here focus on the same fifteen or twenty schools, the insanely competitive ones with brand-name value. Which is why, at fifteen and sixteen, kids like Nellie are popping Tums to relieve their churning stomachs because they can't decide between premed or prelaw, a business major, or to roll the dice on undeclared.

After Nellie leaves, only somewhat mollified, a senior in a cheerleading outfit comes in sobbing loudly. The twelfth-grade counselor, Gary McHatton, is out, and so Wold ushers her into her office, expecting to hear of some horrible personal tragedy, so extreme is the girl's distress. Wold is relieved to learn that the tragedy is nothing more than a failing grade on a preliminary calculus test. "But I've never failed at math before," she wails. "I'm just not connecting with the teacher on this class."

Wold consoles her, then sets up some tutoring sessions with Aisha, who got a five on her calculus AP test. "It's early in the year, a little tutoring, you'll be fine," Wold promises, then sends a much calmer student on her way.

"I wish every problem could be solved so easily," she says. And then the phone rings.

A short time later, an announcement over the school's public-address system summons all teachers to the faculty lounge for a meeting during the morning snack period. The voice is flustered; the explanation for the unusual, unplanned meeting is ominously vague: "It's a matter of some importance."

Coprincipal Patty Hager is standing in the lounge, anxiously surveying the teachers as they file in and glance back at her questioningly. "We've had some very bad news," she says when the lounge is half full, "but let's wait another minute for everyone. So we only have to do this once."

When the teachers all arrive and the tables and booths are full to overflowing, it's Shirley Wold, looking pale even for her, who rises and clears her throat. "We've had some terrible news this morning. Debbie Logan's son, Tommy, was killed in a drive-by shooting last night."

Teachers gasp, shake their heads. A few begin to cry. Debra Logan is the head of Whitney's English Department. She has left the classroom this year to become one of the three grade-level counselors, one of Shirley's partners. She is funny and earthy and many of the kids call her Mama Logan. Mama Logan is always the one who cooks and bustles and keeps things together for other people when tragedy strikes. Her son, Tommy, had been finishing college, pursuing a degree in accounting. The faculty at Whitney had known him since he was a little boy.

Wold clears her throat again. "We don't know a lot yet. We don't even know the city in which it took place. He was standing on a porch, outside, when a car came up and someone started shooting. He was not the intended victim. Tommy was not and never has been a gang member." She pauses. "The school is sending her flowers, but don't inundate her with calls. . . . She knows how we all feel. She knows."

The gathering of teachers, rarely a quiet group, is struck speechless. That same morning, a large contingent of students had departed school on day passes to attend a funeral for the father of the student council president, who was killed by a drunk driver less than a week earlier. Now this: Tommy Logan was twenty-five, with a four-year-old daughter, Debbie's only grandchild. The teachers filter back out to their classes, searching for the words to tell their students about this terrible blow to one of the school's favorite instructors.

"Tommy had some bad friends," Wold says to a few who linger. "That was Debbie's greatest fear for him, that they would bring him down. But he had really turned his life around. It looks like he was just in the wrong place at the wrong time."

The day takes on a surreal quality after that. Gary McHatton is buried under the load of senior recommendation letters and application packets he must assemble and send out to colleges for his students, so Wold takes on Logan's eighth and ninth graders in addition to her own two grade levels. She will not go home before six or seven at night for the next several weeks.

Then the new geometry teacher, who had been receiving mixed reviews from students (and who, despite his formidable math skills, was utterly bewildered by such mundanities as seating charts), abruptly quits. His untimely departure right before comps, refusing entreaties to stay at least until the exams are over, leaves his students befuddled, their grades unrecorded, and the school scrambling to find a long-term substitute. The kids and their parents flood the counselors with complaints. Whitney parents take math particularly seriously.

Then the Mystery of the Missing Transcripts begins—a dozen or so student transcripts, most of them for National Merit Scholars and other honors students, have vanished from a stack of records in McHatton's frequently unlocked office. Pretty much anyone could have done it. The administration area of the school is wide open, a suite of glass-windowed offices and open-air work areas for the school's secretary and receptionist, where kids come and go without restriction throughout the day, using the area as a hallway and gathering place. This is not a school overly concerned with security: A basketful of dollar bills, collected for coffee contributions and other voluntary donations, sits unattended on the front counter, and in three years, no one has ever taken a dime, Brock likes to boast.

McHatton isn't too concerned. He can get new copies, and he feels no one can do anything shady with the missing ones: colleges get student transcripts from high schools, not from students directly. "I don't see how anyone could use them."

Wold disagrees and launches an investigation. "I think someone who doesn't have the grades wants to doctor a good transcript with a different name," Wold tells him.

Suspicion soon falls on a couple of office aides who have been doing miserably in class this year. One of them might not graduate because of failing grades, though she has her heart set on going to a top college. Someone remembers seeing one of them in McHatton's office alone a week or so ago. But when Wold confronts them obliquely, not accusing them but just asking if they know anything, they stare at her blankly and say almost in unison, "No, Ms. Wold, we don't know anything about missing transcripts," which, of course, convinces her they do. She draws up a list of kids she wants to question, others she wants to recruit to relay to her "the word on the street," then puts it aside, where it quickly becomes submerged beneath the piles on her desk, a mystery that will never be resolved.

Next she heats up a Crock-Pot of chili-cheese dip left over from the weekly faculty potluck lunch, which two of her favorite seniors, the inseparable Lisa and Pearl, scoop up, briefly interrupting their discussion of what they consider to be the miserable dating scene at Whitney. "Thanks, Ms. Wold, you're a lifesaver," they say, heading back out to bring the dip to a student event.

They are replaced by an irate mom who comes in to speak to Wold about her daughter, who forged a note excusing herself from school. The mother had initially confirmed that her daughter's absence was unexcused—she had been cutting classes, not home sick—when the school called on the day of the absence. But when Mom learned the forged note could earn a trip to "Saturday School" as part of the new get-tough discipline policy, as well as disqualify her child from attending the senior prom, she changed her story. She came in to swear she had written the note after all, and that her daughter was, indeed, home sick that day.

Wold listens to her politely and noncommittally, cranks down the volume on her computer before Homer can ask, "Is poopoo one word or two?" then points out the contradictions in the woman's evolving story—to no avail. Mom is adamant. There is little the school can do if a parent chooses to lie for their child. "It provides a terrible lesson, really," Wold says, "but in the end, we'll have to let the kid attend the prom."

Next Wold finds out that her biology class will no longer be able to feature an important fruit-fly laboratory experiment on genetics. Part of the lab requires examining live fruit flies under a microscope, which in the past was done by anesthetizing the flies with ether vapors. The Occupational Safety and Health Administration determined that ether, even small quantities of it, was too dangerous a substance to have around a school, decades of past practice notwithstanding. Wold in the past had tried an alternative method, using ice to knock out the flies, but heat from the microscope light invariably woke them up. Her room had a fly infestation for four years after one swarm rose from the dead and flew off. "I give up," she says. "We'll just use a computer simulation. It's not as good, but that's the way the world works now. We can't type blood anymore, either. We used to use sterile lancets on each other. It was easy and fun. But the state says we can't. Liability issues."

Then she has to haul David into her office to speak to him, once again, about staying out all night. His mom called frantic again, but it's all very dicey for the school, because David is showing up for class and doing his work. Yet he hasn't been home in three days.

"What are you doing, staying out until six A.M.?" Shirley asks him. "Are you crazy? And for three days in a row?"

He begins a long explanation, starting with how he was out late working on a group project on Hawthorne's *The Scarlet Letter*—they had to create a newspaper for the Puritan outpost that was then Boston, he says. He just fell asleep on a friend's floor. ("You never heard of picking up the phone?" Wold exclaims.) The next night he was working on building the school Web site at a friend's house when it got late. And last night he was just parking with friends in the vast Cerritos Mall lot, playing hide and seek with the police and security guards, talking. He finally admits that staying out late probably wasn't the best idea. "I just don't want to be home," he says simply.

"So you were out with Jill*?" she asks, referring to another rootless kid angry over her parents' divorce.

David nods. They have a lot in common, he says.

"Am I going to hear from her parents next?"

"No," David says, "her mom's okay."

Wold is incredulous. "She's okay with her daughter staying out with you till six A.M.?"

"No, she was at my house watching videos and fell asleep."

Wold is confused now. "She was at your house but you were out all night?"

"No," David explains patiently. "That's just what she told her mom."

Wold is continually amazed at the cluelessness of so many parents. So many of them are plugged into the minutiae of grades and college applications, yet remain in the dark about who their kids' friends are, who they may be dating (or if they are dating), and even where they spend the night. She shakes her head and tells David he's got to stop doing this. Something bad is going to happen. "I tell you this not as someone who's lowering the boom—your mom, undoubtedly, will be doing that later today—but as someone who cares about you. This isn't good."

"I know. I'm not going to stay out anymore," he says wearily. He's either made the point he wanted to make—if there was one—or he's just too exhausted to keep it up anymore. "It's too hard to study. I think I bombed my history test last period."

She sends him on his way, having already heard from his mother that he would be grounded for a month and subjected to an early curfew (which David accepts with surprising equanimity—a good sign, Wold decides).

The day winds up with a very different sort of conversation with another young man and his mother. They have come to the office to check the eleventh grader out of Whitney in favor of his neighborhood high school across the district.

"Why?" Wold wants to know. They've taken her by surprise. "He's doing so well here. His grades are good. He's a great kid. He's on track to go to a good college, maybe get a scholarship. What's the problem?"

The boy stares at the floor, as his mother looks both pained and proud of her son. The family has an immigration problem, she finally says. They hired a lawyer to work things out, but he just took what little money they had and accomplished nothing. Now, she says, they're afraid that the whole college application and financial aid process will get them in trouble with immigration authorities. Times are rough for immigrants—9/11 has changed everything. She falls silent then. She doesn't want him to give up his dream of going to college, but she's also afraid.

Her son speaks up then. At Artesia High School, the much larger comprehensive high school he can attend, there are many undocumented immigrants, he says. He'll blend in. After he graduates, he wants to go to work and maybe go to a community college part-time. It's time he helped support his family, he says. Going off to school can wait.

"No," the mother says, "you should go to college. We've been poor so long, a couple more years won't matter."

Her son looks up for the first time and says, "It matters to me."

Wold has to clear her throat. She feels overwhelmingly sad and impressed, watching a boy grow up in front of her eyes, far too soon. At this point, you don't try to talk him out of it, she decides. There's only one thing to say: "I wish you all the best and we'll do everything we can to help you. And if you change your mind, you're always welcome here."

The pair leaves and her room falls silent, until Homer Simpson belches, a welcome tension buster. The hackers did her a favor, she figures, deciding to leave Homer right where he is. Next up, she has seven referrals on her desk for cheating, including four kids in the same class who used the same plagiarized report from the Internet for their homework.

They had assumed, incorrectly, that their teacher didn't actually read every paper. Of course, they deny doing anything wrong. She closes her eyes. Most people at the school consider the week of comps to be the most hectic and tense time at Whitney, but for Shirley Wold, it will be a relief that can't come soon enough.

"Wow, Anna! I cannot believe you actually went out there and performed all by yourself. I never would have been able to do that. That takes guts."

I unconditionally love being Whitney High School's mascot. For the past three years people have come up to me sporadically and said, "You're the mascot, right?" These include faces I have never even seen before....I am genuinely touched with their warmth as they say comments such as *Good job!* Or *That was really cool!*

I am the girl who sports furry pants with suspenders and Mickey Mouse gloves. I am the girl who dances with the referee. I am the girl who jumps up onto the referee's spot on the volleyball court. I am the girl who almost gets kicked out of basketball games for being too rowdy. This is my third year as mascot, and I adore every single minute of it.

Cheerleaders, song leaders, and mascots all serve the same purpose—to support athletic teams no matter what the circumstances may be. However, mascots are slightly different. Being a mascot is not about hitting angles or being sharp. A mascot possesses the privilege to go out on a limb and do what she feels. I cannot do a Russian; I am physically incapable of touching my toes—I hardly ever see them. However, being a mascot allows leeway to ad-lib and improvise according to the situation at hand....

I love meeting new people and interacting with those who do not know me very well because I learn so much from them; after all, I yearn to engage in a career that involves helping others. . . . I get to know people by simply performing solo; people recognize me in the halls and embrace me as I embrace them.

—A note from Anna

10

Comps are over, Thanksgiving has come and gone, November has slipped into December, and what passes for winter in Southern California has arrived, which means most, though not all, of the kids (and all but one of the teachers) have stopped wearing shorts to school.

The tests went smoothly enough, three days given over to them, each day divided into three parts: a two-hour test in the morning; a twenty-five-minute break; then a second two-hour test. The process repeats over two more days, until students are tested in all six of their classes. School lets out at 12:30 so they can all go home and cram on Wednesday and Thursday nights, then crash on Friday.

The quarterly comps are dreaded even by the top students because they can account for as much as 50 percent of a course grade, making for a pretty tense three days. Kids who have maintained their 4.0 for four years know that one bad day or one bad test can blow it all for them. Large groups meet after school to drink coffee, eat pizza, and pore over notes, prepping one another on force-and-motion equations and Spanish irregular verbs. Faces in the halls tend to be tired and grim, and snack time is spent hunkered over textbooks and notes and a guzzled Coke or two rather than actual food, as the kids try to keep straight in their minds the difference between the battles of Bunker Hill and Valley Forge, or the Elizabethan's view of the Great Chain of Being that keeps universal chaos at bay. ("It's God, angels, kings, then everything else is below, right?" Tony asks a study mate who's draining a soda and puzzling over Shakespeare's use of the word *fishmonger* as an epithet in *Hamlet*.) The vending machines, which earn thousands for the band and drama programs in an uneasy battle between tight budgets and empty calories, tend to run dry of all but the least palatable flavors during comp week. Even the kiwi flavors disappear.

"I hate comps," Stella mutters on the third and final day, her round, expressive face set in an unaccustomed frown, her sentiment so widespread there really is no need to voice it. Stella does pretty well in school, and what she doesn't have in grades she makes up with her indefatigable good humor and activities, lots of activities—selling ads for the yearbook at a record pace, shuttling kids in her mammoth pickup truck to eat Korean tofu soup in steaming stone crocks, working after school at her parents' business as a part-time bookkeeper. But comps rob her of her humor, not because she really hates the tests, but because she says her parents tend to rag on her most at these times, complaining about her grades and work ethic. "They think I'm stupid," she says. "At least that's what it seems like." When she received an academic award in one of her classes, she recalls her mother's offhanded reaction: "Oh, they must give those out to *everyone*."

"I don't care," Stella assures her best friend and opposite in life, Christine, with her stellar grades and missile trajectory to HYP. Where no thought remains unuttered with Stella, Christine is more likely to keep her feelings to herself, but neither this contrast nor their academic differences have ever come between them. Christine winces at the careless carnage caused by the parental remarks about the award. Stella waves her off with a lie neither of them believes: "It doesn't matter what they say."

For the kids, relief doesn't come when the comps are over. These students won't relax until the quarter grades are released the following week, a process that has its own peculiar ritual. In most of the classrooms, the teacher sits at the front and summons students, one at a time. They approach like Oliver, but they are given a private peek at their grade in lieu of gruel. Some maintain a poker face, others simply display a look of relief, others whoop, holler, and pump their fists. A few slump or mutter. David is quietly pleased when he ambles up to Mr. Bohannon to find his grade is 78, within striking distance of a B, his late-night wanderings notwithstanding. "Just think what you could have done if you occasionally studied," Bohannon remarks dryly.

Pretty much nothing gets done in any class until this process is finished—the tension is just too great. In civics, Stella and Christine pass the time talking about the anxiously awaited debut of the new Harry Potter movie ("Half the senior class will be absent next Friday," Christine correctly predicts), and passing out pictures of the karaoke square-off between the rival staffs of the yearbook, anchored by business manager Stella, and the school newspaper, *Aspects*, edited by Christine. The loser had to dance in the parking lot to bad techno tunes from Stella's pickup truck stereo; *Aspects* lost and the pictures of Christine and her pained staff getting down are suitably embarrassing.

"Stella," Ms. Charmack calls, interrupting Stella's spirited argument that the Potter books are superior to Tolkien's *Lord of the Rings*.

"Ohhh, I don't want to see my grade," she moans. Still, she slowly walks to the teacher, bends, and squints at the grade book—and a smile splits her face. She claps and hoots at the high mark and says, before she can stop herself, "I can't wait to tell my mom."

The time between comps and winter break is busy at Whitney High, especially for the seniors, who are fully consumed with last-minute college application preparations or by the early-admissions waiting game that many initiated by scrambling to get in their applications by November 1.

Early admission, also called early decision, once existed as a convenience for a modest number of decisive kids who knew where they wished to attend and for universities with an eye toward stable and predictable enrollment numbers. But it has mutated in recent years into a huge collegiate dice roll for seniors, a roller-coaster source of additional stress in the application process that is often more about playing the odds than planning a future. Three decades ago, the pioneers of early admissions intended the opposite effect; they hoped to lower the pressure simply by asking students to promise to attend a given college in exchange for getting an admissions decision by December instead of waiting until spring. Everyone was supposed to come out a winner: the schools would be able to lay plans for each freshman class's size and majors earlier, and the students would be spared months of stress and waiting—if they were accepted.

But the program has backfired, growing by leaps and bounds each year, with applications up 68 percent since the mid-1990s.[5] Elite schools use the program to compete with one another, at a time when warfare over top students is intense. (The competition is so extreme that the Ivy League erupted in scandal in 2002 when admissions officials at Princeton pried into a private Web site at Yale, seeking to peek at decisions by such jointly courted applicants as Neil Bush's daughter.) Students, on the other hand, use early admission not to reduce stress but to boost their chances of acceptance. Many go this route even though they may not be certain of the school they want to attend and despite the fact that promising to go to one school kills any bargaining power they might have to leverage a better financial-aid package by pitting one school against another.

Whitney students, like others immersed in the college scramble, use a variety of Web sites to track and compare the enrollment figures for their favorite schools, mulling over the ratios like stockbrokers managing trades. They know, for instance, that the Ivy League's University of Pennsylvania accepted one out of three of its early-admissions applicants who sought to enroll in 2001—building nearly half the freshman class through the early process—compared to an overall acceptance rate of one in five. Yale accepts about 13 percent of applicants overall, but those who go the early-admission route are twice as likely to get in. Similar odds can be found at Stanford and throughout most of the Ivy League, as well as at a variety of other public and private universities, all of which has fueled the flood of stressed-out early-admissions applicants who hope to play the numbers. The theory goes that weaker students stand a better chance of getting into a top school by committing early, while equal or stronger students considering a range of colleges may be rejected or have their application deferred to be considered with regular spring applications. This plays to students' worst fears, generating even more early-admissions applications, even for kids who would prefer to weigh other options in the spring and who realize they are trading away all their bargaining power to a single school. (In 2003, a growing number of schools responded by ending or altering their early-admissions programs, offering advanced decisions without forcing students to commit.)

Of course, the payoff can be sublime. When Christine gets her coveted early admission to Yale University, she's too excited to sleep that night. Kosha races through the Whitney halls, telling all her friends about her early acceptance to Stanford. When it works, and it's really what a kid wants, they feel there's nothing better, despite the terrible deadlines and extra cost.

Others are not so happy with the experience, as better odds don't necessarily translate into a sure thing. Several kids who had their heart set on similar early decisions instead receive the dreaded deferral letters: not rejections, but wait-and-we'll-see-in-the-spring notices. Several girls walk the halls arm in arm, weeping quietly: No Harvard, no Princeton, at least not yet. Aisha, too, is disappointed at a Princeton deferral, but she is more upbeat and inclined to cast it as a positive, her sights now settled on Stanford or Cornell University in Ithaca. "I love the program there," she gushes. "It's just as well."

"I'm not too happy about it," Ajay says glumly as he drops by the counselors' office. The engineering and technology whiz who started his own Internet company back in seventh grade had talked himself into applying early for engineering studies at Penn. He had sought advice for years from admissions officials there, structuring his course load and résumé accordingly. Now he wonders if he wasted his time and effort. He could still get in, of course, but he is in a funk, unsure of anything—a common reaction to the early-decision deferral. "Now I have to rethink everything. I thought I'd get it for sure. Now I may not even want to go there. Maybe I should stay on the West Coast."

During the same week the early-decision letters begin arriving, a very different wave of stress and giddiness courses through the school, though the source is social this time, not academic: Winter Formal approaches.

Some students are stressed out about going to the dance, about asking others to the dance, about being asked to the dance, about finding novel and bizarre ways to ask someone to the dance. (School tradition involves, among other things, a guy hiding near and sometimes inside an unsuspecting prospective date's locker, then jumping out and terrifying the poor girl between classes—a method that has achieved only mixed results over the years.) Whitney is no different on this score than most other schools, except perhaps for the high percentage of teenagers who are forbidden to date by their parents. The kids in this situation fall into three major categories: those who don't know what to do; those who know someone they'd like to bring to the dance but are too afraid to ask; and those who have elaborate feints and excuses set up to disguise the fact that they are attending with a member of the opposite sex.

Dee,* a junior who has never dated in her life, accepted an invitation that arrived on her computer screen via Instant Messenger, and she is now in a complete meltdown over the impending event. "There is no precedent for this," she tells a friend. "I've never gone out with an actual male. Should I sneak out of the window? Or should I just forget the whole thing?" She buries her face in her hands and sits without moving for several minutes in the art room.

The whole matter is complicated by ethnic considerations and parental restrictions related to them. Dee is Korean American, while her would-be date is Caucasian—a combination somewhat rare here, and one that can entail detailed plans and secrecy to avoid possible parental concerns and culture clashes. Whitney parents often look at their children's high grades, consistent achievement, and problem-free behavior at school, and assume their kids have little to hide. Yet here is Dee, a nervous wreck, morose when she should be happy about her first formal, hatching one silly plan after another so that she can date a boy undetected. In the end, she just ditches him.

Angela has laid elaborate plans of her own to leave for her prom with girlfriends and to have pictures taken at the dance posing with a male friend, clearly platonic, as her official escort. She plans to maintain a secret second photo album, meticulously decorated with her formidable scrapbooking and drawing skills, depicting her arm in arm with her actual date, known as "*that* boy," to her parents.

Tony, meanwhile, managed a coup of his own: He went to the prom last year as a junior despite a household dating ban. His solution: He argued that, because he would be "required" to go to the prom as a senior, he needed to check it out a year ahead of time "so I won't make a fool of myself." It worked, and now he has license to attend the formal on similar grounds. "If it is a school requirement, then it's okay, as opposed to just doing it for the fun of it," he chortles to his friends. "Frankly, my parents don't really want to hear about it. There are certain things in my house we just don't talk about, and sex and dating are at the top of the list. If you bring them up, people just walk away. It's weird."

The jockeying does nothing to dampen enthusiasm for the event itself. If anything, the intrigue and plotting add to the fun. In mid-December, as anticipation mounts for the celebration—and for a blessedly homework-free winter vacation—the students file secret ballots for the formal's six homecoming princesses, one of whom will be homecoming queen. A few days before vacation is to begin, teams of students are dispatched at five in the morning to the homes of the six winners, kidnapping them from their beds, painting their faces, hauling them out to a pancake breakfast, and then carting them to school, still clad in their pajamas.

The young women chosen in the vote are all popular and well liked, and five of the six fit the profile one might expect of a prospective homecoming queen: poised, outgoing, fashionable. The five are on the song, cheer, or flag squads or are varsity athletes. When asked by the school paper how they would spend a day if given the power to do anything they wanted, without limits, they choose skydiving and shopping and a glorious day at the beach; when asked which celebrities they most resemble, their choices include Jennifer Lopez, Julia Roberts, Liv Tyler.

But the sixth nominee would never describe herself as glamorous or poised or ready to parachute into anything other than a bowl of chocolate ice cream. The celebrity she most relates to is rubber-faced comedian Jim Carrey. Her day without limits would be to ride up a cloud to heaven to visit her father, bringing along some of her chocolate birthday cake so she could celebrate her turning eighteen a second time, this time with him. Then they'd both dance like Gene Kelly in *Singin' in the Rain*, except, "In heaven, I'd never step on his toes."

Anna is charmingly flabbergasted at being voted a finalist. She is so flustered when the kids roust her from bed and try to paint the word *Hottie* on her face that she flees the room and ends up going through the day with a blurry scrawl that appears to say *Hotl* instead. She cannot stop grinning, and when she is later selected as the surprise winner of the homecoming queen competition, some of the sadness that has shadowed her ever-present smile for the past year seems to fade as she imagines her father standing beside her. Her teachers are delighted, though few expected her to win. This is not because Anna is undeserving—she is, as are each of the other nominees, a great kid, with her own talents and special qualities. It's just that Anna is not the obvious choice in a contest that could easily boil down to the most superficial, Barbie-doll qualities. She doesn't fit that mold of the typical high school homecoming queen. Yet she proves to be a perfect choice, radiant in her gown, her smile dazzling.

"Just when you're convinced that teenagers are the most shallow and superficial creatures on earth," Shirley Wold says afterward, "they go and do something that is just so cool, so wonderful. I'm so happy for Anna. And it reminds you that there's nothing typical about this group of kids. At almost any other high school, she doesn't win. But here, sometimes, anyway, it seems like anything is possible. They actually got it right."

The next day puts a brutal twist on Wold's words—a difficult reminder that Whitney High is in no way immune to the troubles that afflict other American schools.

Charles, a popular figure on campus, slinks into the school office early, right after first period, to see the seniors' counselor, Gary McHatton. Charles is not himself, McHatton can see: The normally wisecracking, easygoing kid is looking pale, fearful, jumpy. He won't look his counselor in the eye, and though the man has been Charles's teacher, counselor, coach, and friend for years, he did not see this coming. As Charles haltingly explains his problem, the color drains from McHatton's open, ruddy face. He gets up and closes the door, then picks up the phone. Soon Carey Lin, the college-student counseling intern who knows Charles well, is also hunkering down in the office with the distraught student, the door still closed. Passersby look through the large window in the corner office curiously; even at a cursory glance, it's clear something is very wrong.

Soon the other counselors and administrators are buzzing. Someone calls Charles's home and asks his mother to come over as soon as possible. Kay Cottrell keeps trying to reach Dr. Brock, who is sick at home. He usually switches off the phone, and Kay is wondering if she should send somebody over. She worries that Charles has to be watched, that he may even be suicidal, he's so beside himself.

"He was *tweaking*," Carey explains when she emerges from the office later and plops down in a chair in Wold's office. "Crystal meth. He came in for help—his heart started racing in class today and he said he thought he might be dying. He says he's addicted and he doesn't know what to do." She thinks a minute, then says, "None of us really knows what to do."

Tweaking. Crystal meth. Methamphetamine. The words horrify Wold and the others. They always knew some of the kids attending Whitney, as at almost every other American public high school, have experimented with drugs. But it's the sort of thing that's easy to put out of mind—the kids here are so good, no student ever looks or acts high or drunk on campus. If they were doing something outside of school, it was surely limited to the occasional joint, a beer here or there, kids being kids—that was the assumption. But crystal meth is another story, insidious, tough to spot, the drug of choice for power studiers intent on pulling one all-nighter after another and willing to play Russian roulette with heart and brain and blood pressure. A little tweak here, a line or two of powder snorted there, and the drug provides a rush of well-being, an erasing of sleepiness, the ability and will to stay up all night. Night after night if your supply holds. Tweakers can go three, four, five nights with little or no sleep. Just don't let it run out. Because, after a while, after your tweaks have become constant, running out becomes unbearable. But then, so does staying awake.

"He says he's not sure how to stop, but he wants to," Carey continues. "It's great that he came in for help. He started out just using to help study. But now it's out of control. The bad part is, his supplier is a former student here. So we're trying to talk to him, too."

In McHatton's office, Charles's sister and mother are standing next to him now. Brock has arrived and is in there, too. Charles has his head down on the desk. He is a leader, a trendsetter, a cool kid. Students look up to him, follow him. In the office, the staff looks vaguely ill, dreading what will come next, but also trying to get ready. Charles has merely broken the ice.

"This is bad. We've had our eyes closed," Carey is saying. "There are other students doing stuff."

"It's going to be a rough Christmas," Wold agrees. "We've got our work cut out for us."

The best about life and learning at Whitney:

Basically all the academic courses in themselves? Unimportant. While they do play (some?) part in helping you in academics in college I suppose, they won't stick with you the rest of your life. What is the most important, I think, is the discipline you have to learn when your teachers force you to do this assignment or read that book; it's the fact that you've had to do it that will be most important in college because when mom and dad aren't there strangling you and chaining you to your Math Text, you will get the lock and chain out yourself and force yourself to work....

The worst about life and learning at Whitney:

The worst is probably the fact that it's so competitive academically that teachers forget to teach people life beyond the books. In other schools, there are shop classes, cooking classes, home economics classes; those prepare you better for when you have to eventually live on your own. Whitney doesn't provide that so they end up sending out students who are for the most part bookworms but street-smart-wise, useless....They are not in the least bit well-rounded. They know how to do tangents and they can probably tell me how many heart compartments a fish has (two), but if I mention *Beowulf* or modern literature, Ethnic and Asian studies, the

Kashmir crisis, or the oil spills in the North Sea, I only receive
huge blank looks.... If people become that shortsighted, they
will eventually not understand what is going on in the world,
and it is this girl's humble opinion that not all the physics in the
world can bring an end to international hunger.

The Stress Issue:

You deal with it. End of story... Even when there're a
thousand things to do, you can only really try your best, tear
your hair out, buy an extra-shotted cup of Macchiato, and start
getting to work on it. Sure, I stress, I worry, but the thing is,
you can't suddenly turn life off and let it go by while you're
busy wilting under the heavy load of school. Basically, all you
can do is spend an hour crying about The Injustices of My Life
before you shove yourself in the grinder and start working
frantically. Hysterics and commiseration with friends don't solve
a thing...they're just really fun to indulge in once in a while....
When I actually was stressing over homework, grades, weight,
it was mostly from my parents' expectations. Parents expect a
lot from their kids. They want them to set goals for the future,
stick by the goals, and then go on to cure AIDS and the
common cold in between work hours....I guess the stress
comes most out of knowing what your parents want and
striving to please them, yet also knowing what you want and
trying to stay true to yourself. Much of the time, the two refuse
to reconcile....

What I would never change:

Something that I've liked about Whitney is its small,
intimate nature. It is theoretically possible to know every single
person in the school, know all the staff members on a personal
basis, which is something that you'll probably never find in any
other school. There's a kind of familial atmosphere in Whitney
where people look out for one another whether they know
them or not, just because they come from the same school....
In Whitney, it was possible to find people who were like me,
and liked me, rather than merely tolerated me. People who
were interested in who I was. They showed me that I wasn't
worthless because I was a girl, because I couldn't get high

enough grades, they were there for me when home life was
rough, and held my hand walking forward in my life. They
showed me that it's possible to trust someone unconditionally
and not get stabbed in the back.... Whitney gave me
something that really nowhere else has truly given me:
acceptance.

—Cecilia, on her years
at Whitney High School

PART II

Cow Towns and College Boards

*I have never let my schooling
interfere with my education.*

—MARK TWAIN

11

When it opened a quarter century ago, Whitney High School was the last place anyone would have tagged to become a center for scholastic excellence or stress, having entered the world less a home for academe's stars than a dumping ground for its drop cases.

Best known for training short-order cooks and florists, the original Whitney was born to a community where the commitment to learning was so meager its leaders refused to pay a modest annual sum to support the county library system. Instead, they fulfilled their legal obligation by tacking up a shelf at City Hall with a few of the city manager's dog-eared paperbacks and a self-service sign-out sheet. This would be the city of Cerritos's sole gesture at providing a public library for nearly two decades.

It is difficult for those who live outside of Los Angeles— and even for many who call some part of its vastness home— to reconcile the improbable history and geography of Cerritos, California, a community whose name is derived from the Spanish word for "little hills," though this city built on an ancient seabed is utterly flat. (In fairness, misleadingly named communities are a California tradition, begun most famously

in 1887 with the founding of Hollywood, which featured neither holly nor woods.) As late as 1970, Cerritos still clung to
a rural existence that had largely vanished elsewhere in the
sunbaked bowl of the Los Angeles Basin, and given the concrete and asphalt, auto mall and tract home reality of Cerritos today, that past now seems little more than a mirage.

Yet there it was, newly incorporated a decade after the
end of World War II, the last-ditch brainchild of dairy farmers, most of them Dutch and Portuguese immigrants and
their descendants, pushed off their original spreads by a post-
war explosion of suburban growth, home construction, and
the birth of a newfangled enterprise called high tech. They
had watched the nearby city of Lakewood (no lakes, no
woods) rise from nothing on the inland fringe of what was
then the navy town of Long Beach, 3,400 acres of prime
farmland and dairy center paved over in a single season, the
construction crews moving in even as the last harvest was
gathered. One developer alone put up 10,000 houses in two
years, built assembly-line style to accommodate the burgeoning, G.I. Bill–fed demand for homes, part of an enormous
decimation of productive farmland that was unprecedented
in human history and that laid the blueprint for the sprawl of
modern Los Angeles.

So the dairymen moved east, settling in what was then a
sparse farming corner of L.A. County with plentiful water
from shallow artesian wells and a few neighboring towns
built around railroad terminals. They named their city Dairy
Valley, a last stand against encroachment on the agriculture
that once was L.A.'s economic engine but which was looking
increasingly anachronistic in this new landscape of aerospace
and celluloid.

Dairy Valley's unofficial census at its founding listed
3,439 people, 100,000 cows, and 106,300 chickens. The closest thing to a "little hill" within the city limits was Manure

Mountain, a three-story, 6.5-million-cubic-foot mound of cow flop, standing within smelling distance of what would later be the site of Whitney High. The city founders defiantly adopted ordinances to keep suburban sprawl at bay: Building a home on less than five acres was forbidden in Dairy Valley. For a decade the tactic worked, a legal line in the sand that kept the developers at bay while 217 dairies cranked out $100 million worth of milk a year, chicken and turkey farms squawking and stinking next door—all within a short drive of downtown Los Angeles. City council meetings convened at ten A.M., right after morning milking. This was the era in which a single bookshelf was called a library, and the citizens of Dairy Valley considered it a right smart way around the law.

But Southern California's future could be staved off only so long: The era of orange groves and family farms that had sustained Los Angeles since the end of the nineteenth century had played out. The Red Car Line with its twenty-five-cent fares, a model of public transit simplicity L.A. has been spending billions to replace ever since, was being ripped out of the ground right along with the uprooted orchards and demolished packinghouses. All were replaced by subdivisions and suburbs knitted together by six-lane freeways, designed to bear a new generation of commuters with no patience for sitting at train stations when they could sit in their cars instead. There was no longer a reason for a downtown to be a center for anything in this new Los Angeles, with people, commerce, jobs, and culture moving to outlying areas, leaving behind a wasteland of government offices, courthouses, jails, and the cardboard sidewalk shanties of skid row. Dairy Valley sat directly in the path of this march, an increasingly rare and irresistible slice of virgin territory for the bulldozers and Realtors. Surrounded by increasingly dense development, the old immigrant farmers finally gave in and cashed out on land that had become worth far more than the milk and poultry it could produce.

Dairy Valley ceased to exist then, as the sprawling feedlots bought for $600 an acre before the war sold for $30,000 an acre or more by 1965—an enormous sum for the times. After a brief flirtation with renaming the town Freeway City (when the name summoned images of a rosy concrete future rather than dystopian montages of gridlock and road rage), the name Cerritos captured the townspeople's imagination (especially once Manure Mountain was shoveled into oblivion). The name seemed anchored satisfyingly in the region's Spanish land grant, Wild West past, notwithstanding the fact that the actual historic Rancho Los Cerritos is located west of the city; Cerritos actually occupies a corner of another Spanish land grant, Rancho Los Coyotes, though no one cared for a more historically accurate town name linked to the scraggly desert scavenger. No sooner had the city changed its name and lifted its development limits than the tract homes began going up. Within five years the population had doubled, then doubled again, then yet again—topping 15,000 in 1970 and 37,000 in 1972, making Cerritos the fastest-growing city in California at that time. Now with more than 50,000 people, the city has become a model of suburban planning, with more parks and green space than any of its neighbors, a world-class performing arts center, and, finally, a large and lavish public library. The remade city adopted strict laws forbidding unsightly aboveground power lines and drive-through fast-food windows, along with tight regulations on signage (the chain Toys "R" Us, with its famously backward R, was for years ordered to set the letter straight, though the city finally relented on this one point). The amenities were financed through turning a good portion of the old dairy land into a regional shopping center flanked by one of the world's largest and busiest auto malls—twenty-one dealers and acre upon acre of shiny new cars and pickups where herds of cows once tromped, funneling millions in sales tax receipts into the city's coffers every year.

Old and new worlds clashed for years during the transition, with the mayor still trotting out his "educated cow" to chew through ribbon-cutting ceremonies, and livestock sometimes busting loose to nibble the freshly planted lawns and flower beds of newly minted suburban homes. But there was no longer any question about the future of Cerritos. It was destined to become, like most of Greater Los Angeles, a suburb in name only, inoffensive and prosperous rather than glitzy and affluent, blending into the vast, contiguous patchwork of borderless super-urb that covers the region from mountains to sea, a place where municipal boundaries are imagined on maps and in the tabulation of votes and taxes, but rarely exist in any physical way. There are few rivers, mountains, bridges, woodlands, wetlands, or pastures to serve as barriers and dividers in today's L.A. landscape—just the concrete canyons of freeways snaking like blood vessels, tying it all together rather than pulling it apart. Driving across the Los Angeles Basin with its eighty-eight separate cities, where Cerritos lies close to the geographic center, the formerly distinctive Dairy Valley can be distinguished from the next town only by virtue of the green-and-white freeway signs posted to announce that another set of city limits has been crossed.

It was during this uneasy transition from agrarian past to urban future that Whitney High School enrolled its first students, entering an educational world rocked by just as much clashing of values and history as was roiling the former town of Dairy Valley and the new city of Cerritos.

12

Whitney opened its doors at a time when the nation's confidence in public education had been shaken badly (once again), with leaders of all political persuasions expressing fears that American children were being left behind, unable to compete in the global economy. The new high school was conceived as a response to those concerns.

That these complaints about public education's failure closely mirror today's, three decades and six presidents later, is not particularly surprising. Each decade for the last century in America has had its own education "crisis," in which it appeared certain that the schools were failing and in dire need of reform. Each generation of parents and leaders seems to believe this crisis is its own and that their ideas and outrage are original. Yet the cycle of concern followed by reform followed by certainty that the reforms were wrongheaded is remarkably repetitive. (Will Rogers adroitly summed up Americans' peculiar view of public education across the years as eternally falling short of some mythic past golden age: "The schools ain't what they used to be and never was.")[6]

A quarter century ago, critics of public education made the now familiar argument that the failure of public schools owed its roots to the countercultural 1960s. This era, the critics argued, ushered in a "dumbing down" of traditional studies of literature, language, history, science, and math, with the era of hippies and war protests an ever-popular whipping boy for every public education woe from math illiteracy to declining SAT scores to a perceived elevation of self-esteem building over rigor. This take on the decline of public schools and the need to go "back to basics" has been enshrined as conventional wisdom and lies at the heart of many current government policies. But though some of these criticisms are valid, other, much earlier decisions are responsible for the current shape and failings of American schools—decisions that date back to the dawn of the twentieth century and the Progressive Era, when the so-called "basics" everyone wants to return to were first conceived. If failure in American schooling had a birth, it was then, in the cold light of the young Industrial Age, not during the flowery haze of the sixties.[7]

Compulsory education and the public school is only 150 years old in America, pushed into being almost single-handedly by the humanitarian Horace Mann.[8] He envisioned the public school as a "great equalizer" and a "ladder of opportunity" that should teach the same classical, rigorous, academically oriented course of study to all students, rich and poor alike, thereby narrowing the divide between the privately schooled elite and the average American.

These ideals still resonate today (and continue to influence the structure of public schools). But they came under harsh criticism early in the twentieth century from business interests and the progressive movement's leaders, who had legitimate concerns about standards and quality in the patchwork of locally controlled schools, but who also derided classical "book" learning as an impractical and inefficient waste. Like the end of Cerritos's cow-town days, change in public education had become inevitable by this time: The schools Horace Mann envisioned were conceived to serve an agrarian society of overwhelmingly Anglo-Saxon citizens with a shared language, culture, history, and values. But the industrial revolution had transformed the nation, and now this same system of schools was being asked to do its job in an urban, factory-dominated landscape populated by a melting pot of immigrants with different languages, backgrounds, religions, and expectations. Bilingual education, religion in schools, and other hot-button issues of today were causing a stir in the schools debate a hundred years ago as well (but the foreign tongue in question then was German, the language of preference in the United States's first kindergarten classes, opened in the 1870s in St. Louis to help give a head start to immigrant children).

Criticism emanated then from bastions of free enterprise such as the Carnegie Corporation, backed by a cadre of influential university professors, who slammed the public schools not for doing too little, but for trying to do *too much*. The classical, academic program Mann envisioned as an engine of equality for all should not be taught to every student, these critics insisted, but should be reserved for an elite with the intellect capable of using that knowledge. The majority of young people—conveniently enough for the industrialists who needed cannon fodder for their burgeoning production lines and sweatshops—should be channeled into the "basics" of vocational training. Why teach "useless" subjects such as history and literature when a home economics course or lessons in mechanical drawing could be taught instead to children who would never be more than laborers anyway?

Schools should be more like factories, it was decided, efficiently sorting and molding their products—the students—into the forms society needed. In the 1920s, the sort of high schools that fill our educational landscape to this day were built; students no longer stayed with a single teacher but moved from classroom to classroom like products on an assembly line, and were tracked through IQ tests and other measures into college-prep or various nonacademic and "practical" courses of study. Junior high schools were invented primarily so this sorting process could begin at a younger age rather than allowing elementary schools to retain children through eighth grade as had always been done in the past (and as many private and parochial schools continue to do). A child's future, then, could be determined at age twelve instead of fifteen, not for his or her delight or benefit, but in the name of social efficiency.

This new educational philosophy provoked a barrage of criticism and, by the 1940s, the same sorts of studies that trouble today's theorists and parents began popping up, revealing too many high school seniors incapable of saying when George Washington was president or why the Civil War was fought or where Italy is located on the world map. And though the proportion of American teenagers who graduated high school continued a steady climb (from 6.4 percent at the turn of the century to 25 percent in 1930), dropout rates also remained quite high through the 1950s, when four out of ten high schoolers failed to earn diplomas. This record of dropouts, coupled with poor achievement for those who did make it through twelfth grade, persisted for years. Yet it was not perceived as a crisis by the general public. Most American adults did not at the time possess a high school diploma, nor did they consider it an essential milestone in life.

This attitude abruptly changed one day in 1957, when the *beep-beep-beep* signal transmitted by the first man-made satellite was broadcast around the world—and it was a Russian, not an American, beep. The successful launch of *Sputnik* by the Soviet Union and the advent of the cold war have often been cited as turning points in American public education, when outcry over a perceived "brain gap" led to the first direct federal involvement in public schools, the National Defense Education Act, which beefed up science, math, and foreign language instruction. The old reforms of the Progressive Era were now seen not only as wrongheaded, but as a danger to national security. Doing well in school and aspiring to go to college became, for the first time, a matter of national pride. The law also spelled the end of full local control over schools and launched the now universal practice of high-stakes tests to hold schools accountable.

The cycle of educational reform, followed by criticism, followed by new and often contrary reforms continued after *Sputnik*. By the 1960s and 1970s, a new breed of progressives began complaining that American schools were uncreative and "irrelevant," too heavily focused on rote learning and out of step with the Civil Rights movement and other forces of social change. For good or ill, a time of experimentation had begun in many school districts, with some dubious results, including the demise of history in favor of the more ambiguous "social studies," and the advent of self-esteem programs that perversely sought to boost the self-images of students *despite* their poor performance in school, rather than linking self-esteem to improved academic prowess. There were also some excellent and subsequently proven ideas pioneered: small group instruction and project-based learning among them.

Considerable interest was also focused on small, less bureaucratic alternatives that offered novel ways of learning for kids poorly served by large comprehensive high schools. The "school-without-walls" concept, pioneered by the Parkway Program in Philadelphia, briefly flourished in the 1970s as one such model. Accomplished businessmen, scientists, doctors, lawyers, political leaders, and other members of the community partnered with experienced teachers to mentor and instruct in their areas of expertise. (Thirty years ago such ideas were derided as overly liberal concepts; they were abhorred by teachers' unions, which feared job loss, and bureaucrats who prized formal teaching credentials over real-world skills and knowledge. Today, similar proposals are derided as overly conservative and abhorred by teacher unions and bureaucrats for precisely the same reasons.)

In Cerritos, the superintendent of the ABC Unified School District had heard of a similar program in Texas, a community learning center for children of all grade levels and abilities, with instruction for adults offered as well. He wanted something similar for ABC—a learning hub of sorts, intimate and flexible. The new school he envisioned would fill some of the gaps left by the district's three large comprehensive high schools, with their mishmash of sometimes contradictory mandates to separate kids into appropriate tracks while providing all students with a rigorous academic course of study. The new campus would be designed as both an alternative school for smart kids with untapped potential and a remedial program for struggling students in danger of dropping out. Dropouts were considered a huge crisis at the time, although the national dropout rate hovered near its all-time low of 23 percent when Whitney was conceived, a marked improvement over the *Sputnik* era. (The dropout rate has since climbed back to 30 percent in 2002.)

When Whitney opened, the school offered eclectic classes and practical training unavailable at any other school in the region. The culinary arts department was run by the former executive head chef of the Ambassador Hotel in Los Angeles (voted chef of the year by California's Chef de Cuisine Association the year before coming to Whitney), and it featured a fully functional commercial kitchen and a working restaurant open to the public, which served gourmet meals at cut rates prepared by apprentice chefs (the six-month course, free to high school students, cost thirty dollars for adults). There

were floral-arranging classes designed to encourage entrepreneurship directly after high school graduation. The students
learned architectural drafting (the graduates of this era still
use blueprint-style printing, their handwriting near type-
writer perfect, a composition teacher's dream come true).
There was a preschool program with intensive reading instruction for the district's pre-kindergartners, with older students providing some of the day care and learning about
educational theory, child development, and psychology at the
same time. And all of this took place in a radically new kind
of school building—a wide-open warehouselike structure
where the very walls could be moved to construct new classrooms, labs, and performance areas according to the needs of
the students and the evolution of the school's mission. The
structure was to be both practical and a metaphor for the
school's essence: nimble, flexible, ready to adapt to its constituency and the marketplace. When the Whitney Community Learning Center opened its doors in 1976, it was hailed
as revolutionary in every way.

And it was an utter flop.

13

The beautiful metaphor of the movable building, it soon became clear, did not work in the real world. Flexible architecture with moving walls is great in theory. Actually living with it drove everyone crazy.

The walls proved too heavy and awkward to move (except when a small army of prank-playing students decided to turn the place into a doorless rat maze). Yet they offered no soundproofing: Despite their considerable heft, the walls were paper thin, nothing more than burlap-textured cloth stretched on a heavy metal frame, allowing the sounds of one classroom to drown out the next. Teachers joked that, in the event of a fire, the emergency exits were everywhere: Just run through a wall.

Wiring for phones and electricity also turned out to be a nightmare. Nothing could go inside the walls, creating an instant fire-code debacle of extension cords snaking through the building. Odd little columns humming with electricity and studded with light switches and outlets appeared in the middle of rooms, the only architectural alternative to the conventional wall switch and plug. It took three muscular people to manipulate the elaborate grapples and clips necessary to mount a chalkboard in a classroom.

Meanwhile, the air-conditioning system rained water down on the students—that is, when it worked, which was rarely when it was needed most. And plans to build a gymnasium and auditorium were scrapped for lack of money, leaving a muddy grass field for all outdoor activities.

Yet the physical shortcomings were the least of Whitney's problems. Plenty of schools have lousy buildings, Principal Bob Beall knew. What Whitney really needed was students.

As Whitney's first principal walked the halls near the end of his school's first year, Beall grappled with a mixture of pride and fear that the school he helped create, and that he felt certain could become something great, would die. The ghastly orange lockers, so ugly they were almost cool, would be emptied and stay that way. It was that simple.

He paced past the mostly empty classrooms, the long stretches of open space, searching for the inspiration that would stave off closure. He had helped bring into the world a unique place to learn: Students labored in a ceramics class with a new, energetic, big-haired art teacher just out of college herself, while four-year-olds in the pre-K program were already learning to read. Delicious smells wafted in from the Hutch, where student cooks prepared the best and healthiest school meals in the district—and turned a tidy profit with their adjacent public restaurant, a favorite among local businessmen and single male teachers who raved about the full-course gourmet meals that cost less than four dollars. Beall was the one who thought of bowling and racquetball in place of conventional physical education when the schools' facilities fell short, and he made holding proms in the Hutch and graduation ceremonies on the field where the gym was supposed to have been built seem a fun-filled virtue rather than a slight. Beall always seemed to finagle some sort of solution, a way around the rules (or a way without them, when need be).

The only quantity he couldn't seem to produce were enough regular high school students to make the program fly. The school felt empty and deserted much of the time. Most of the space was still wide-open rather than contained by classrooms; many of the available walls remained stacked in a corner, since there was no one to use all the additional en-closed space they represented. It seemed more convenient to leave it all open, anyway. There was only one telephone line in the school—the budget left no room for more wires or phones—and without walls in the way, it was easier for the secretary to dash through the building to pass on phone messages or summon someone to take a call. It also helped compensate for the antiquated school bell system Whitney inherited from some district scrap pile. The cumbersome wood and metal device hulking in a corner of the adminis-tration area like a cheap prop from an old movie never man-aged to sound class-ending bells at the right time. Kay Cottrell, the principal's secretary then (as now) finally just switched the thing off, relying instead on the teachers to figure out class had ended by actually looking at the clock or by being jolted into action after seeing other classrooms emptying elsewhere in the wide-open school.

"You've got to get the enrollment up," the new superin-tendent told Beall as summer break approached and prepara-tions for Whitney's second full school year were about to begin. The superintendent who commissioned Whitney and hired Beall—Charles Hutchinson, whose name is enshrined in the Hutch—had retired. His successor, while supportive of the new school, was under pressure to relieve overcrowding at other district schools. Beall had managed to attract an en-rollment of just over three hundred—fewer than a third of the one thousand students the school had been designed to accommodate—while the district's other high schools were brimming full. The superintendent told Beall bluntly, "We can't afford to keep an empty school open. We have to fill it up or close it up."

It was a tough spot for Beall, cast as the executor of a departed superintendent's vision. Beall knew there were flaws in the concept from the start, but he had not considered them fatal, at least not until Hutchinson retired and support for Whitney's innovations and quirky charms evaporated.

Beall came to Whitney already a controversial character, with a devoted following of teachers and parents who considered him a visionary, and an equally devoted body of detractors who felt he rarely behaved as a team player within the larger world of the school district. Before Whitney, he had been principal of a nearby elementary school, where he had pioneered a successful year-round curriculum with an innovative menu of courses of study for parents to shop. He hammered through a then-unusual (and now thoroughly mainstream) proposal to make kindergarten a full day rather than half a day, which many parents and teachers initially opposed. He also insisted that teachers keep accurate, detailed, and up-to-the-minute records of classwork accomplished and planned, so successors in any classroom could pick up without missing a beat should a teacher get sick or depart. This had the potential for stirring dissent because Beall made it clear that such records would also impose a new level of accountability on teachers, as he would use them to reveal just what was—and was not—going on in each classroom.

Full-time kindergartens and detailed lesson plans/grade books are common today, even taken for granted, but Beall's insistence on them twenty-five years ago was in many ways groundbreaking and highly controversial. Parents, by and large, and most of his teachers as well, were pleased in the end because their children did well. But doing better by kids is not always the only measure and purpose of educational reform;

Beall's reputation among some district higher-ups as a trouble-maker who went out of his way to stir the pot had taken hold, and it followed him to Whitney.

Unimpressed by his predilection for open collars and gold chains, Beall's colleagues from that era say he could be pushy and impolitic. Most considered him a true educational visionary however—even his critics concede that—some-one who glimpsed the future of education and, after initially faltering, found a way to turn Whitney's original amalgam of disparate programs into a model of success.

But to get there—and in those first years, simply to stay alive—Whitney had to change. Beall felt it was essential that his new school stop trying to exist as a supplement to other schools, and instead offer the full gamut of high school courses every student needed to graduate. He had been stymied, however, by the principals of the three other com-prehensive high schools in the ABC District, which serves Cerritos and several surrounding communities. They ob-jected to a full educational program ever being offered at Whitney; they wanted their high school students to go to Whitney for electives only, not required courses, while stay-ing enrolled in their original comprehensive school. When Beall tried to offer standard algebra classes, the other princi-pals threatened to pull their students out and shut Beall's school down. This was at root an economic issue: schools get money from the state based on each student enrolled. So long as the students' original high school issued their graduation credits and diploma, those students could spend all day at Whitney, but the money would still go to their home high school. By keeping Whitney from offering a full high school program, the other schools guaranteed their coffers would stay full and that Whitney would never become a serious competitor for students or accolades. Sooner or later Beall's school would be forced to close.

The other high schools piled on further by referring only their least successful, least motivated, and most problematic students to Whitney, using the new school as a dumping ground for the kids they didn't want to deal with anymore. Beall had tried to increase Whitney's drawing power with unique offerings—child care, photography, interdisciplinary programs, businessmen brought into class as mentors—but those attracted more adult learners and very small children than high schoolers. The regular high school students stayed away.

"You would think innovation would be welcome in the educational world," Beall mused to his staff, "but it's not. It's treated like an invading organism in the body. All the other educators surround it and try to remove it from the system." Some of his teachers would laugh at the image of Whitney as a virus under assault by a bureaucratic immune system, but not Beall.

Just when he figured he had exhausted all possible solutions, his wife, then a counselor at another school, posed a simple and direct question: "What's the difference between your school and a school *everyone* wants to go to?"

"You tell me."

"They're *selective*. Kids have to choose to go to Whitney—it's not automatic, like a neighborhood school. If you want people to choose to go to Whitney, it has to be selective, too. There has to be the possibility someone *won't* get it. Who wants to go out of the way to pick a school that *anyone* can get into?"

Beall remembers just staring at her, agape at the wonderful simplicity of it—and the sheer ballsiness it would require to pull off what would amount to an educational coup d'état. This would be school reform on the fly, without studies, official approvals, or a chance for naysayers to say nay, and it would involve crossing a dicey line: creating a public school that would not be open to all the public. But he knew she was right. Beall describes this as a lightbulb-over-the-head moment, and though the story is not precisely a secret, the students who many years later treasure Whitney's high standards and pedigree have no idea that the top-rated school in the state owes its genesis more to marketing concerns and sheer desperation than any lofty decision to build from the outset an academic powerhouse.

Given the environment of sabotage Beall felt Whitney faced at the time, a grandiose plan that openly sought to construct a world-class academic magnet school could well have died stillborn. The other high school principals could hardly have been expected to suddenly change their views and willingly surrender their best students if asked in advance. On the other hand, Beall figured a backdoor, end-of-the-school-year, grassroots plan, conceived at the principal's kitchen table and launched with as little fanfare as possible, might actually work. And so, with a new enthusiasm, he began to cobble together a selective-admissions high school and to lay plans to get it up and running almost before anyone even knew it was there.

This seat-of-the-pants rethinking of an entire public school by the school's own staff probably couldn't happen today in such a sweeping manner: Only today's bureaucracy-purged charter schools approach that sort of autonomy. Principals, stripped of the sort of power Beall once exercised, now have a largely thankless job, which may be why there is a national principal shortage. A quarter century ago, though, public high school principals had real perks and power, running their schoolhouse kingdoms for good or ill with an impunity long gone in today's environment of standards, laws, litigation, and risk-management guidelines. The other high school principals had been throwing their weight around to keep Whitney in line; Beall figured it was his turn. As the school year drew to a close, he pulled his brightest and most loyal teachers together and began to lay plans to remake Whitney as he saw fit.

"The summer is to education what midnight is to the castle," he would later recall with a plotter's cackle. "It's the best time to get things done—things you might not be able to get away with when everyone is around."

Once the idea of an admissions process at Whitney took hold, there was no real question about the sort of student the school should set out to select. Vocational programs were fast becoming dinosaurs, Beall decided. He wanted a school filled with bright, independent, academically capable boys and girls who were either college bound or who appeared to have that potential.

And he wanted to get those students early—seventh graders, maybe younger. The artificial midstage of junior high school was just getting in the way, a relic of the industrial revolution Beall decided to sweep aside, using Whitney's original mandate to take students of all ages as justification. The faculty knew from experience that the broad span of ages could actually be a plus, allowing a kind of buddy system to evolve in which older students mentored the smaller kids, benefiting both.

Combining junior and senior high would play to another of Whitney's selling points as well—its intimate scale—and run counter to the conventional wisdom of the era, that when it came to public schools, bigger is better.[9] With room for a little over one thousand students, Whitney was half the size of the district's other high schools. By filling that school with six grades instead of four, Beall could keep each grade level's enrollment below 170—quite small in comparison to larger schools, particularly in California, which leads the nation in the enrollment size of its high schools.

The mission of Whitney from this day on would change radically, Beall told his bewildered faculty, which at the time was still teaching floral arranging, restaurant services, and remedial reading. Now they would focus on creating an educational culture of high expectations and aspirations, featuring a curriculum rich not with the crafts and electives, but with rigorous classical academics, bolstered by plenty of individualized instruction and attention. They would launch the college-preparatory process in seventh grade, before adolescence and teen angst had even kicked in, so that the kids would walk into the door *knowing* they were going to college. Whitney could then fill a niche other public schools were then ignoring. If school quality and achievement were the ailments, then Whitney would be presented as the cure.

Public schools of the era were being pummeled by two opposing trends, as Beall saw it, and for Whitney to succeed, it would have to be positioned to use both of them to its advantage. The first trend was obvious: Public concern about lagging student achievement once again was on the rise, commanding headlines and politicians' attention. "If an unfriendly foreign power had attempted to impose on America the mediocre educational performance that exists today," read one U.S. government report of the era, the controversial, *A Nation at Risk,* "we might well have viewed it as an act of war."[10] In Beall's view, Whitney would be the place parents could turn if they were concerned about mediocre schools.

The second trend Beall sought to exploit was a curious corollary to the claims that public education was failing: Despite the declining test scores and achievement in high schools, aspirations for obtaining a college degree were rising, not falling, among students and their parents. College, as never before, was being viewed as a necessity, even a birthright. Part of this stemmed from a changing economy: corporations once willing to train high school grads for skilled technical and professional jobs in return for decades of loyalty had increasingly focused on short-term earnings and cyclic layoffs as a means of competing in the new global marketplace. The days of getting out of high school and hiring on at the phone company—back when there was only one phone company that mattered—and receiving training and a job for life were coming to an end in the seventies. The same industries that lobbied earlier in the century to limit purely academic curriculums in public schools to a select few were now clamoring to have them back. College degrees were becoming a requirement for a far wider spectrum of jobs, the information economy was suddenly on the horizon, and public schools were being called upon to prepare more kids for college than ever before.

And here was the real reason for the declining test scores decried in *A Nation at Risk*: They were not the product of a sudden drop in the quality of public schools so much as a response to a new mission for the same old schools. Suddenly a much broader cross section of America had begun enrolling in college-prep courses and sitting for the SAT than in decades past. A drop in scores was inevitable once college prep stopped being dominated by a privileged elite. This crucial part of the equation is often overlooked when schools are criticized for declining achievement since the early sixties.

With more kids seeking college degrees, a new cycle of heightened competition began at the nation's colleges and universities. Public schools interested in academic excellence, Beall decided, should be doing what private schools have always done: marketing themselves and their students to the top colleges and universities. It would no longer be enough to keep a dusty shelf of college catalogs in the back of the guidance counselor's office. You had to get in the game.

So Beall settled on a goal for Whitney far ahead of its time: to become a public school dedicated to the proposition that all of its students would go to college. Such an ambition is exceptional even in the twenty-first century, when two-thirds of all high school students in the nation pursue a post-secondary degree. Back then, it was all but unheard of in a public school. Barely 10 percent of adults had a college degree at that time, and fewer than half of all students in high school (public and private combined) then aspired to get one, even with university enrollment artificially pumped up by the Vietnam War and the desirability of college draft deferments.

Beall recruited two of his teachers to devise the admissions test Shirley Wold would be among the first to take. Beall is the first to admit it was not a scientifically assembled and sanitized exam, but a rough-and-tumble, highly subjective slice of what the teachers figured a new Whitney student ought to know—and ought to be like. The school was going to be making itself up as it went along, and it needed students who could handle and enjoy that. And that test couldn't be *too* hard, at least at first: They needed a good-sized group of incoming kids. Beall had seen enough anecdotal evidence in his career to feel certain that telling students they were special and expecting them to perform at a high level would help generate superior achievement.

Next, Beall dispatched a young English teacher named Dennis Brent to San Francisco to study the curriculum and philosophy of California's top-ranked school at the time, as measured by standardized testing. Lowell High School, the first public secondary school in California, also boasted a very high percentage of graduates accepted into four-year colleges and consistently high average scores on the SAT. Beall's instructions to Brent were simple: Go up and find out what they're doing. Then come back and tell us how to do it here. We'll steal what works and make up the rest.

Lowell's administration and teachers seemed happy to help the upstart school, never guessing they would be supplanted in the rankings by their new rival in the not-too-distant future. With the help of Brent's intelligence gathering, the Whitney faculty assembled a new curriculum offering such college-prep classes as Latin, trigonometry, and honors English, though none of the Whitney teachers had previously taught those subjects. New instructors were recruited and old ones received new assignments: The floral arrangement teacher became a middle school science teacher; the adult pottery class teacher was put in charge of fine arts; and Debbie Agrums found her career for life.

Students would have to step up, too: In the new Whitney, they'd be expected to maintain a grade point average above 2.5; if it dipped below, they would go on academic probation and receive intensive help and tutoring to bring their grades up. Two consecutive semesters of probation without improvement and students would be asked to check out of Whitney and return to their home schools. There were four possible grades in any course: A, B, C, or F. Sports team members would have to maintain grades no lower than a B-minus in every course and do their homework before practice, or leave the team. Drivers ed and sex education would be moved to a special summer session so they wouldn't cut into academic offerings. The old Whitney assortment of offbeat electives remained to serve the current crop of students, but the curriculum had to be beefed up to feature all the required courses for a full-service middle and high school.

Beall also called in a few favors at the University of California at Irvine, where several professors agreed to work at Whitney over the summer to help design the college-prep program. Study-skills training and classes in SAT preparation were built into the offerings as a result. Long offered at private schools, this sort of training to take the college boards had always been a pay-to-play extra for public school kids. But Beall needed every edge he could get in order to drive up college acceptances and SAT scores for his students, the best means of marketing the revamped school. And Beall made it clear to his staff that marketing would be crucial, that fostering successful students and a successful school had as much to do with image and reputation as anything else.

"Colleges want the best cherries," Beall would say. "The colleges wag the tails of education. And the feet and the head and everything else. If we're not ranked well by the colleges, people are still going to look down on us. And we'll be gone."

In their senior year, Beall announced, all students would be required to apply to five colleges—not just the University of California campuses, but at least one private school and one Ivy League school. The more acceptances the kids garnered, the higher the rating would be for the school, thereby enhancing Whitney's statistics and its reputation. The college-prep process would start in seventh grade and not end until the kids packed off to the university: that would be Whitney's promise to parents. The intentions were honorable, even groundbreaking. But the seeds, for many years invisible, of a generation stressed had been planted even before Whitney accepted its first college-bound student.

14

Reaching the top meant the image of a broken school for bereft students had to be purged for good.

And so the architectural disaster of a building became a virtue, evidence that the school was focused on substance over form. Of course there was no gym—that would be superfluous in a school where academics were the priority. Calisthenics in the field were just as healthy and less of a distraction. Even the haywire school bell system became a plus as Beall crafted his pitch: Whitney students didn't *need* bells to remind them when to go to class. They were expected to be responsible enough to keep track of time on their own, just as they would have to do in college and in the workaday adult world beyond. To this day, there are no bells at Whitney (although the school finally got its gym in 1996).

The original Whitney students would be grandfathered in to the new program, which retained for several years its culinary institute and other exotic offerings, though no longer requiring students in those programs to remain linked to their original high schools. The mix could have proven contentious or even explosive, but it turned out to enhance the Whitney experience: The new students, who tended to be from more privileged and sheltered backgrounds than the old-timers, got to know and be mentored by kids with far fewer advantages in life. Many of the older students, meanwhile, thrived in an environment of higher expectations in which they found themselves anointed for the first time in their lives as leaders. Many went on to college though few had entered with that expectation. When Beall began the Whitney tradition of reading college acceptances over the public-address system for all to hear during morning announcements, it was to honor these older students who had defied the odds and excelled; the tradition was also intended to influence the youngest kids listening in their classrooms, so they would come to think of having their own names read in this way as a necessary rite of passage.

Finally, word went out about the new Whitney through parent groups and trusted colleagues at some of the local elementary schools, accompanied by invitations to take the new admissions test on one of several Saturdays spread throughout the summer. Families at Beall's old elementary school still remembered him fondly from his kindergarten and curriculum innovations and they showed up in a large group to take the first Whitney test, ensuring a passel of new students.

As Beall expected, the other high school principals were furious when September rolled around and the new Whitney greeted them as a *fait accompli*. But the battle-hardened principal had cannily organized in advance an enthused cadre of parents ready to respond to any complaints to the school board. He recruited smart, articulate, well-heeled parents, the sort who are not shy about going to the microphone and pointing out how desperately a school like Whitney was needed in Cerritos—the sort of community leaders school board members are loathe to offend. When questioned about the remaking of Whitney, Beall simply said he was following instructions from the superintendent to save his school and boost enrollment. He had, in fact, accomplished the stated goal: Beall had made Whitney a school parents wanted their kids to attend. In the end, over the objections of administrators and teachers at the other district high schools, the school board retroactively approved the creation of a new sort of academic magnet school, and the learning center was renamed Whitney High School.

By 1983, Whitney's scores on statewide tests put it among the top three high schools in the state. By 1987, it reached the number one ranking, and that same year was named a Blue Ribbon School of Excellence by the U.S. Department of Education (the first of three Blue Ribbon honors awarded the school). Whitney has been the top-ranked high school in California ever since and, for much of that time, the top-ranked public school of any grade level in the state, with test scores routinely exceeding those published by other college-prep public schools in the nation and many elite private schools as well.

This became a point of community pride, but also pain: Every time the local newspapers published yet another story on how Whitney out-tested all other schools in the district and state, the teachers at the other Cerritos-area schools, particularly those running college-prep and Advanced Placement courses, grew more resentful. Whitney was accused of "stealing" the top students from other schools; it was derided as elitist and antidemocratic—a "brain drain." There was retaliation of sorts, both momentous and petty. The district closed the restaurant, and the fresh-cooked, balanced meals served students were replaced with the current high-calorie, high-fat, high-priced fare of preheated burgers, soggy submarine sandwiches, chips, and sodas. Whitney students who signed up to play varsity sports at their original home schools— as they were entitled to do, so long as Whitney lacked a gym—were often forced to warm the bench, regardless of their abilities. The school responded by begging time at a community gym and fielding a basketball team that won the regional small schools division title two years in a row.

Hostilities grew especially intense at Cerritos High School, less than a mile away and the perennial academic leader in the district before Whitney came along. Its college-prep program had been hardest hit by the Whitney transformation, though its test scores remained well above the state and national averages and the number of its graduates going on to college was a healthy 65 percent. Nevertheless, Cerritos High became a center for a petition drive to close down Whitney as an unnecessary duplication of programs and classes already offered at the other comprehensive high schools. Among the petitioners were two teachers who would later join the Whitney faculty—calculus teacher Steve Murray and a young science teacher by the name of Rod Ziolkowski.

"You have to understand how the teachers at the other schools felt—and how they still feel," Mr. Z recalls of that time. "You're trying to build a program, to improve the level of academics, and then along comes this new school and you feel like they're stealing all your very best students. These are the kids every teacher wants in their classroom. It's easy to shine, to be the best, if that's all you have in your class. It makes the other teachers mad. They feel it's unfair, and unfair to the majority of students."

Some teachers suggested at the time—and continue to suggest on occasion, usually after annual statewide test results are published—that their schools could vault to the top in test-score rankings without changing a thing, except for swapping student populations with Whitney. This view holds that Whitney's success came solely through cherry-picking top students from other schools. Of all the criticisms of Whitney High School, this one angers Beall and others who were around for the school's rocky birth the most, because it is based on a false assumption. Whitney, they say, became a great school *before* it could attract the greatest students, first rising in the ranks to become one of the top schools in California and only then becoming the academic magnet for the district. In its first years, recruiting students and teachers for the fledgling school, whose existence had to be ratified almost year to year, proved difficult. In those first years, Whitney took a far larger percentage of those who applied, and its student population resembled that of every other school in the district. Yet it entered the top ten and then the top three in statewide test-score rankings, helping to cement Whitney's reputation. A certain mystique began to surround the homely little school with the bare-bones campus, and only then did the competition to get in begin to mount.

"If there is dissatisfaction with the other schools, they should be looking at themselves and finding ways to raise up their programs and raise up their students, not bring down young people who are succeeding," Beall responded to the critics. "That's what we did at Whitney, one of the most important things we did: We expected great things from the students, and they did great things in response."

Aside from the question of which came first—the great school or the great students—by the time of the petition drive, Whitney wasn't just taking students who would have otherwise gone to the district's other schools. People had begun moving to Cerritos and surrounding communities for the express purpose of getting into Whitney. Cerritos had become a majority Asian city largely on the back of Whitney High. Many Asian immigrants and Asian American families would not have come here otherwise: Whitney was a big draw. "Our school isn't a brain drain," Beall railed at the petitioners. "It's a brain magnet."

Beall and Whitney's parents staved off closure efforts for years, along with several thinly veiled poison-pill plans to alter the school so severely it could not survive—by ending admissions standards, ousting the seventh and eighth graders, or folding Whitney into another campus. One proposal even called for carving up the school's eighteen acres and selling it to developers. Each proposal was defeated in the end. But in the early nineties, opponents found their best opening, when the district faced a $3 million budget shortfall, an immense sum for a medium-sized school district of only 22,000 students. A majority of teachers signed petitions at the other district high schools and middle schools demanding closure of Whitney's "duplicate" program rather than cutting other educational services. Board meetings were packed with noisy crowds who would burst into applause when one side or another scored a point. The district seemed torn, the debate affecting everyone from the school board, to the top echelons of the administration, to the teachers and students on the street. The superintendent at the time backed Whitney, if tepidly. But critics, some of them in offices next door to the superintendent, waged a media campaign, some speaking anonymously to the press about Whitney's "elitism" and how blacks and Latinos were underrepresented there, while Asian Americans were overrepresented. "It's just not right to siphon kids off," one "high-placed district official" told the Los Angeles Times. "Who said it's right for a public school to exclude kids?" And an anonymous sixth-grade teacher weighed in: "I'm very opposed to what Whitney does to my children. It's a very negative thing. I watch it destroy kids. I watch it pit one kid against the other.... They think their whole life is ruined or made by their scores on that test at eleven years old."

But where some (typically those families who did not get into Whitney) saw a school that harmed the aspirations of children through one high-stakes test, others (typically those families who *did* get into Whitney) saw an opportunity to soar. Behind the anti-Whitney sentiment, they perceived a seldom-recognized brand of bigotry that they asserted is all too common—and universally tolerated, even celebrated— in American culture: bias against the intellectually gifted. No one complains when star athletes or artists or performers get scholarships because of their innate ability, or when the third-string quarterback warms the bench so the more skilled player can win the game, the Whitney supporters argued. Indeed, most high schools would have their coaches' heads if they acted otherwise. Why should kids who excel at their studies be treated differently? Aren't they a group themselves, adding to cultural diversity?

"Success is ignored and failure is funded," Whitney math and physics teacher Sandy Bruesch told the *Times,* a sentiment she still holds today as one of Whitney's most senior teachers.

In the end, the closure movement fizzled, with Whitney parents rallying forcefully on behalf of the school, pressuring the school board to keep its hands off (for the most part). The critics' arguments were largely dismissed by the school board as flawed,[11] although the opponents of a separate college-prep school still won their small victories: Plans for building the Whitney gym were delayed for several more years because of the budget crunch, and the campus was put at the end of the list for renovation, computer networks, and other new equipment. But Whitney's future was secured and would not be subject to future challenges, as long as the achievement stayed high.

There was one last battle, however, this one over race and ethnicity. The growing Asian American majority in Cerritos, coupled with the propensity for Asian American kids to outperform other ethnic groups when it comes to gaining admission to elite educational institutions, had spawned concerns that the Whitney student body was not sufficiently representative of the entire school district. There had been more of a balance struck when Whitney used its own admissions tests and selection process, but once the district took over the admissions test, the imbalance seemed to grow. Compared to the school district's overall population, Whitney's student body, about two-thirds Asian American, had twice the proportion of ethnic Asians; blacks were underrepresented by a factor of five and Latinos by a factor of six.[12] Bowing to criticism from members of the community who felt their children were being denied opportunity, and sensitive to charges of elitism, school board members voted to impose racial quotas at Whitney, hoping to strike a balance that the multiple-choice tests used for admissions were not achieving. The quotas were designed to boost white enrollment along with that of other ethnicities; every group would benefit, in essence, except for Asian Americans. ABC became one of the few school districts in America in which whites argued for and enjoyed the benefits of affirmative action while a group normally regarded as a minority found itself in the position of arguing in favor of merit-only considerations. But the affirmative action program for Whitney never really succeeded in significantly altering the demographics, and the quotas came to an end in 1996 when California voters approved Proposition 209, which banned all racial preferences in public schools, universities, and government operations. From there, the school district adopted the sort of method since championed by George W. Bush as a "race-neutral" form of promoting diversity: geographic preferences.[13] At Whitney, this proved to be even less effective a tool for diversity than the old racial quotas.

Bob Beall fought hard against this quota system when it was first proposed, lashing out at its advocates as hypocrites who were afraid of admissions standards based solely on merit. "Asian students of the 1980s are the Jews of the 1940s," he said, making few friends in high places and losing the few that he had. "They are being mistreated because they are successful. Since when does the American dream preclude success?"

Beall argued in vain that the wrong approach was being taken—that instead of reducing the role of merit in the admissions equation, other schools in the district should adopt Whitney's model, building a culture of high expectations that begins at home, where the Asian American families particularly shine, and is then woven into the fabric of the school, so that everything—sports, social events, clubs, activities, *everything*—is subordinate to academics. The synergy between high expectations at home and at school is crucial, Beall argued.

"It is almost like magic. You have to share the dream, express the dream—nobody can walk around in your dream if you don't talk about it. The dream at Whitney is you want to be the best, in the nation and the world. That there is no end to improving."

Beall is a natural storyteller, and he has one to illustrate why changing other schools, not Whitney's admissions program, should have been the board's approach. It's one that has made its way around educational circles for years, and may or may not be apocryphal, but it sums up neatly the power of expectations and high standards as he sees it: A sixth-grade teacher in a major city was at her wit's end because of the bad behavior of her unruly class. The students were noisy, disruptive, disinterested. Many refused to do their work, and when they did do it, the product was dauntingly below grade level. This class lagged behind its peers in every subject. The teacher feared many of these students were in need of special education services, that they might be suffering from learning disabilities or other problems, and so she went fairly easy on them with schoolwork. But one day, she ventured to take a peek at their confidential files in the principal's office. To her astonishment, she found her students were not candidates for special ed; they almost all had tested out with above-average IQs, far more capable than she had ever dreamed. This waste of potential horrified the teacher, who returned to class and announced an end to coddling. She doubled the workload in class and on homework, punished swiftly and severely when students misbehaved or failed to produce, and began tackling subjects vigorously and appropriate to their grade level, all the while assuring the kids that they were very smart children who could succeed if they would only try. She told them they could do it, every day. And, just as she expected once these smart children had their feet held to the fire, things began to turn around.

By the end of the year, the class had made great progress, the quality of their work had improved, as had their behavior and their grades—a stunning change. When the principal asked her how she had worked this miracle, she confessed to being inspired after perusing the confidential files. Only then did she learn that she had not, after all, managed a peek at the kids' IQ scores when she cracked open those secret records. She had been looking at their locker numbers.

"The power of the dream," cackles Beall.

The quotas battle would be one of the few Beall lost as principal at Whitney, but it would prove to be his last at the school. He left for another assignment at an elementary school a short time later, expressing the hope that his departure would "take the heat off" Whitney.[14] It did not. An entirely different sort of controversy soon erupted about the school, this one over testing—and cheating.

15

As Whitney's reputation and stature grew, demand for the limited number of slots each year became feverish. Competition fueled demand further: The school began affecting the real estate market as agents used Whitney's record to sell homes, which drove the area's changing demographics and influenced immigration decisions by families halfway around the world.

Word that a public school education with a fast track to top colleges was available in ethnically diverse Cerritos spread first among Filipino families, then Chinese families from Hong Kong and Taiwan, and finally among families from South Korea, where pursuit of educational opportunities is renown for sometimes reaching near-obsessive intensity. Soon, more than five hundred academically eligible students from the district wanted to enter Whitney's seventh grade each year—nearly four times the number that the school could accommodate. If the ABC School District had not imposed an absolute rule against accepting students to Whitney from outside its boundaries, applicants would have numbered in the thousands.

Given that sort of demand—and the high stakes many families created for themselves by moving to the area expressly because of Whitney—it was inevitable that the annual sixth-grade testing used to determine admission to the school would become a much anticipated and dreaded event. Children felt enormous pressure to perform for the parents who had moved halfway around the world for their educational opportunities. Some got sick as the tests were handed out. Every year a few burst into tears from the stress.

Those who had their hearts set on Whitney but missed the mark were crushed—or, at least, their parents were. Some families felt they were being relegated to a second-class education, one of the things that most riled the teachers at other schools and helped drive the desire to close Whitney. Determined parents would show up at Bob Beall's office, making veiled—and not so veiled—offers of payment to alter an unfavorable admissions decision. "I'm very wealthy," one father assured the principal during one especially tight admissions year in the eighties. "I'll be happy to make a large donation once my son is admitted. What amount would you like?" A mother with a child on the waiting list, meanwhile, took a different tack: "I'd do *anything* to get my daughter into Whitney," she said, closing Beall's office door, leaning close to him, and staring meaningfully into his eyes. "Anything."

With that sort of desperation in the air, the private sector soon smelled a golden opportunity: Professional after-school tutoring. A virtual cottage industry sprouted up around the school, at first catering to sixth-grade students, then fifth, and finally rolling back to first grade and even kindergarten. Storefront academies appeared seemingly overnight, unregulated operations needing little more to open than a location and a city business license ($160 at City Hall, checks accepted). Their numbers shot up from a handful to more than twenty in the space of a few years. Some called themselves education centers or learning centers, but others, striving for a friendlier face or a marketing edge, incorporated in their titles words like *handsome, smart, elite, Einstein.* This academy industry became increasingly competitive and aggressive in promoting itself in the early 1990s, moving beyond the more typical after-school tutoring and raise-your-score-by-100-points-or-your-money-back SAT courses (although these programs remained huge draws) to specifically advertising "secrets" of the Whitney admissions tests for up to one thousand dollars per student.

Immigrant families in particular flocked to these academies, anxious to protect their investments after being enticed to Cerritos by the promise of a prep-school education with no tuition. Some academies earned sterling reputations as excellent tutoring services, but others have been criticized over the years for their ethics, or lack thereof. One academy printed an ad so explicit in a special edition of Whitney's school newspaper—which was to be sent home to parents at all nineteen elementary schools in ABC—that officials scrambled to seize the papers before they could be delivered. The advertisement asked the rhetorical question: "Do you want the answers to the Whitney entrance exam?" Four of the other twelve pages of the issue were devoted to private academy ads offering Whitney test-prep classes.

The academy insisted its ad was a poorly phrased solicitation for customers interested in preparation for the *type* of test used to select Whitney students, not an offer for the specific questions used on the actual exam. But the advertisement struck a nerve among Whitney teachers and the parents of prospective students. Rumors began circulating that some of the academies had a knack for getting copies of the admissions test in advance, allowing them to rehearse their students and give them an unfair advantage—for a steep price some anxious and desperate parents were willing to pay.

Allegations of cheating on the test were never a problem for the first dozen or so years after Whitney imposed its entrance-by-exam admissions system. The school's original teacher-authored test cost nothing, could be altered every year, and employed numerous essay questions rather than the ubiquitous multiple-choice questions typical of the off-the-shelf commercial tests more commonly used by schools and school districts. It was graded by Whitney teachers and was just one component in a relatively flexible and subjective process that also took into account a student's academic record in elementary school, the relative difficulty in scoring high grades in one school versus another, and that student's perceived potential for doing well at Whitney. Beall had wanted to consider "the whole student" rather than simply selecting for the top test takers—admissions methods more reminiscent of elite private colleges than public schools. There were no quotas back then, but the marching orders were to strive for geographic, ethnic, and economic diversity whenever possible. In the early years, this posed few dilemmas because not every eligible seventh grader in the district applied to get into the fledgling school, and so a greater percentage of prospective students could be invited to enroll than would later be the case.

The door to cheating opened in the late 1980s, when the district decided to strip Whitney of its autonomy and assumed control of the testing and admissions process. A district-sponsored committee of parents and community members had recommended a more objective, standardized test, the Curriculum Frameworks Assessment System from educational publisher McGraw-Hill (currently CTB Macmillan/McGraw-Hill). The multiple-choice test would be given to all 1,600 sixth graders in the districts, with the top 25 percent eligible to apply to Whitney. A separate essay test, based upon a literary excerpt students would have to read and analyze, would also be given. The multiple-choice test would count for 70 percent of a student's score when applying to Whitney, with the essay test worth 30 percent.

Complaints began almost from the start, with irate parents whose children did not qualify alleging that some of the test takers appeared to recognize many of the questions on the test and were able to cruise through them while other students struggled. This was dismissed as little more than rumor, however, until 1994, when scandal erupted in the form of a formal complaint by a sixth grader named Melissa, who described a disturbing scene in the classroom where the test was administered: Several students appeared to have memorized the answers in advance, breezing through the pages of the test in record time. One of them smugly announced, "I've seen this test before," the girl told district officials.

The cheating allegations were at first met with disbelief and characterized as a hoax or sour grapes from a family whose sixth grader missed the Whitney cut. Months later, however, McGraw-Hill officials revealed that they had sold a copy of the test to one of the Cerritos storefront academies that had been prepping students for the admissions test. An exam the district had believed to be secure had been, it turned out, on sale for years, readily available to any educators in public or private settings who could dial a phone and order from a catalog. Although the academies all denied misusing the test materials, mortified district officials concluded that some test takers had indeed been given the answers to the test ahead of time. Even so, a follow-up investigation by the district was unproductive and ultimately toothless. No crime had been committed. No legal action could be taken. The academies, as unregulated businesses, had only the marketplace to answer to, which posed little problem for them, given the success of their students on the Whitney test. The district offered no estimates of how many students got an unfair edge on Whitney admission in this way over the years—a handful, dozens, hundreds? It was impossible to tell.

With only anecdotal evidence of cheating, the district declined to redo the exam, and instead commissioned from

McGraw-Hill a scrambled version for the next year's test, with some different questions from the company's other commercially available versions. When this failed to satisfy security concerns the following year, the district asked the company to impose an embargo on the test, so that it could not be sold in California before the district administered it. Uneasiness persisted even with that assurance in place, and the district finally scrapped the entire practice of a separate Whitney admissions test in favor of using scores from the standardized and more secure California Achievement Test, which was then given to students throughout the state and not available outside the public schools. Once again, a separate essay test was added by the district to create a middle school placement test, but this left room for yet another security breach. A copy of the essay portion of the test was obtained by one or more of the academies—it had been distributed a week in advance to the elementary schools—and once again some kids caught an early peek. Another cheating scandal erupted, followed by another district investigation.

In January 1999, the district's director of curriculum, instruction, and schools was forced to write a letter to the parents of every sixth grader in the district, all 1,600 of them: "There is widespread evidence that the security of the writing portion of the Middle School Placement Test has been compromised. This evidence comes from students, parents, teachers, principals, and a private academy owner. It is clear that some students had the essay question at least one day before the exam. It is also clear that some students received improper adult assistance in the construction, wording, and editing of the essay before the exam."

This test was used to determine placement and programs for all middle school students, but no one doubted that the impulse to get kids into Whitney lay behind this latest cheating scandal. The upshot: Every student would have to retake the essay portion of the test, and the security would be beefed up further, with tests kept under lock and key until the day of testing.

Even these precautions left room for the academies to confer an edge, because students took the essay test over the course of three days, with the first two spent reading and discussing a literary passage in class. On the third day, the students were given their essay question and asked to write about the passage they had previously read. This system gave the academies ample time to interrogate their students about the reading so that they could attempt to predict likely questions and provide suitable answers. Ten years of doubt, missteps, and problematic ethics had resulted from one seemingly reasonable and simple decision to remove authority over the admissions exam from the local control of the school. Security had been compromised and Whitney's reputation sullied, all because of a test that the school's teachers viewed as inferior to their original.

The daily newspaper serving the Cerritos area, the *Long Beach Press-Telegram,* fumed over the scandals that tarnished the school's image, editorializing about the dangers of "Whitney obsession" among parents, who were sending the "wrong message" to kids. "Impressionable youngsters are told that it's permissible to get exam questions and answers in advance. If our best and brightest are doing this on a sixth-grade exam, what will they do when they assume leadership positions?"

But even the paper conceded that zealous parental pursuit of Whitney admission is understandable, especially in an era when most public schools have been criticized incessantly by national leaders. Once Whitney had established a track record of maximizing students' chances of getting into great colleges while at the same time minimizing their exposure to drugs, gangs, and the other social ills plaguing so many schools, demand was bound to become great. Many parents turned a blind eye to the methods of the academies so long as the results were good, while others were well aware that they were participating in the stacking of the admissions deck, choosing to do so anyway because they saw it as a necessary means of achieving a desirable end.

"I'd do anything for my child," one mother later explained. "I have no guilt. No laws were broken. It's only one test, but the results will last a lifetime."

Other parents were outraged by such justifications. They obtained only legitimate prep and practice for their children and felt they had been unfairly tarred by the actions of a few less-scrupulous parents. And then there were those families who lacked the resources to pay for any sort of academy preparation, legitimate or otherwise, and so felt their children did not get to compete on a level playing field for those precious slots in Whitney's seventh-grade class. The same sort of divide that exists between private and public schools—a gap Whitney was intended to bridge—seemed to be opening anew.

Affirmative action and, later, geographic preferences, attempted to address some of these concerns, however imperfectly. Because the scandals involved students *applying* to Whitney, rather than kids already attending, the school's reputation remained intact. Outrage over the series of test scandals soon faded into the background, even as the academies kept prepping record numbers of little kids.

Still, the episode marked a turning point for Whitney. The obsessiveness of some parents in preparing their children for the school does have its positive side: Strong parental involvement in any school is a source of strength, and Whitney parents have been generous with their time and their checkbooks in an era when few schools can maintain quality without outside sources of money. The high expectations, as Beall and his successor, Tom Brock, argue, do seem crucial to the school's success.

But the fervor over gaining entry to Whitney and then pushing the achievement envelope ever higher also ensured that the school would change in fundamental ways. Inevitably, it evolved from the quirky place of Shirley Wold's youth, where coffee was a drink for old people, to its current, far more serious, far more stressful, far more caffeinated incarnation.

Or, as wise-beyond-her-years seventeen-year-old Cecilia observes, "When your family moves from another city—or another country—so you can go to Whitney High School, the pressure is on. And you better not screw up."

PART III

Finding the Lucky Pants

It's not that I'm so smart.
It's just that I stay with problems longer.

—ALBERT EINSTEIN

16

"If I shake this back and forth," Rod Ziolkowski asks the class, "what will happen?"

By now, the students in honors physics know a Mr. Z trick question when they hear one, and they hesitate to blurt out the obvious answer. Their teacher is holding before them a strange-looking model: It has a flat wooden base, about one foot long, anchoring three vertical metal rods of varying lengths, from less than a foot to about two feet tall, each topped by a small, rounded block of wood. The effect is less physics experiment and more like the spindly Dr. Seuss trees the kids remember from kindergarten story time.

The topic today is wave motion: water, sound, light. The class eyes the unlikely model warily as Mr. Z gives each thin metal rod a slight push with a finger, one at a time, making them sway slightly, so the class can see they are all flexible. "If you shake it, they'll all move," several students finally volunteer. Sometimes the obvious can be right.

"Well, let's see," the teacher says, and he begins to shake the model back and forth, very fast. Only the short rod sways. He stops and switches to a long slow motion and immediately the long rod moves as the others stand still. Then he strikes a motion somewhere in between; the medium rod moves in syncopation while the other two remain motionless.

"Whoa," one student says loudly, accompanied by a dozen other *ooohs* and *ahhhs*.

"He's a magician!" Sam calls out, for it does look like a parlor trick.

"Come on up and try it," he says, and they do, kids with a cool new toy, fascinated and perplexed, then quick to grasp this visual demonstration of the dry discussion of resonance and frequency they read last night in their textbooks. The model illustrates a host of principles and equations the class will use over the next few weeks, explaining everything from how wind can make a suspension bridge collapse (one very cool video), to why green light and red light combine—in apparent contradiction of everything they've been taught in the past—to make pure yellow.

Mr. Z could have just given them the technical explanation of light waves and electromagnetic disturbances and resonance and the natural frequency of objects. He could have had them memorize the right equations, and they could have passed a test on wave theory just as handily. But long after those equations are forgotten and the exact wording of the underlying principles grows hazy, they will remember those magic metal trees and understand, viscerally, how one tiny piece of the universe ticks.

"As a teacher, you live for those oooh-ahhh moments," he reflects after class. "It is a rush, every time. Maybe it's the performer in me....Or maybe it's the idea they might be walking out of the room with something they'll keep."

This idea of what students "keep" is a concern that has weighed heavily on Mr. Z this year, and not only because he worries about his physics classes. He also frets about the education of his own son, a junior at another high school in the neighboring city of Long Beach. He's a smart kid, a good kid, but Ziolkowski has worried he's underperforming his potential and has ridden him a bit in recent years for bringing home Bs and Cs instead of As and Bs. It's a familiar tale: Perhaps it's a father remembering his own experience of trying to skate by in high school and almost missing out on life's opportunities. Perhaps it's just wanting the best for his son, to see him succeed, to get the legion of As he'll need to get into UCLA or beyond. Whatever the reason, things grew a bit tense between them, and Mr. Z (prodded by his wife) has had to make a conscious effort to back off, to be more approving and less judgmental, with the surprising result that his son's attitude and grades and willingness to talk about schoolwork have all improved this year, like one of Mr. Z's counterintuitive lab experiments that do the opposite of what common sense dictates. He is taking his first AP class this year, European history, and he loves it, he's been working his tail off and doing well. The workload is huge, but it is matched by his enthusiasm.

And then, the other day, it happened. They're riding in the car and his son is saying his grades are coming up, he's got a GPA nearing the mid-threes now, and Mr. Z just can't help himself. He says, "And now if you just change one of those Bs to an A, then you'll..."

As he speaks, he looks in the rearview mirror and sees the expression on his son's face, the spark just draining out of it, replaced by the grim look of a kid who's thinking, *Nothing I ever do is good enough.* Suddenly, Mr. Z sees—no, feels—with perfect clarity for the first time just what so many of his students at Whitney have to deal with, how they are too often made to feel less than what they are by the pressure and the demands, and he knows, with gut-punch certainty, that he does not want to be that kind of teacher. Or that kind of dad.

———

Bob Beall is right: A school is like an organism, living, breathing, complex, impossible to know in its entirety. A thousand
dramas unfold daily, endless storylines, alliances, jockeying,
heartbreaks, victories, and secrets—oh so many secrets—
small and large. The physics experiment unfolds, some kids
are rapt, others are discreetly working on another class's
homework, one kid is playing Uncle Worm on his computerized calculator, another is daydreaming about next year while
her neighbor is dreading next year—and this incredible
human mosaic, rich and unwieldy and only sometimes expected, repeats in every other classroom, every period, every
day.

Parents very often have no idea what life is like in an
American high school today; their own high school journeys
of twenty or thirty years ago might as well have been a century earlier. Their experience is utterly divorced from their
children's, these schools of the Internet and chat rooms and
sexual imagery everywhere, of junk-food lunches and Starbucks dinners and laughable television ads beamed into
every classroom, telling kids that buying pot supports terrorism and that cola should be their drink of choice and that
one big, cool adventure is waiting for them right around the
corner if they would only join the "life accelerator" and sign
up for four years with the U.S. Navy. High school today is
perpetually in motion and, contrary to what so many students and teachers say, never boring. What governmental or
social endeavor is more vital? Does anything that goes on
in Pentagon war rooms or corporate boardrooms, hospital
operating rooms or White House conference rooms, have a
greater impact on our nation's future and potential and
dreams than what goes on in a classroom? And yet the tools
we have to measure and understand this most important of
institutions, this haven for our most precious commodity, are
hopelessly inadequate: the test scores, the SAT averages, the

graduation rates and college acceptances and PTA meetings and legislative studies give only the faintest of caricatures of what Whitney High School, or any high school, is really like. "My parents think they know," Nisreen says. "I mean, my mom teaches here, right? So if anyone should know what life is like for kids like us, she should. But she has no clue."

No wonder a century of educational reforms has failed to accomplish their goals, these piecemeal approaches that seize on a single problem, a single symptom, a single cure—whether it's phonics instruction or self-esteem building or more computers in the classroom—without ever considering the effects on the whole organism. Class-size reduction is a perfect example, perfectly commonsense: Who could argue with the goal of making classes smaller? Smaller classes mean more attention can be offered each student, and surely that has to lead to better learning, better test scores, better schools. So in 1996, Pete Wilson, then governor of California, called the state superintendent of public instruction into his office and gave her twenty days to lower class sizes from thirty to twenty students in kindergarten, first, and second grade. Legislation followed, and just like that, on a political whim from yet another governor with presidential fantasies, a $1.6 billion annual program to make classrooms more intimate in California was born. It soon expanded to include third grade and select secondary-school classes as well (at Whitney these included ninth-grade science and English classes) involving over 1.5 million kids, all of which demanded the immediate hiring of some thirty thousand new teachers.

Only problem is, there was a national shortage of qualified teachers, a profession long accorded little respect and less money. So California did what many other states have done since: Even as the reforms were giddily trumpeted as ushering in a new era in education, the state quietly filled many of those new positions with uncredentialed, novice, or emergency-credentialed teachers with little or no experience in the subjects they were being asked to teach. It took six years for the bad news to finally surface about this costly but wildly popular program: The smaller classes had no effect on student achievement in the state. A consortium of think tanks led by the RAND Corporation found that, overall, schools participating in the class-size reductions did no better as a group on standardized tests than schools that opted not to pony up the money to join the program.[15] Perhaps the classes weren't small enough at twenty, the researchers suggested, or perhaps the underqualified and inexperienced teachers who marched into those smaller classes were not as effective as well-qualified teachers instructing larger numbers of kids. Whatever the explanation, $9 billion and counting had been spent, portable classrooms were constructed by the hundreds to accommodate greater numbers of smaller classes, school districts were bankrupted—with no evidence that classrooms of twenty kids are any better or more effective than those of thirty. (Which isn't to say that the idea is bad, just its execution: A smaller-scale controlled experiment in Tennessee has linked higher test scores to class size, but only when the classes were reduced to *fifteen* students, and all teachers were *fully* credentialed—details that somehow eluded Governor Wilson.)

The same sort of well-intentioned but flawed attempts to reform education have brought us math textbooks with no math in them, computers in the classroom that are more distraction than learning tools, school accountability laws that encourage a lowering of standards, contracts to for-profit education companies that cannot make a profit, and reading-instruction programs based on outmoded and discredited theories. Enormous sums of money are spent on such remedies for our public schools, yet it is rare indeed for any reformer, advocate, president, or legislator to actually sit down in one of those schools, to spend time observing and listening and finding out what works and what doesn't in the real world. No one who really understood how a school works, or even how a single classroom functions, or what an incredibly arduous and unnatural process it is to teach a young person to read, or to understand fractions, or to appreciate the beauty of a John Donne couplet, would ever advocate hiring thirty thousand new teachers, virtually overnight, then throwing them into action. California still has not recovered from that debacle.

Tom Brock has decided to take a different approach. If any school should lead the way on this score, to take a close, reasonable, informed look at what works, what doesn't work, and what needs to be improved, he figures it should be Whitney High School.

As part of the same initiative that created the three new grade-level advisor positions, Brock has brought together for a luncheon meeting a collection of parents, students, teachers, counselors, and members of the school's various parents' associations and fund-raising groups. He has asked them to discuss the areas each grade level at the school would like to see addressed, fixed, expanded, or quelled. Their suggestions will be used to help decide the priorities for each grade-level advisor over the next several years. The participants seem to think that Brock's cooperative, open approach to school counseling and administration is both refreshing and unusual.

On the same day in which Mr. Z engages his class with the natural frequencies of steel rods, Brock has pulled together several large, round tables inside the Multi-Purpose Room, the largest meeting space available in the building (there is no dedicated auditorium or performance area at Whitney, where the drama class gets by with fifty kids crammed in a classroom with a plywood platform in one corner for a stage). The MPR is crowded with stacks of brown metal folding chairs and a chaotic herd of black, bristling music stands along one wall, with assorted other boxes and disused movable walls stacked to the side in anticipation of the long-awaited remodel planned for the summer. It's a humble, jumbled setting, but there are sandwiches, fruit, soda, coffee, and doughnuts for the participants, and every Whitney constituency is represented in the room, even the little kids. As the gathering separates into a mix of table-sized groups, each equipped with a large notepad and markers to create a list of concerns, Brock summarizes his reason for inviting them all.

"Whitney has been the top-ranked school in the state for three years in a row. Our vision is for Whitney to be the best college-preparatory public school in the world. We think that is a realistic vision, but one that will require much hard work. And that's why you've been asked here today."

As each group begins to discuss individual concerns, the divide between the constituencies quickly becomes stark: Parents and kids are on different pages, almost as if they're discussing different schools, different lives.

Michael, a slim, dark-haired eighth grader, complains about the quality of classes and teachers in seventh and eighth grade. "We keep hearing that eighth-grade grades don't matter. The colleges won't even look at them. So a lot of kids aren't trying. It makes it hard for the rest of us." Jessie, a tenth grader, has a related concern: rampant procrastination in doing schoolwork by her peers. At home, kids sit down at their computers and begin chatting with Instant Messenger instead of doing their homework, she says. Hours pass, and then panic sets in. "Procrastination leads to cheating. There's a lot of 'Can I borrow your homework?' right before it's due. And, you know, you can't say no. And you feel like a fool for doing your work."

"I have kids falling asleep in class and when you ask them, they joke about being up all night on IM," eleventh-grade English teacher Sue Brannen agrees.

Two Whitney moms at the table are staring, astonished. "I had no idea," Nancy, the mother of a ninth grader, says. "I've been concerned that when I ask my daughter what does she want to be, she doesn't know. But maybe there are other things I should be worrying about."

"Parents give us a lot of pressure," Luke, another student, observes. "They want us all to be doctors and lawyers and they don't want to hear anything else....Maybe that's why your daughter says she doesn't know. Because she knows you only want to hear one thing."

"It may sound strange to you," the mother replies, "but I never thought of that. My daughter never said anything." Which is, of course, Luke's point.

The groups begin to list their concerns in order of importance. Homework turns out to be a top one, but for different reasons: The kids say they are concerned that cheating is rampant and that many kids copy their homework from friends, ingeniously splitting up tasks and doing it piecemeal (and, therefore, learning only pieces). The parents, on the other hand, worry there is just too much homework, and that the quantity, rather than a real desire to cheat, might be contributing to "sharing." This is pretty mild (Whitney parents generally approve of lots of homework), a far cry from the "homework revolts" that have gripped some other suburban school districts around the country. Still, the teachers there scoff at both notions. They seem certain the kids are exaggerating their homework load and that they simply need to manage their time better, though they agree that homework sharing is so commonplace they can't even begin to police it. Kids who say they would never cheat themselves cannot say no when a friend asks to copy their homework, nor would they turn somebody in for doing so. "So I guess that does make me a cheater, in a way," one girl muses. "It's too hard to say no."

Second on the list of parent, student, and teacher complaints is SAT stress. "Everyone wants to go to the same few colleges," Luke complains. "So the pressure to be brilliant on the SATs is huge. Many kids are unaware of other choices for college, though. We need to hear more about them. And parents need to be open to them, too. A lot of times, they aren't." Behind him, several of the moms are shaking their heads and making Luke's point for him: Their Ivy League dreams are too firmly entrenched to be so easily diverted. If the name of the school doesn't carry a certain weight of familiarity and reputation, it often is discounted.

Sleep deprivation; Internet overtime; other forms of cheating; pressure from parents; lack of communication between kids, teachers, and parents; and overscheduled student lives round out the list of concerns. Shirley Wold stands up and writes them with bold black marker on a big sheet of poster paper at the front of the room. Brock seems pleased at the results of this first meeting, and he starts to explain how they'll refine the lists each table submitted, pulling out the top concerns, and then begin looking for ways to address them. "It seems like stress and time management are big issues, followed by cheating and career paths..." he starts to say.

"Just so that we don't have to worry about it," one father interrupts a bit sheepishly, "can you speak to something else that hasn't come up? Can you tell us there are no drugs or crime problems on campus?"

Brock looks at the man and takes a deep breath. It would have been tempting to simply say yes, but he doesn't. "I cannot say that we do not have a problem with drugs on this campus. I cannot say we don't have a problem with criminal activity on this campus. Are we better off than most schools? Yes."

"So our children are safe here?" the dad asks, anxious now.

"They're safe here," Wold interjects. "But some kids are doing things off campus, and we can't control that. Are kids using drugs on campus? Not that we know of. Are they doing it off campus? Yes. Some are."

The kids, so vocal during the rest of the discussions, have fallen silent now. They feel certain Whitney compares favorably to most other campuses when it comes to drugs and crime, but they are equally aware that it is not perfect. No one is completely satisfied with that answer. But there is none other to give.

A short time later, the guests gather up their papers and books and filter out of the MPR, the kids heading back to classes, the parents bound for home and work, a few lingering to chat or to make a last point. As they leave, one mom leans over and whispers to her fifteen-year-old daughter, "So, when are you going to start thinking about what you're going to do with your life? ... You need to pick a major!" The daughter just keeps walking.

When he looked into that rearview mirror and saw the crestfallen expression on his son's face staring back at him, Mr. Z wished he could suck those words back in, make it so they were never uttered, but all he can do at first is silently berate himself: *Dammit, Ziolkowski, you said the wrong thing. Again.*

But then he does something he doesn't often do: He stops himself in midsentence. It's not easy to do because, in his heart, he feels he's right, that in the best of all possible worlds, his son would try just a bit harder and would earn those extra As, and would get to go to some top university. But he also knows that's exactly what his students' parents say to him when he tells them their kids are doing great, and that there's nothing wrong with a B. He knows his prodding is dead wrong if it saps the joy of learning his son is just rediscovering now that his dad has backed off, and he knows that his wife is right when she says: "Rod, he is a great kid. And he's going to have a good life and a successful life no matter what college he goes to."

And so he cuts himself off and looks in the mirror and starts over again, as if he hadn't said a word: "You know what? You're doing great. And I'm proud of you." Then he just keeps on driving, the tension drifting out through the open car window.

You spend a whole year building kids up, his friend Steve Murray, the calculus teacher, likes to say. *Carefully, slowly, you bring them along. And then someone else comes in and with one careless, hurtful comment, can just destroy them. That's the power teachers have, to build up or bring down.*

Mr. Z knows what side of that equation he wants to stay on, at school, and at home.

17

The first morning that school reopens after winter break is cool and colorless, the sky a dull gray—January 7, a staff development day, just faculty, no students. Teachers finish their meetings and putter in their classrooms, catching up on paperwork and grade books. The building feels hollow today, every scrape and rustle magnified by the fluorescent emptiness. The shabbiness of the place shows most when the kids aren't around, the solitude exaggerating the drabness of the beige walls with their burlap texture and the stains on the industrial carpeting in the hallways. Mike Mustillo, the science teacher and tech-support guru who is masterminding the logistics of modernizing the place, scuttles through the building in his trademark shorts and baseball cap, toting a clipboard and trying to hold Whitney's frayed infrastructure together a few more months. "You really see how much we need a face-lift when the kids aren't around," he sighs. "I can't wait."

In the front office, Tom Brock has assumed his old role of psychologist, gathering the school's counselors around his desk for a ninety-minute crash course on detecting, preventing, and dealing with substance abuse. He tries, as is his way, to keep things light, but it is a fairly grim meeting. The pre-holiday crisis with Charles's methamphetamine tweaking has left them all shaken and feeling caught off guard—something Brock is determined to remedy.

There is some good news for the group to consider first: Things seem to be going well with Charles's recovery. His family has come through in a big way—supportive but not accusatory, concerned but not angry, firm and resolute in laying out new rules for him, but willing to let him slowly rebuild trust. Sometimes families fly apart at these moments, Brock says; but Charles's came together. His sister's regular reports to Gary McHatton suggest he's remained drug free since that day almost three weeks ago when he sat shaking in McHatton's office. The family decided against checking him into a residential program, but he is seeing a doctor and is under close supervision at home. Charles is exercising, working on the homecoming float with the other seniors, spending time with McHatton, and steering clear of any friends who tweak or who use other drugs. "Mom is watching that very closely," McHatton says.

Charles's supplier, a recent Whitney graduate, has also been persuaded to get help; the Whitney network of friends, teachers, and alumni has extended its reach in an effort to bring him back from the brink as well. The college freshman was angry when first confronted by his mother (who had been alerted by a call from Shirley Wold). At first, he denied everything. But when his mother persisted, his face crumpled and he broke down, saying he was afraid he would die soon if he didn't get help. He took a leave from college and checked into a treatment program.

Now the larger question remains, Wold says to the group. "How do we respond here? What do we do when the next Charles comes along?"

One of the next steps is obvious. Brock and the others all agree they must make certain there are no drugs, and no drugged kids, on campus. Perhaps they can arrange some training for teachers to recognize the warning signs of drug intoxication in their students. But they all agree that's not really much of an issue. They have seen no signs that on-campus drug use is even a small problem: It's the kids who could be using after school, outside their view and jurisdiction, that they're worried about.

That was Charles's story. He didn't use drugs at Whitney, and no one really saw his meltdown coming except, perhaps, his closest friends and an ex-girlfriend in whom he confided. Here was a kid with scholarships in the works, who seemed happy and carefree, whose grades had slipped a little bit, but not so much as to raise any alarms—just another case of se-nioritis after the big push of junior year. Everyone knew Charles, and everyone figured he would do well in life. In retrospect, his cyclic bouts of energy and exhaustion seem like obvious clues, but in truth, his teachers chalked it up to just another kid pulling too many all-nighters and chugging too many lattes, his behavior indistinguishable from that of a host of his classmates. There's always someone crashing and falling asleep in class, particularly among the seniors—that doesn't mean they're tweaking, Brock says.

The principal makes it clear he is very uneasy about launching anything that could be construed as a witch-hunt. This is not the sort of school that would start drug testing its kids (a practice declared legal by the U.S. Supreme Court in 1995, but employed by only 5 percent of the nation's schools). Nor does he want the counselors to take on the role of cops hunting down drug users, which he feels would be counterproductive. "Why," Brock asks, to drive home his point, "did he come forward at all?"

"Because he trusted us," McHatton says. "And because a friend he spoke to about his fears of addiction and dying told him that we were okay."

"I rejoice in that," Brock says, "because it means part of

what we need to do, you're already doing....We don't want to lose that trust."

Realistically, a drug-free school is probably attainable, Brock says. But a drug-free student body? Not likely, he says. They can and should preach abstinence, he adds, by urging kids to stay away from drugs and drinking as the surest way to stay healthy, whole, and out of trouble. But they have to recognize the limits of that sort of message. "The truth is, that's out of step with most adolescent behavior. It's like saying, don't have sex and you can't get pregnant. It just doesn't work."

The counselors shift uncomfortably at this. Knowing what to do about drug abuse, casual or otherwise, is a challenge that has confounded schools and governments for decades. Billions of tax dollars have been spent on prevention programs, from the ubiquitous but statistically irrelevant police-sponsored program DARE, to a series of equally ineffective and sometimes laughable television ad campaigns ranging from "Just Say No" to "This Is Your Brain on Drugs," to recent attempts to link buying drugs to funding terrorism (in which kids are depicted defending their right to get high, then announcing, "I helped kill a judge" or "I helped terrorists build a bomb"). Despite such efforts, a quarter of all eighth graders and more than half of all seniors surveyed nationally in 2002 reported using some kind of illicit drug, with even more owning up to boozing.[16]

Whitney students and recent graduates give a similar ballpark estimate of drug activity at the school, at least for marijuana and alcohol. They seem to think Whitney students are less likely to experiment with other drugs than the national average, but it's pure, if informed and insider, guesswork. It's hard to know for sure, they say, because students here are so adept at concealing pretty much everything from their parents, who are invariably tempted to assume that a high-performing, low-crime school like Whitney has little in the way of drug problems. Charles's family had no idea of the secret life he was leading. School officials never thought Whitney was immune on this score, but even they hadn't given it much attention before Charles forced their hand. Now the idea that kids like him might feel so pressured that they take speed to keep up has added a new wrinkle to the equation; the potential allure of stimulants in this land of all-nighters has the counselors worried.

"My question," McHatton says, "is how do we identify our other kids with a problem? Because I don't think this is a one-shot deal. Even though he says he wasn't doing it with friends on campus, I'm not sure we can accept that at face value."

"He may be protecting people," Shirley Wold agrees.

Brock pulls out a sheaf of papers and gives a set to each person in the room, a kind of mini-course on evaluating kids for potential drug abuse that outlines the physiological, sociological, and psychological risk factors. Among the factors particularly significant for Whitney, Brock says, are over-demanding parents and, ironically, *overprotective* parents.

"We have students whose parents never let them make a mistake or take responsibility for anything..." Brock starts to say.

"So when they get to their first big party," Debbie Logan interjects, "and there are kids smoking pot—look out!"

Brock nods. "We've had enough seniors come back after three months and tell us they felt totally unprepared for life at university. They are overwhelmed, and they have no skills for making choices. And then there's the other end of the spectrum, where some of our kids are at greater risk because our parents can be so demanding, they ask for so much. And their children cannot cope."

Just this past week, Brock had to talk to a troubled young woman who comes from a family of physicians, gifted musicians, people at the top of their fields. The expectations were so high she began to rebel by wearing startlingly heavy makeup and trashy clothes, all very much out of character. She stopped doing her work and started hanging out with older kids from other schools, and the buzz among concerned friends was that she might be into drugs. When the principal called her in to ask what was up, she told him she realized she could never measure up to the expectations at home and that she had decided to leave Whitney and embark on a new career—as a hooker in Las Vegas. The staff isn't sure how serious she really is, but they have been talking to her daily ever since, trying to persuade her that she has better options than selling herself and getting high.

"To me, it blows me away that eighth or ninth graders are drinking coffee to pull all-nighters," Debbie Logan says, shaking her head. She is back after a long leave and throwing herself into work after the loss of her son, whose murder remains unsolved. "And to me, that's the start of it....I never drank any coffee in high school. It just blows me away that they say they need this to keep up. And that may be leading to all sorts of other things."

"I think a lot of this all-nighter stuff is legacy. They think that's what they have to do—that this is the Whitney way," Wold says. "Staying up all night to get the work done, showing what you're made of: It's such crap!"

The others are not so sure, however, and Brock suggests it might not hurt to talk to the teachers about making sure homework loads are doable, and also to offer guidance to students—and their parents—on time management in some upcoming newsletters and classroom sessions. They also agree to bring in someone to talk to the faculty about how to spot the warning signs of drug abuse. Wold says she already has several students she thinks are having a problem for whom she's going to set up parent conferences.

In the end, though, the meeting leads to little in the way of concrete action, and the teachers break up feeling like they are helpless to put a dent in a problem they aren't even sure how to define, much less solve. "I'm not sure anything is going to change," Wold tells her colleagues after the meeting. "I'm just afraid that, once this blows over, we're going to go back to where we were. And I'm not sure that's good enough."

The uproar over Charles seems to have brought other simmering problems to the surface. A few days later, Wold finds herself in a conference with the mother and stepfather of Jill, one of the stay-out-all-night kids. Jill is a tenth grader who did well in her first years at Whitney but began struggling enough last year to be placed on academic probation. She barely passed all her courses in ninth grade. Wold has always found her to be a good-natured kid, intense but easy to talk to. Everyone figured she'd snap back this year.

Instead, her anemic grades have plummeted to her worst ever, she's been staying out until dawn, every conversation between her and her mother seems to erupt into a huge argument. Jill's parents fear she is using drugs and Wold thinks they may be right. She's noticed Jill's personality has changed, that she flies off the handle over the least irritation, she's overemotional and manipulative, and that she seems to lie about things without compunction or guilt, simply spinning a new and more creative tale once she's caught. She had her marine biology teacher alternately furious at her for refusing to do the work (the *Moby-Dick* assignment so many in the class despised), then consumed with guilt when she burst into tears and told him the reason she didn't do the reading was that she couldn't afford the book—her family's too poor, she told him. The first-year teacher, Chris Williams, was so stricken he gave her a copy and put a long note of apology and encouragement inside. Wold hated breaking the news to him when he confessed how awful he felt for being so hard on

Jill: "Chris, her family's got money. She's just shining you on." When Wold told Jill how wounded her teacher had been when he learned the truth, the girl just shrugged.

"I used to think of her as the best person I know," her stepfather says forlornly during the meeting with Wold, without Jill present. "I loved being with her."

"She denies doing any drugs, but we don't believe her," Jill's mother says. "We think she might be using speed, or maybe ecstasy."

"Well, she is showing a number of the warning signs," Wold agrees.

It turns out that Jill's parents have already made up their mind about what to do: They're taking her for a blood test— today. "At least then, we'll know," the stepfather says.

Wold wishes them luck, arranges for Jill to come to the office after class, and sees the parents out with their unhappy daughter. If the test turns something up, Wold thinks, maybe Jill will come clean and start to talk honestly with her parents.

But the results of the test are negative, which solves nothing, because it only proves Jill hasn't imbibed narcotics or alcohol within the last few days. Little is accomplished except to further boost Jill's anger and alienation and her parents' frustration with their daughter and the school. At least a positive blood test would have given them something concrete and specific to fight, something to try and fix. Now they are left wondering: What happened to our little girl? Why is she acting this way?

Debbie Logan, meanwhile, has been counseling an eighth-grade boy with behavior very similar to Jill's, though it turns out drugs are not a factor here, either. When confronted, he admits he's tanking on his schoolwork on purpose. This is a phenomenon unique to Whitney: A handful of kids go this route every year; it's the only way they can think of to get out of a place where they don't want to be. This boy wants to return to his friends at his neighborhood middle school. He wants to relax, without looking over his shoulder all the time for the next test. A ninth-grade girl who misses her old cheerleading squad is doing the same thing. These are two kids whose parents desperately wanted a Whitney education, even when their children did not.

In both cases, the parents first asked the school counselors if drugs or mental illness might be the causes of their kids' decline in academic performance, which had once been fairly high. Maybe they need treatment or therapy or mood-altering drugs, their parents speculated. Gentle suggestions from the counselors that another school might be a better choice are met with disbelief and anger. They will not voluntarily withdraw their children from Whitney, they say.

So one of the students will stay and be miserable, at least for another semester. Another must leave anyway, over parental objections, because of failure to pull up his grades. The parents are furious, but kids attend Whitney on a special permit that excuses them from attending their neighborhood schools, a privilege, not a right; the school can pull the permit for cause whenever necessary, for academic or disciplinary reasons. Logan took the boy aside on his last day and told him he'll always be a Whitney student, and he would always be welcomed back. "You might find you'll miss us," she told him, and he almost smiled at that. But he smiled more when he headed out the door.

Next, on the heels of the conference with Jill's parents, comes the very angry, very adamant, very mistaken mother of one of her classmates. Early in the year, Alice* had been failing honors chemistry. She wasn't getting the material, and she wasn't clicking with the teacher. After several miserable months, she transferred to the slower-paced college-prep chemistry course, where the turnaround was immediate and her grades improved. Her new teacher wanted to reward and encourage her at report card time, and so averaged her semester grade out to a C, giving greater weight to the more recent A-level work in college-prep; counting her work in the two classes equally could have resulted in an F.

When the girl found out what her grade was going to be, her reaction was not one of relief at not failing. Instead of being pleased, she burst into tears and insisted she should receive an A. Her parents would freak, she said, real fear, almost hysteria, playing across her face. It seems she had never revealed her struggle with honors chemistry to them. Sure enough, mom was on the phone the next day, demanding that the grade be changed, arguing that only the college-prep scores should count, then insisting on a face-to-face meeting to argue in person when she was told her request was impossible. The meeting does not go well: Wold explains that the girl's grades were what they were, and that she already has gotten a big break. The mother walks in angry and leaves angrier. And a kid who should have been happy about turning things around and who could have worked toward that A next semester is left feeling like a failure.

The scene is emblematic of a larger problem afflicting Whitney: A week rarely goes by here without several students, parents, or both arguing, cajoling, and demanding that one grade or another be raised. Parents have come in with their sheepish senior children and demanded that a B be raised to an A in some tenth-grade course two years earlier, not because there was a mistake, but because "fixing" that one grade can allow a kid to achieve a coveted 4.0 or valedictorian spot at graduation. Teachers have refused such requests at Whitney; others have acquiesced. Such pressure can be relentless, a barrage of pleas, notes, and phone calls. Rod Ziolkowski has been pursued for weeks by one junior so desperate for an A that she has presented him a series of pleading letters and written proposals to justify a grade change, including a kind of "deficit grading" scheme that would allow her to borrow points from next semester's grade in order to boost her grade this time around. Very original, he told her, but no way.

"Can't you just change it to an A? Her whole future is at stake," the girl's mother asked the next day in a tortured phone conversation that ended up lasting an hour. "Just two or three more points, what can it hurt?"

Mr. Z closes his eyes at the memory. These are the moments—there aren't many, he says—when he questions his decision to leave acting and become a teacher. "That kind of pressure would be very tough on a new teacher. Actually, it's very tough on me. She's a great kid, you want her to succeed, but when you've been doing this for eighteen years, you know you can't go there. You just say no."

The girl had been provisionally accepted to a prestigious university program for the summer, but she fears that her physics B will be a sore thumb on her transcript when there are straight-A students waiting in line for the same program. In most subjects, she is a top student and she's a gifted writer, but it's clear she has little affinity for physics, Mr. Z says. She is in the most basic course available at Whitney, college-prep, and despite her voluminous notes, long hours of study, clear organization, and admirable work ethic, she simply cannot apply the physics knowledge she's recorded in her notebook. As long as Mr. Z poses a problem in exactly the same way each time, she can find a solution. But change a problem even slightly, which is the only way to test understanding of the underlying concepts, and she's lost. She was fortunate to get a B as Mr. Z sees it—a grade she earned by working harder than just about anyone in the class, with a couple of makeup tests thrown in. But her work is not A work. Ziolkowski believes he has to draw the line or the grades are worthless. "I'll write a letter of recommendation if you want," he tells the girl, "but your grade is your grade."

Still the pleas and phone calls persist. And hers is only one of many. Frantic parents call regularly trying to talk him into a higher grade, offering the kids up for extra-credit work, time after school, any bargaining chip they can think of, as if they were negotiating a business deal.

Grade pressure is not unique to Whitney; it is a national phenomenon, and one that has led to nationwide concerns about grade inflation, from ordinary high schools to the halls of the Ivy League. This dates at least as far back as the Vietnam War, when failing grades could put an end to draft deferments, leading some professors to artificially raise some men's grades. Concern about the problem of grade inflation peaked in 2001, however, when a group of faculty members at Harvard University went public with a study showing that nine out of ten seniors graduated with honors at Harvard, and that 70 percent were getting grades of B-plus or better in all their classes. That figure was 15 percent in 1950, when the grade of C, now a rarity, was the most common mark given—back when the average grade was really the average grade. At the high school level, a study by the College Board found that the number of twelfth graders with GPAs in the A range in 2001 was 41 percent, compared to 28 percent a decade earlier. Yet, during the same span of years, average SAT scores for straight-A students dropped, leading the people who administer the SAT to conclude that it had become easier to get straight As in the nation's high schools than ever before.

Whitney seems to navigate these treacherous waters fairly well: The grades are high here, with Bs more common than Cs, but the standardized measures of high-level work are also well above average. Unlike the national picture, SAT scores here have climbed over time and are consistently several hundred points above the national average. Still, some teachers at Whitney believe the parental pressure has some impact.

"Grade inflation happens all the time," Dave Bohannon tells his class during a discussion of his grading policies. "I've been around long enough that they don't ask me too much anymore—they know I'll say no. But not everyone can resist the pressure. An A should mean something, in my opinion, but that's not always the case."

Three weeks after report cards go out, when the calls stop and Mr. Z finally feels he can relax on the question of grades—at least until next quarter—he hears a small voice behind him as he strides to lunch. There's his B student, holding out a shopping bag, a wrapped gift inside.

"I want you to take this and put it back in your locker," he says gently. The girl's mother is genuinely kind, and Mr. Z recognizes the gift as a thank-you for all the extra time he spent working with the girl, not as part of the campaign to raise her grade. Still, he would feel uncomfortable accepting it. "Thank you very much. But for me, the greatest reward is for you to be successful."

She smiles, if wanly. She ends up not getting into the university summer program. But, with the pressure off, things get better for her: The next semester her hard work in physics continues, and this time, she earns the A (with a healthy dose of lunchtime and after-school labor with Mr. Z).

And when the girl's grateful mother again offers him a generous present—a restaurant gift certificate—Mr. Z can't say no.

On the day Charles returns to school, a far more encouraging scene plays out than the one preceding his departure, reminding Shirley Wold that she needs to get out of her office more and not just focus on the problems that wander in her door.

Charles, she sees, looks fit and healthy, his attitude good. He carries with him a large jug of water and guzzles it constantly in class—purging his system, he explains. A few weeks later, word comes in about a number of scholarships Charles has received. He will be able to attend his first-choice college, almost without cost.

But what strikes Wold most is how the other students react to him and his crisis. Whitney is a small community; there is no keeping this sort of thing quiet and she has no doubt that many of the kids who know Charles, and quite a few who don't, have a pretty good idea what's been going on. It's not every day that a kid bolts from class in a panic, pale and sweaty, his heart pounding so wildly that he believes he is about to die.

Yet the other kids seem to be treating Charles with un-qualified kindness and respect. There is no obvious gossiping, no overt stares, no stage whispers. His friends seem to be be-having as they always have, and if they harbor any questions about the water jugs or his absences or the weird scene weeks earlier in Gary McHatton's office, they keep it to themselves. And Wold realizes that there was a piece of the puzzle they neglected to consider during the meeting with Brock to dis-cuss the drug crisis: the support Whitney kids in distress get from their fellow students.

If the tests and the college admissions race and the home-work and the parents sometimes overwhelm, even to the point of becoming risk factors for drug abuse or worse, there is an antidote: the school itself, its student body, the idea that Whitney is a community, a place that takes care of its own—cause and cure, rolled into one. The kids talk about this when-ever you ask them what they really love about the school; the answer is almost always the same. "I feel safe here," Aisha says, while doing some computer work for the office staff. "I feel like I can be myself here. That it's okay to be strong aca-demically and it doesn't make you a nerd. That's what I'll miss. Kids here say, 'Oh, we have no lives,' but then when they leave, so many people say they miss the life here."

The academics, the Ivy League admissions officers who come a' courting, the opportunities Whitney offers—that's all valuable and important, Aisha and her friends say, but that's not what they love or what they remember or what they'll miss when they leave. This is why so many other high schools are ghost towns when the last bell rings, but Whitney remains full at the (no bell) end of the day, a hub of activity and hanging out. Other schools in the district forbid it. Whitney wouldn't work without it. The counselors comfort themselves with this notion: If Charles's drug problem did, indeed, begin with Whitney's weaknesses, at least part of the reason for his recovery will be Whitney's strengths.

18

As I stood in line at the market, I couldn't help but giggle under my breath at the sight in front of me. A little girl about the age of five was restlessly pulling on her young brother's shirt as she whined, "Let me see! C'mon...MOM...look'it. He won't let me see!" Her brother at this point was holding a *Disney Adventures* magazine high above her head and sarcastically exclaiming, "Wow...Whoa...Cool!" I have to admit, I had to give him credit. A bustling supermarket and a mother who is frantically trying to unload groceries is a perfect opportunity to unleash havoc on a younger sibling. Being the older sister, I know these things. My moment of reminiscing was cut short when I glanced up and saw the children's mother, with a stack of too familiar papers in her leathery brown hands, waiting patiently as the checker read the fine print of her food stamps.

Both her fears and mine were realized when the checker explained that the stamps had just the day before expired...

The essay-writing workshop is off to a rocky start inside Whitney's spartan conference room, which, due to the architectural oddities of the building, is not only cramped and uncomfortable, but also serves as a makeshift hallway. My spiel is repeatedly punctuated by apologetic passersby and the occasional maintenance worker or deliveryperson, a problem that Mike Mustillo swears will vanish with modernization.

"Your college essay should be a story—a story of you," I manage to say between interruptions. "It can focus on a big event in your life, or a very small one, it doesn't matter, so long as it's quintessentially yours, and it communicates something you think prospective colleges should know about you. Something special."

I see I am drawing blank stares at this point—especially when I get to the "story of you" part—except from the kids bent over their loose-leaf binders scratching notes as I speak, something that makes me nervous, as if I am imparting actual wisdom.

"Think of this essay as the closest thing to a personal introduction you're going to get. I'm no expert on the college admissions process, but I did read an interesting column written by an admissions officer at Carnegie Mellon University." At this point, I can't resist mentioning the fact that a surprising number of applicants blow their first impression by misspelling the school's name, as if they were applying to a large summer fruit. None of my workshop members seems to think this is as amusing as I do, and I push on. "Anyway, each year Carnegie Mellon has about fourteen thousand applications to go through, and ten or so people to read them all. In a week. So you don't want to write an essay that *anyone* could have written, and probably already did. They'll just toss it aside or go to sleep. You want something that only your name could go on top of."

I've really scared them now. They have to write something personal *and* unique? We have just finished reading everyone's first drafts aloud—except for those of the inevitable homework procrastinators, who were still scrawling their essays when the workshop period began. ("I meant to get to it," Nicole explains. "I've just had so much other work to do.")

They look at me suspiciously when I say that's fine, there are no grades and no recriminations here. This is the problem: If there is one common element among a majority of the pieces read today, it is that most of these kids will go to enormous lengths to avoid revealing anything remotely personal or insightful about themselves.

I have been handed essays on the trials and tribulations and life-altering decisions of...cousins. There are essays on successful siblings, essays about unsuccessful siblings, essays on parents and politics and poverty. And, invariably, somewhere near the end of these, there will be a sentence or two in which some small phrase is grudgingly added that finally includes the word "I," wherein the author explains the valuable life lessons learned from observing these other folks. (*I know now to avoid using drugs like my screw-up cousin; I will never let myself fall into a deep clinical depression like my mom; I will never push my kids so hard to excel the way my dad pushes me.*)

Angela has worked through several weeks and three drafts, and I continually urge her to insert more of herself into her piece about driving lonely and stranded underclassmen home from school. She has managed to add only three additional sentences that could be considered even remotely biographical, though they remain sketchy and stripped of context, and they would undoubtedly sound alarming to someone who didn't know Angela: "I had tried to run, but I found that I could never get away, that life came faster than I could ever run. Some people have told me that life is not worth living. It is worth living if there is something to live for." I put a note on this latest draft yet again suggesting she put in some positive details about herself.

I started as a volunteer writing coach by working with Angela and some of the other seniors on a one-on-one basis. Now, as their deadlines are passing, I have moved on to some of the juniors in a group workshop setting. This is something new for the school, a bit of antiprocrastination. The counselors figured getting them started a year ahead of time on their college applications might relieve their stress, although by the looks of them, it's not working.

The problem isn't just an adolescent reluctance to engage in self-revelation. Though Angela's inability to see her own best qualities is not uncommon among teenagers, there are plenty of kids at Whitney—probably a majority—who are happy with themselves most days and who feel confident in their abilities and their prospects. They know they're a good bet to get into their first- or second-choice colleges and that their futures are bright, yet many of their essays still fail to tell a positive story about their lives or activities or outlook—or to tell any real story at all.

As we work through their drafts, it becomes clear that the underlying problem is as basic as it gets: Many of these students simply don't know how to write a logically constructed essay, or how to unfold and develop a story, and this is only complicated by their discomfort at being their own main character. Many of these students, though they are impressively advanced and sophisticated in their academic pursuits, well-read, and possessed of vocabularies that would shame most adults, have never had to develop their writing skills. Writing just isn't considered crucial during much of their schooling, it isn't tested for, and their preferred mode of communication these days—the barely literate venues of e-mail and online chat—is only making matters worse. Even the kids see that. "I used to write better before Instant Messenger," David says. "Now I don't always remember to use complete sentences—you don't need them online."

Which isn't to say all of the essays are bad. There are gems in the mix, and they become the models I present to the rest of the workshop writers.

...In a soft shaky voice all the mother could say was, "Oh, I'm sorry." Her tired glistening eyes looked over at her children and then at the rest of the audience in line. Without warning she was forced by poverty to exit the supermarket and leave the bread, milk, and eggs she needed behind, but taking my heart and the sympathy of an entire market with her.

That night, I say with much difficulty, I cried for her. I cried for her children, and I cried for myself. It brings me to tears thinking that a mother cannot feed her children and imagining how she felt being embarrassed in front of her peers in such a manner. How I prayed. I prayed and asked God to turn back time so I could have said, "Don't worry, I'll pay for it." I am ashamed to say that I said nothing. I stood there and watched her pride get beaten to a pulp while a twenty-dollar bill burned a hole in my pocket....

Ann Palmieri thinks she knows one reason why a majority of her seniors' writing skills aren't as advanced as their other areas of scholarship: Group projects. The widespread classroom practice of letting groups of students produce their major papers and projects has left many of them ill-prepared to write individual papers or even simple punchy essays on their own.

"They complain about the workload," Whitney's newest English teacher says, after a particularly tendentious round of griping from her AP seniors. "But I'm really not asking that much of them. They should at this stage be able to string together a few well-written paragraphs. Many can't. There are some good writers in here, but many of my seniors are going to be eaten alive in college if they turn in papers like this." She holds up a sheaf of essays. "I was really quite shocked."

Palmieri has observed that her students excel at the toughest multiple-choice tests she can find, and that they are close, good readers with excellent comprehension, even with notoriously dense works such as *Heart of Darkness*. Consequently, she has dismissed her initial theory that language barriers in a school of many immigrant families might be causing the writing difficulties. Language isn't the problem, she says, and that leaves simple lack of practice as a likely cause.

"I think this is a problem. I graduated college with honors, but I can't multiply two times two. If you can write, you can succeed. This is a college-level class, but these kids are not writing at a college level."

Palmieri did not realize that group projects were the default mode in many Whitney classes until her seniors started pleading to be allowed to do their work in groups every time she made an assignment. Several of her students, when forced to write on their own, resorted to copying passages and papers obtained on the Internet and presenting them as original work—a problem sufficiently worrisome that the school has begun relying on a teacher's Internet service called TurnItIn.com to detect plagiarism. The kids like group projects because they allow them to stay up all night with their friends, hanging out, going online, eating pizza, and doing only a modicum of work. (Parents have repeatedly complained, Shirley Wold says, about the pizza bills for these constant—and constantly voracious—group meetings.) The best writers in the group can do the lion's share of the wordsmithing, while others do most of the research or reading, which means there are fewer temptations to bootleg papers from the Internet. In an English class, however, the group approach might mean dividing up *Hamlet* or *Catch-22,* rather than each student reading the book in its entirety (contrary to the teacher's instructions). Palmieri is so concerned about her students not actually reading the required texts that she has her seniors reading aloud in class. Yet many of her fellow teachers prefer—or at least tolerate—group projects and papers because five or six group projects are a lot less work to grade than a detailed research paper from each of twenty or thirty or more students.

"I don't believe in group papers," Palmieri says, "but I am a lonely voice in the wilderness. I give forty grades per pupil in this class, and I feel like it's too few. But some of the other English teachers here give less than half that number. That's a workload issue for teachers, not students.... The result is they are not prepared as well as they should be for a very important aspect of college work: writing a clear paper."

Dave Bohannon has made a similar complaint, and he finds that the twelve-page formal research papers he assigns to all his juniors are the first ones many of them will have done in their high school careers. Bohannon is indeed an anomaly on this score; a nationwide survey of high school teachers by the *Concord Review,* a publication devoted to high school history papers, found two-thirds of history teachers have given up assigning research papers to their students for lack of time.

"We've never really had to do anything like this before," Angela tells me as we go over her essay.

It is only later that I hit upon an idea that ends up helping some of the kids in the workshop loosen up and inject some life and self into their work. I ask how many chose their topics not out of desire to write about them, but out of a belief that they were choosing something their colleges wanted to hear, something that meshed more with the latest college-admissions intelligence than with something they truly believed in. About half the kids raise their hands, and I know I have at least part of the answer. I tell them about Irene's story of lucky pants and rubber-band erasers. I tell them about Vivianna's story of standing in line at the supermarket and not helping someone in need. I suggest to them that their application forms, their transcripts, their test scores, and their recommendation letters already contain all the objective measures of their academic and life accomplishments, all the big-picture stuff—but none of the heart. That's what their essays are for. I tell them to find their lucky pants, and the writing would take care of itself.

Funny thing is, for quite a few of the kids, this works. They start looking for the little things, the stories they actually tell real people in real conversations, not because they're trying to sell themselves or close a deal, but just to be entertaining or funny or because they want to pass on a certain feeling. The clinically depressed mother stopped taking up an entire essay and is instead relegated to a single sentence of background in a piece about finding joy in a dance. The political diatribe on diversity becomes a single paragraph in a lovely piece about the challenges confronting an American girl studying the ancient tradition of Bengali folk music. The somber essay on being one of the only "responsible" members of student council shifts its focus to a hilarious exploration of why one of the writer's eyebrows bears a slight but distinctive scar—an essay that ended up communicating far more about responsibility than the first, lifeless attempt ever could. The kids still struggle with the conventions of writing in their essays, but little by little, the stories at their root get so much better. They are very quick studies.

...The next day I talked to a leader of a volunteer club at my school and began helping at a local Salvation Army. My guilt was the driving force, but the satisfaction in helping someone less fortunate has compelled me to compensate whenever and wherever I can. Whether it is my weekly visits to the Salvation Army, my frequent trips to my mother's low-income school, or my current job as a tutor that helps ease the memory of that one day, I cannot say.

What have I done outside of school that has personally affected me? What if the thing that has affected me most was something I did not do?

—Vivianna,
senior essay

19

The students of sixth-period honors physics know something is up as soon as they filter into Mr. Z's lab. They find brand-new computers sitting atop the smooth black surfaces of their lab tables, where previously there had been only chrome gas nozzles and old stained sinks bearing DO NOT DRINK signs. Mr. Z sounds like a proud dad introducing the compact new PCs: "They've got plenty of power, and you're going to need it over the next six weeks. No one else will touch them. They're for this class only—so please, please, take care of them."

Standing at the front of the classroom, he waits until the stool legs stop scraping and the papers and books are settled, then he reaches up with a green marker and writes on the white board in large letters: "There is only room for one teacher in this class. And that is me."

He underlines the words, and recounts the story of the university professor who introduced himself to his students with those two sentences, the friend who immediately dropped the class in disgust, and Mr. Z's gut reaction that a good teacher would never say such a thing.

"But then I started thinking about this class and the stuff that we do. And most of the time, you come to class, I have a projector or a lab set up, and I determine where we're going every day. And you're doing great. Probably one of the best classes I've ever had. You do consistent, high-level work.

"But this one-teacher idea is nagging in the back of my head. And somewhere in my heart, I feel you are going to leave here knowing some physics, that you'll do well, I know that.... But you'll be missing out on something."

Mr. Z pauses, looking at his students, searching their faces. They are silent, intrigued, not sure where this is all going. A couple kids are fingering the new computer mice, itching to fire up the machines ("*They have Internet access!*" Kevin whispers). But they control themselves. Mr. Z resumes in a very quiet voice. "I feel, and I've talked to classes from past years, that none of these things we're doing are what stays with you for the rest of your life. I'm talking about the kind of things where you do it all, the times when you didn't think you could do it, but in the end, you do. And it's really something when that happens, something life changing. We're wasting something here. We've got the best and the brightest, and we should be doing more.

"So this quarter, *you're* going to teach *me*. There's got to be room in this class for a lot of teachers."

He slaps his palm on the countertop at the front, a punctuation mark ending the wistful tone that has crept into his voice. Now he enters what the kids call his Mr. Wizard mode, when he becomes a businesslike gadgetmeister with a drawer of surprises. He reaches into a cardboard box and pulls out a clear plastic 35-mm film canister, the kind with a lid that fits inside the canister, rather than snapping over the outside, and closes with a snug, airtight seal. Then he pulls out an Alka-Seltzer tablet, drops it into the canister, pours a dollop of water inside, snaps on the lid, and slides the whole thing upside down into a piece of plastic PVC tubing. The tubing sits at a forty-five-degree angle, a miniature cannon barrel, mounted on a wooden block. In three or four seconds, the gas pressure inside the canister from the frothing bicarbonate tablet causes the lid to pop off like a champagne cork. Half the class can't help but recoil involuntarily at the tiny explosion, as the PVC tubing turns into a miniature rocket launcher and the canister flies across the room, trailing water droplets and foam as it passes.

"There's a tremendous amount of physics in that," Ziolkowski says admiringly as the canister clatters on the floor and comes to rest. "And you're going to spend the quarter finding out about it."

"We're going to spend six weeks on *that*?" Albert asks, incredulous. Cher, one of his tablemates, shushes him, but he only grows more gleeful when Mr. Z goes on to explain that, as they work on this project for the quarter, there will be no homework and no tests. There will only be weekly updates on their progress, in which *they* will teach *him* about their findings, then answer his questions about their experiments. In order for this to work, for the students to become the teachers, Mr. Z had to choose a problem for which he did not know the answer. "I have never done this before, so I will be learning right along with you," he says. "For the next six weeks, we will reverse roles. And you will be responsible for setting your pace and staying on track."

"No homework?" Albert and his friend Brian whisper simultaneously, unable to contain their delight. "No tests? This is gonna be great!"

But Mr. Z sees the wheels turning out in the classroom, and he gives them fair warning: "This is going to be hard. You will spend all your class time working on this, and you will be expected to work outside of class as well, or you will not get it done. This is not the sort of thing you can wait to the last minute to do, the way some of you do other projects here at Whitney." He gives them a knowing look. "Because if you do, you will fall flat on your faces."

As he explains the particulars, it becomes clear that, although the experiment is deceptively simple, the problems they will have to solve are essentially the same ones NASA must tackle in trying to calculate the path of a space vehicle. The only difference is scale. Mr. Z says they should break into groups of three or four students each. First they will experiment with their canister rockets, figuring out how far they travel, how the distance varies with different amounts of water or Alka-Seltzer or changes in temperature. Do the experiments however you see fit, Mr. Z says; alter the canister to make it aerodynamic, modify the launcher—whatever you want, so long as, at the end, you can create a formula that will allow you to calculate how far your canister will fly and where it will land, every time, no matter how much water or Alka-Seltzer is placed inside.

Separately, each group must also create a computer model built not on test flights, but on the fundamental laws of physics: gas pressure, momentum, force, thrust, inertia—whatever the group decides should apply. The model must show what is going on inside the film canister every one-thousandth of a second, from the time the lid is shut to the moment it falls to earth. And this model should also be able to predict where a canister will land, depending on the amount of "fuel." Reality and theory should meet in the middle and match perfectly if everything is done just right, he says.

At the end of the six weeks, they will make a PowerPoint presentation of their models, equations, and experiments, then prove they know what they're talking about by firing their rockets in the gym and landing the canisters inside a target. They'll get three tries. Hit it at least once, and you've got a shot at an A. Miss it, it's like bombing on a test. The remainder of their grade will rest on their presentations, where communication skills and an ability to explain and teach will be just as important as the underlying science. The presentations will be judged not by Ziolkowski, but by a panel of professional and retired engineers he has recruited from the Southern California aerospace industry—"real scientists who will give you real feedback, and who will not spare your feelings."

"Here's the thing to remember, ladies and gentlemen. You cannot fool these people. They are professionals. If you do not put in the time, it will show. I know: The first time I had to do a formal presentation like this, I wasn't prepared, and I spent my whole hour trying to answer a professor's question—that he asked after my first sentence. I never got past the introduction. So if you are thinking six weeks sounds like a lot of time, think again."

A few minutes later, the class has divided into groups and walked outside, laughing in the sunlight as they shoot film canisters across the school yard. It's a hoot. Today they are just getting a feel for what their little rockets can do. Tomorrow, Mr. Z says, the experiments and measurements must start in earnest.

Later, Group 5 is back in the classroom, huddled around their computer, a tray of crumpled Alka-Seltzer packets and wet film canisters next to them. Albert and Brian, two juniors, and seniors Cher and Irene (of the lucky pants) have decided to partner up. They are among the strongest students in the class, and Mr. Z is concerned that they may have an unfair advantage over the others, especially when he sees that Group 4 is composed of three students who struggled much of the year, though not for lack of trying. But he decides to let it alone, especially when Group 4's members approach him about coming in to work over lunch periods in order to stay ahead. He likes their work ethic—and the look of determination on their faces as they hunker over their computers and begin gathering information on the physics of rocket engines. They are nervous and scared they won't get it, but they are also unexpectedly eager. He has not decided if this project

SCHOOL OF DREAMS   231

will be a breakthrough or a bust, but Group 4's initial burst out of the gate is encouraging.

He can't see Group 5's computer screen and so misses how they spend the last half hour of their first day on the rocket project: For the remainder of the period they search the Internet for a cheap used car (Brian wants a Toyota but has only one hundred dollars to spend), download Britney Spears images, and locate MP3 files by the rapper Ludacris.

At the other end of the school, a very different sort of independent study is gearing up. This one unites ninth-grade English and biology classes for an exploration of the literature and science of Ayn Rand's dystopian 1937 novella *Anthem*.

This is the sort of interdisciplinary meld of disparate subjects that Whitney relied on in its early days, and that Brock has been advocating more recently. The kids must spend two periods each day "living" in a society that mirrors the crushing collective culture of the book they are reading. Uttering the word "I" is a crime—you have to say "We" or the teachers feign incomprehension, which makes for some confusing conversations. ("We don't want to do this," says student. "Yes, we do," says teacher. "Well, I don't," says student. "We don't understand what we are saying," says teacher. "Huh?" says student.)

There ostensibly is no freedom to choose in the society of *Anthem*, and so everyone's genes determine their job, whether they like it or not. The teachers, using a DNA analysis of their students, assign them appropriate lots in life, from the leader castes, to the street sweepers, to the House of the Useless, where only the old (over forty-five), the feeble, and the disobedient end up. Members of the lower caste may not speak to their betters, and the two lowest castes may not speak at all. The students learn their fates one at a time, when they walk into a darkened lab, where the results of their DNA tests are revealed by one of the members of the "World Council"— the teachers, looking appropriately solemn and pompous.

"You see this marker here, in lane 2 of the RFLP analysis?" a teacher explains to one girl. "This is the specific DNA banding pattern of a farmer."

The girl, Annie,* is appalled. Farmers are only one step above the Useless and must do the most menial and unpleasant tasks (raking leaves and pulling weeds in Whitney's version of the *Anthem* world). Annie leaves in shock, mortified to be wearing her caste name tag, but afraid to refuse to do so. Losing the tag or failing to wear it is a crime; the offending student may be banished to the House of the Useless. "That can't be right!" she hisses to a friend once she leaves the lab. "I'm no farmer!" She could be banished for talking as well, but none of the ruling class is around, so she gets away with it. "This sucks!" another farmer agrees.

The kids know DNA technology has advanced enormously in recent years, though most are suspicious of the interpretations being made about their career tracks based on some strands of genetic material. Still, few seem to guess the teacher's secret: the tests are completely bogus. They are using store-bought DNA films unrelated to the kids' and simply inventing the results. For good measure, they are deliberately tweaking the students by putting a good number of them in role reversals, placing natural leaders and cocky types in the lower castes and the more retiring and quiet kids in the leadership roles. Just to push them a little, English teacher Susan Brannen explains later. Just to get them thinking.

After one day, the kids are in an uproar.

"I refuse to take part in your experiment for *Anthem*," read one angry note from a boy named Chico. Debra Logan finds it stuffed in her mailbox. "We are paying for an education with our taxes, and all I do all day is pick up trash. I feel that is an injustice."

Logan has the boy report to her office, where she lets him rant in person about how awful it is to be told all he is capable of in life is to be a street sweeper. "It's wrong to tell that to somebody. How do they know what I can be?" he complains. "I don't care what some DNA test says."

"So you think that's an injustice, do you?" Logan asks with a big smile. He nods curtly. "See? You learned something."

He looks at her blankly a moment, then his mouth drops open, followed by a sheepish grin. "Ohhh," he says. "I get it."

"Good. Now get out of here. Go pick up some trash."

Others are not so easily placated, however, unwilling or unable to grasp the lessons in social justice and empathy that are part of this project, or, absent that, to simply go along with the gag. One girl is so outraged at her farmer designation that she refuses to wear her name tag or to observe the restriction on speaking, at which point she is sent to the House of the Useless. She is so upset she pulls out her cell phone and calls her mother, who says under no circumstances is she to wear anything that defines her as "useless." The mom lodges a complaint with the school and then follows up by forbidding one of the teachers to even talk to her daughter unless a parent is present, although the teacher in question previously had a close relationship with the girl.

"I didn't know what the point of this was except to tell me that I was lower than other people, that we weren't all equals," the girl later wrote in her essay about the project. "And this went against everything I had ever been taught by my parents, that no one should make me feel inferior. ... I always had a ton of self-confidence and being called Useless made me *feel* useless."

The teachers seem unprepared for this strong—and literal—reaction from dozens of students. Earlier, they had lengthy classroom discussions about the questions of justice, self-determination, and selflessness explored in *Anthem*, and they figured this would be the ideal way for the kids to empathize with the characters. Combine that with some cool lessons on the genetic code and inherited characteristics in man and beast, put the kids outside in the sun instead of in a stuffy classroom, and it should have been fun, the teachers figured. Instead, there has been a steady flow of kids complaining to their counselors, the principal, and anyone else who will listen about how they were being unfairly treated and banished to lots in life that they believed were far beneath them.

Not everyone is in open rebellion, of course. Many of the participants do get the point of it, catching a glimpse of what stereotyping and oppression can be like: "I learned sort of what the Jews in the Holocaust and African slaves would have felt like to have their freedom taken away," one girl concludes. Others just see it as a big goof—a chance to sit outside and role-play instead of enduring more intensive schoolwork. "What I really enjoy," Jeff says, "is sitting back and watching all the *cool* kids go ballistic when they have to pick up a piece of trash. They hold it between two fingers like they had never touched an empty soda can or food wrapper before. I love it!"

But just as many seem to be focused solely on their own discomfort, saying they are being traumatized by the whole experience. Many do indeed express anger at having to get their hands dirty "touching other people's dirty rotten trash," as one girl writes, or by raking leaves, which is apparently a new experience for many. "If I *wanted* to do chores, I could clean my room or help my mom around the house," one indignant boy complains.

In the end, the teachers decide to halt the four-day project a day early, but it is already too late. By then, the office is flooded with phone calls from angry parents, and some of the teachers are wondering if the *Anthem* project, which had gone over quite well the previous year, should be scrapped.

The teachers are shocked that the point of the exercise has so thoroughly eluded so many kids who, on other occasions, are quick to complain about Whitney students being stereotyped by other school kids as nerds or cheaters, or about Asian students being typecast as whiz kids, an impossible image to live up to.

"I'm really pretty disappointed," Sue Brannen tells biology teacher Eileen Palmiter, who has had to have two parent conferences over the project already. "The kids are just too pissy. And the parents, too. We didn't have all this last year. It probably means these kids need it all the more. They need a little humility. But it's just not worth it."

Two weeks have gone by for Mr. Z's rocket experiment and Group 5—Cher, Irene, Albert, and Brian—seems to be lagging behind the other groups, although they remain confident that they can pick up the pace and catch up whenever they choose.

"There's plenty of time," Brian assures his teammates, when they inquire about his work developing equations for the computer model. He has promised to pull the key information out of some textbooks and Web sites, but he hasn't gotten to it yet. "I've been pretty busy. I mean, we all have been."

Despite two weeks of experiments, the foursome are nowhere near understanding how to develop a reliable method of hitting a target with their little rocket. Their test launches have failed to produce much usable data—even with the same amounts of water and Alka-Seltzer, the canister rarely lands in the same place twice, traveling twenty-four feet on one trial, then thirty-two feet the next.

"I never knew we were the stupid ones!" Albert says, as he lays prone on the gym floor after a particularly unproductive series of launches. He is exhausted from a week of SAT cram sessions, and he has been content to just sit and watch this round of experiments. The highlight so far was a pause in the action so Brian could consume a large and messy submarine sandwich. "This project will kill us before it's done," Albert says. No one else says anything.

The truth is, they know they are *not* killing themselves. The other groups have encountered similar initial failures and, by the end of the first week, had responded by streamlining the canisters with nose cones and other modifications, creating sleek devices that travel in consistent paths instead of tumbling wildly through the air like Group 5's. Mr. Z stayed late, showing the other kids the ins and outs of hot glue guns, while another group had him dig out some special gauges and tubing with which they devised a more accurate way to calculate the amount of pressure needed to pop off the film canister cap. (One group even used stop-action photography to record the launch in fractions of seconds, producing a very cool short film that, nevertheless, failed to help solve the problem.) Group 4, the three girls Mr. Z initially worried about, has taken one wrong turn after another, but science's oldest tool, the process of trial and error, is getting them a bit closer each time—and building their confidence with each new variation. Yet Group 5 has been strangely inert. They put in less time in class experimenting than the others, they rarely meet outside of class, and when they do, they end up eating pizza and wandering the Internet. While most of the other groups have taken to coming to the lab during lunch and after school several days a week, Group 5 has yet to make such an appearance. "We're not really comfortable with all this independence," Albert says. But they're not sure what to do about it. Mr. Z has noticed, but has said nothing to them—so far.

"There's always a group that has a hard time hitting its stride," Mr. Z says later. "But I would never have picked this one for that role."

It's a peculiar thing, because individually, each of the students excels. Cher, a senior hoping for admission to the University of Southern California's pharmacy program, is hyperorganized: She maintains all her parents' business records for them, and her notes look like they've been professionally printed. She excels at math and science; she's unfailingly pleasant and respectful, a runner-up in the homecoming queen vote, and a member of the school color guard, which requires her to toss, twirl, and juggle dummy wooden rifles with precision. Albert, meanwhile, is the dry wit of the bunch, the kid who always has a jovially sarcastic quip in class, a leader on the tennis and basketball teams, with high grades in his junior year and an initial SAT of 1470. The Whitney average this same year is 1343, the national average, 1020 out of a possible 1600. So Albert did quite well, yet he signed up to retake the test the same day he got his scores, then hit up his parents for tuition to go to one of the local cram academies. "Got to get an extra hundred points," he says. Brian is also an A student in his junior year, adept at math and chosen as the student representative on the school site council because of his levelheaded, responsible nature. Brian also achieved a level of fame this year for his election stunt during an unsuccessful run for student president: He performed in a barbershop quartet before the entire student body, then had his extremely full head of hair shaved bald for the crowd-pleasing finale. Rounding out the group is Irene, struggling a bit in her senior year, but still getting As and Bs, and still intent on getting into a college with a good premed program. Or journalism. Or maybe both.

Their first progress meeting with Mr. Z ten days into the project did not go well. "I am seeing four very smart people who are doing the minimum amount of work. Let me clue you in to the fact that you need to spend more time on this outside of class. Not to compare groups, but there is a range. Most of the other people here are much farther along in the process, and much clearer on the next step they need to take. You will never complete this project at this rate. This is first gear.... We want to get into overdrive."

"There's plenty of time," Cher says afterward, a phrase that soon becomes the group's unofficial mantra. But her tone seems to lack conviction. The group is floundering; they all can see it. But none of them is sure why.

This is pretty much a first for them: They have always had success in their academic careers. But now they are on unfamiliar terrain, with no tests to ace, no one riding herd on them every day with incremental lessons, no spoon-feeding. They are used to cramming at the last minute, not setting a pace for six weeks of sustained investigation, Irene complains.

She describes her last twenty-four hours of life at Whitney as far more typical and, despite its whirlwind quality, far more palatable: After school yesterday, she helped run a blood drive. Then she went out to dinner, raced home by seven, spent an hour downloading tunes on the Internet so she could have something to listen to while working, then studied until dawn for AP calculus and biology tests. She slept about forty-five minutes. Then she took a cold shower and raced in to school, took the two tests, came to physics for more experimentation, and is now trying to tame her butterflies in anticipation of an upcoming soccer game in which she's playing. Then she'll grab some fast food and go over to Brian's house with the rest of the group for yet another all-nighter to ready their next presentation for Mr. Z. "It's busy," Irene says, "but it's what we're used to."

Somehow, though, their tried-and-true methods of all-nighters and seat-of-the-pants, gut-it-out test taking aren't cutting it now. "Science the way we teach it here, and doing real science, like you'll have to do for this project, have almost nothing in common," Mr. Z has told the class, remarks that this group, at least, found cryptic. They liked and long for the old way of doing things. "For some reason," Irene says, "we have four very good students near the top of the class, but we are not clicking. Why are we having so much trouble? Maybe Albert's right, there's just too much freedom."

"It'll be okay," Albert says. "We really do have plenty of time."

But two more weeks go by, and there always seems to be a very good reason why they have to concentrate on another class or study for some other test or surf the Internet on those new classroom computers instead of concentrating on rockets and momentum. They are consoled when other groups seem to hit roadblocks, until they overhear Mr. Z praising another group for making a breakthrough during the next round of presentations. Group 4 also wins high marks on their presentation. "I'm not surprised," Mr. Z says. "You're doing everything but sleeping here. Keep it up. You're on the threshold of a door. Now you just have to walk through." The three girls walk away smiling, exultant.

"Maybe we should be copying them," Albert whispers.

"Maybe they'll let me take a look at their presentation," Cher says. "Not to copy, just for inspiration."

When it's their turn to make another progress report a few days later, the group fires up their computerized slide presentation and their group's chosen name flashes on the screen: "The Physics Superstars." It's an unfortunate choice, because this presentation is a worse disaster than the last. The slides look like the product of an all-nighter by exhausted kids running on empty: The graphs have errors in them, crucial data is missing, an important value—the initial velocity of the canister—is a negative number, which can't possibly be. They've measured different variables, but they can't explain their significance.

Mr. Z looks at them one at a time, then asks quietly, "Can you even tell me what makes this thing fly?"

They stare at him in silence. This most basic of questions about what actually exerts the force that makes the canister fly—is it the water, the gas, the force of the cap popping off, a combination of all three?—has barely been discussed by the group members. Cher says, "We're not really sure if it's the water or the gas from the Alka-Seltzer that is the fuel for the rocket."

"That's a really important question," Mr. Z practically yells at them. "We're three weeks into a six-week project, and without answering that question, you can't solve the problem."

Mr. Z decides he has to take drastic steps. "Let's go outside for a private talk," he says ominously. Then he gets up and, without a look back at them, strides to the door and walks outside. The other students in the class look up from their work, mildly curious. The Physics Superstars feel their faces burning as they trail after the teacher, Albert whispering, "Oh, this is gonna hurt."

Susan Brannen decides she, too, has to have a heart-to-heart with her ninth graders after the premature end of the *Anthem* project. She is another Whitney graduate among the teachers, having entered as a seventh grader in 1978, and she tells her students this sort of project would have been considered a fun diversion back then, a way of discussing new ideas, of putting yourself in the next guy's shoes. "Everything wasn't taken so seriously then," she says. "Everyone is so uptight now."

She waves a sheaf of essays written by the kids on their experience. "So many of you got so angry. And I don't really see why."

Brannen sighs. She had been looking forward to a stimulating discussion about the kids' immersion in the twisted values of *Anthem,* and the parallels they might find with their own society and world. She even talked to them about her hopes and fears for her youngest son, who is disabled and faces an uncertain future in which others will try to decide what he is and is not capable of. They seemed to be getting it, until they got a little taste of that powerlessness themselves. Now she can't hide her disappointment from the kids. "Why did you have such a volatile reaction? Why so much extreme anger? I just don't understand that."

No one speaks, but Brannen waits, knowing sooner or later someone will fill the silence. "We objected to having people call us useless," one girl finally says.

"But we had to have the useless," Brannen responds. "Not just because they're in the book, but because *our* society has people perceived as useless. We even talked about it before: the homeless, the elderly, the handicapped, the welfare recipients.... You guys are the future movers and shakers in our society. You are the future leaders and scholars, and goddammit, as your teacher, I want you to be good ones. I don't want you to treat people as useless when you are in positions of power and authority. So you got a little taste of what it's like. That's the point. Do you understand what I'm talking about?"

A few kids rather sheepishly say yes, but most have returned to a stony silence.

"Was it really that horrible pulling a few weeds? Was it so terrible that you had to touch a little dirt? When I was growing up, every Saturday, I was out there on the lawn on my little tush pulling weeds with my mom. We had to. It was a chore. I think you guys could do with a little more weed pulling."

The class is stirring restlessly now. Someone says, "No thanks. That's for gardeners."

And finally, the teacher understands the anger better. She's got a roomful of fourteen-year-old elitists. They aren't against a caste system—so long as they're on top. Some of her students have told her stories over the years about some of the traditions practiced by the various cultures represented at Whitney, in which kids are exempted from household chores, they're not allowed to have after-school jobs, they are permitted and even encouraged (the firstborn boys, at least) to yell at and disobey their mothers. In one ceremonial birthday celebration, little firstborn sons are dressed up in kingly robes and feted like royalty. And there is the larger issue of continually hearing that Whitney is the top school. Who wouldn't have a big head after all that?

"That's for gardeners, is it?" Brannen says, letting her own anger show now. "Well, you know, in our social hierarchy, I'm pretty low, too. In *Anthem,* I'd be just one step up from street sweeper. I know that's how some of you think. I get students who come back to visit and they say, 'I would *never* be a teacher.' And they say it with such contempt. I know, somehow, it's in jest, that they don't mean to be hurtful. But beyond the joke, there's some truth in it. I don't make the bucks of a lawyer or a doctor, we all know that. And the kids who say that, they can't see beyond the money."

Brannen pauses. Kids are looking at their desktops. "It's just that we aren't used to being treated that way," one girl says.

"We're pretty spoiled," a boy ventures.

"I thought we were being graded and that if we were useless, we'd fail," another says. "And I need that A."

"It's just that I felt like I had so much more to offer," Annie says.

"Oh," Brannen says. "And you hated it when someone said, 'You will *never* be anything useful,' didn't you?" The girl nods. "Well, maybe it wasn't such a waste of time, after all. Maybe some of you are getting it."

The class ends up having a spirited discussion about the project and its goals, and though not all hurt feelings are assuaged, most of the kids seem to appreciate, finally, that there was a point to their discomfort beyond making them miserable. Brannen is heartened by something else, too: Apparently there were parents unperturbed by the exercise, the calls to the office notwithstanding. One boy explains how he went to his mother and demanded that she file a complaint about his useless status, earned after he twice lost his name tag.

"My mom just laughed at me," he complains. "And she said, 'Serves you right.'"

Mr. Z came to teaching late. He had worked as a sales and technical rep for Standard Oil for five years out of college. It was a good job, good money, he had a nice house and car and a promotion in the works. But he found the work unrewarding, the routine numbing. He would come home in his shirt and tie, take off his pants so they wouldn't get wrinkled, and just plop down in an armchair to watch TV and drink beer in his undershorts, too exhausted to even undo his necktie. "I was dying," he says. "They were very good to me there, but I was just dying. And if I had taken that promotion, the money was so good, I would have never left."

Instead, his first wife did something for which he's remained grateful, long after their marriage ended. She said he should quit. He was miserable, and she could see it, and they just didn't need the money that much. They'd get by. He should follow his dream. And he took her up on it, pursuing something he'd thought about for a long time—a career in acting. To make ends meet, he did some substitute teaching, waiting to see if the acting career took off. Eventually he landed some parts onstage, not much money, but good experience and exposure. And then he started finding roles in television commercials, as surreal a world as his old job with Big Oil was mundane.

He'd get an audition call and he'd walk into a studio and there'd be one hundred women sitting around in bikinis waiting to be cast as "the California girl in the bathing suit." They'd wait around all day, knowing that ninety-eight of them would go home, cast aside because of the shape of their breasts or abs or belly buttons. But they'd do it and then come back and do it again because when they get to be the lucky one or two, the money is remarkable, far better than for most acting roles.

Getting the role was no less dehumanizing than losing it, as far as Mr. Z could tell. Once he was cast in a food commercial. He arrived at the appointed hour and sat and waited. No one spoke to him, which is typical, and he had nothing to do—until someone yelled, "Get the Talent." No name, no title. He was just "the Talent."

He sat down on the set, and the director said, "I want to see you swallow." Mr. Z is a tall man with a long face and neck and a prominent Adam's apple, which is what earned him the part in the first place. It had to be a forceful, visible swallow. So, with the camera inches from his face, he swallowed hard. And swallowed again. And again.

By the time he was up to twenty times, with no end in sight, he started having trouble. It doesn't sound like much, sitting there swallowing hard, but kick on about three thousand watts of light overhead and try it sometime. It's not so easy. The thing about being the Talent is that, when you're in front of the camera, you're king. You need a cool drink, or your sweat dabbed or your chair adjusted, someone flies across the set to serve you. Whatever you want, you get. So he took a drink and kept going. Then, after about a hundred swallows, when he thought he would pass out if he heard the word "again" one more time, it was done. The director yelled, "Cut!" And everyone walked away without a word.

"You don't exist anymore," Ziolkowski recalls. "You're the Talent."

At that point, as he found himself being typecast as the tall guy with the Adam's apple, relegated to a lucrative lifetime of doofus roles, he decided it wasn't much of a dream to follow after all, and that there had to be a lot more to life than this. By that time, his true job-related joy was coming from the classroom, not the studio. "I get to do more acting in a day at school than in any commercial," he says. "So I made the leap."

Tom Brock, an unabashed Mr. Z fan, calls him a natural teacher, someone who is always finding new ways to reach kids. The district superintendent, Ron Barnes, comes around now and then just to sit in and watch "a master teacher." But Mr. Z says it's all just self-preservation: He can't bear to do the same class the same way twice. It's too boring—for him, not the students (they only have to sit through it once, after all). He has to feel fresh, or he can't be an effective teacher. Which is a problem, because after ten years of finding new approaches to chemistry, he ran out of ideas. The only way he could continue teaching, he says, was to switch to physics (and, more recently, to teach a filmmaking and media class). The rocket project is just his latest idea for keeping himself fresh and for challenging his kids' thinking and complacency.

So far, he feels the project has been a qualified success. As it has evolved, it has accrued other benefits he barely imagined at the outset: lessons in leadership, independence, resourcefulness. His kids are learning more research skills than many college graduates possess, and they are enjoying themselves in the process. Getting away from focusing on tests and grades and doing something real once in a while is important for all students, he believes, but especially high-achieving ones. If the test grades are all that motivates a student, nothing sticks. That's what's wrong with the SAT academies, he believes: They show you how to shine on the test, but they don't teach you anything of substance.

But this project is bringing physics alive for his students. They are working phenomenal hours, doing college-level experiments, learning what it's like to be scientists. And with it all, they are learning physics, as well or better as his other

classes following the traditional curriculum. It has been a joy
to watch. Except for Group 5. Which is the reason he considers it a *qualified* success.

Now he leads his four sheepish students to one of the old
metal picnic tables scattered outside the school, where kids
eat and work during breaks, and where the denizens of *Anthem* sat while in the House of the Useless. Mr. Z makes sure
the door to the classroom is shut.

"It's interesting to me to see how different pupils react to
this project. You guys are really good when you're told what to
do. But now we're on a new level. No one's telling you what
to do anymore. And frankly, I don't see the drive to succeed
here. We have people in this class who didn't have a clue but
they're pushing every day, talking to each other, sharing, they
keep trying things. And it's incredible to watch. But you guys..."

He looks at them, then suddenly pounds the metal table,
hard. All four jump.

"You have a reluctance to take risks, I can see it; you want
everything laid out for you so you can connect the dots. Well,
that's not how science works, and that's not how life works."
Mr. Z has raised his voice now. His eyes are wide, his mouth
is compressed—he has that look the kids hate, the one he
gets when he's just completely disgusted with someone. This
is the first time this look has been directed at any of them.

"You come in here winging it, as if I am a fool. You're
thinking, Maybe we can fool him into thinking we did something. Well, let me make this perfectly clear: The emperor has
no clothes. When you show me a graph that tells me the initial velocity is negative, that pisses me off."

The kids are wide-eyed now. They have never seen this
side of Mr. Z, his teeth clenched, his voice harsh. "This is
work that you threw together at the last minute—and it's
crap. I can't begin to tell you how embarrassing this is. It feels
like you're trying to bullshit me. And I don't like to be
bullshitted."

The kids flinch at the colorful language. They hear that sort of talk and much worse all the time in the school yard— a couple of them might use stronger words than that themselves. But not coming from a teacher aiming it right at them.

"It's still not too late. You have the firepower to turn it around, if you make the effort, although now it will take a huge effort. But I will work with you. I will take you where you want to go, but I need to see you are making the effort. Just don't bullshit me anymore."

He stands up and prepares to leave. "Now you need to have a heart-to-heart with one another. You need to talk, figure out what you expect of each other. You can make me the bad guy, call me a son of a bitch, that's fine. But you needed to hear this."

Without another word, he turns and stalks back to the classroom, leaving four very stunned teenagers behind. For a very long minute, they sit in silence, unable to find anything to say. "That was bad," Irene finally says. "But, you know, it was, I hate to say it, fair. I mean, we totally screwed up."

They lapse into silence, faces forlorn. No teacher has ever spoken to them that way. "I guess he was trying to motivate us," Cher says quietly.

"He cursed us out," Albert says with amazement, as if he has just realized it. Then he finds his own outrage. "You know, I need an A in this course. If we all get Bs, our parents are going to complain to the administration."

It is not the reaction Mr. Z hoped for. He had hoped they would come to him with some sort of plan, maybe an apology. But, instead, when class ends, they depart without a word.

"I don't know if it will help, but it was worth a shot— they needed a kick in the rear," he says after class, when the kids have moved on. "Like I said, I do more acting in one day at school than I ever did when I was doing it professionally. Now we'll see what happens."

20

Cecilia arrives in her best black pants and jacket for the interview, looking calm but feeling unnerved. Gary McHatton is talking to every senior, one at a time, as if he were a college admissions officer and this was the make-or-break interview for each kid's number one college choice—their "reach" school, as it's called. When he's done, he'll use the information he gleans from these chats for letters of recommendation, and even though she knows this is just practice, that Mr. Mac is a friendly audience and that there's nothing to be nervous about, Cecilia is worried her voice will shake like the soft noodles she had for lunch. She hates this sort of thing, this talking about herself. Nobody's harder on Cecilia than Cecilia.

"Harvard, Stanford, and the UCs, those are my top choices," she tells McHatton when he asks about where she hopes to be next year. "But Harvard wasn't really my choice. Harvard is my parents' pick, not mine."

McHatton nods, thinking he's heard that too many times from his kids, but he makes no comment. Instead, he asks about her interest in art, knowing this will animate her, and she talks to him about the merits of the art programs at each of the schools she is applying to (Stanford University: good but not great; University of California, San Diego and UCLA: very good; UC Berkeley: okay; Harvard, dunno, but I won't be going there anyway, so it doesn't matter). She doesn't mention the ongoing battles with her parents on this topic, the hurling of her portfolio into the street, the insistence by her parents that she not major in art once in college.

"How do you get along with your parents?" he asks mildly.

Cecilia forces a smile. "I can't tell anything to my parents anymore," she says simply, making it sound like the usual teenager-parent stuff.

And maybe it is, she thinks. Except for the times I locked myself in my room and wouldn't come out, and the way I used to comb my hair in front of my face in ninth grade, hiding myself, because my family had told me that I couldn't accomplish much in life, being a girl in a man's world and all. My grandmother actually pulled me aside and explained it to me, trying to be kind, but cutting like a knife: she said not to worry, they loved me, it was just that they loved my brother more, because he was a boy. But I can't tell Mr. Mac that. And I can't tell him that my father doesn't know me, and doesn't seem to want to. I can't tell him I have no memory of my father ever saying, "I love you."

Instead, she says simply, "Everything I do is designed to show my family that I can succeed, no matter what they think, no matter what obstacles I have to face."

"So what obstacles have you had to overcome?" Mr. Mac asks.

"The main obstacle is myself," she answers, without having to think about it even a moment.

He looks at her quizzically, then taps a few keys on his computer and stares at the screen a moment. "Well, I don't know how that can be. You're a commended National Merit Scholar. A California Governor's Scholar. An AP Scholar. Your SAT scores are a combined 1450. You took three AP tests and got a perfect five on each. Your GPA is 3.8. You volunteer at a nursing home, you're in Model United Nations, you were part of the design team that won the NASA Space Set award last year for Whitney. You write fantasy and science fiction. And you are in advanced art this year. Where do you get that kind of drive?"

"I consider myself pretty average," she says. "I actually have to *study* for my grades, unlike some of my friends, who seem to do all this effortlessly. I have to pull all-nighters. Sometimes I get sick of it. Other people here say how easy it is. Not for me."

McHatton shakes his head and starts complimenting her then, but Cecilia doesn't take it in. She is wary of praise and thinks of herself, sometimes at least, as a bit of a fraud. She has an academic record that puts her in the top 5 percent of kids in the nation, but she will look you in the face and say, "I'm really pretty stupid," and she is not kidding. She draws incredible anime and pointillist pictures, which are prominently displayed in the art room and around the school, but she runs away from acclaim and harshly criticizes her own work. This has been a habit since the seventh grade, when she had her worst moment as a Whitney student, which, perversely, comes to her now, in the midst of this interview, though she says nothing.

When you're in seventh grade, you don't really know about cruelty, words just kind of fly from your mouth helter-pelter without letting your brain screen over them first. I liked to draw, drew on anything that had a flat surface, and Sean always complimented me on my scribbles. I never thought it was good; it embarrassed me when he would say it.

I don't know if I thought he was mocking me or just because I was unused to being continuously praised like that but it made me very uncomfortable. I wasn't a great artist. I was learning, but I could only do so much. My mother didn't want me to go into art; my dad said that only true artists could really capture a picture and draw it from the mind. I couldn't do that. It made me resentful and I hated the fact that this boy thought it was so great.... My parents told me it was nothing, weren't they always right? So why did he have to say this kind of thing? Why did he have to predict that I was going to be an artist when it was probably not going to be possible?

Well, it was this mixture of resentment and confusion that made me one day burst out, "Don't say that! I don't even like you!" Shit. When you're in seventh grade, you don't know how to say these things, how to ask him not to say these things. You don't know how not to hurt people's feelings. You don't really mean what you say, but you don't know how to say what you mean, so words like these spill out, all venom and malice. Later, it made me ashamed, but I didn't know how to say, "I'm sorry." How do you apologize for something like that? I couldn't talk to him after that; he never did talk to me again, not in the next six years of middle and high school.

They say that time makes you forget, but it really doesn't; it just gives you time to mull over those times you want to forget until every moment is clear and crystal sharp in your mind. Even now, when I think about it, I sometimes clamp my hands over my ears and think, "Shut up shut up shut up."... It never works, of course. Your conscience is much stronger than you are.

"I consider myself pretty average," she tells McHatton again, "except I'm okay at art."

McHatton has to laugh at that. But then he realizes Cecilia's modesty is sincere, and it pains him that this kid should have no idea how truly special she is. Later, he writes her a strong recommendation letter in his plain, no-nonsense prose, and he does not shrink from talking about Cecilia's struggles with her parents and her fight to further her study of art. "She is living in the midst of two cultures at war with each other," his concluding paragraph reads. "The important thing is that she does not intend to be a casualty."

Last year, Gary McHatton was teaching marine biology and middle school science classes and preparing for retirement in June. But then the stock market tumbled and his retirement funds took a big hit, and Mr. Mac, much to his students' delight, decided to stay on.

This is his first year as a full-time counselor, and his interviews have been an eye-opener. He has tried to go beyond writing letters that tout his students' accomplishments and instead has focused on revealing something essential about their lives and struggles, to somehow bring them to life for the college admissions officers who receive, literally, bales of applications every year. The result is a collection of letters that celebrate some amazing accomplishments, but through which runs a surprisingly deep vein of sadness.

When Angela comes in for her interview, McHatton is no longer surprised to hear that the abilities and ambitions of one of Whitney's most gifted young artists are unappreciated at home. Unlike Cecilia, however, Angela is not so circumspect about her sometimes trying home life: She recounts for him, and he includes in his letter, the loneliness and stress of her youth, of being forgotten after school and forced to wait for hours for a ride home—one time until half past ten in the evening.

"She was forgotten once again," McHatton later writes. "From that point on, Angela decided to depend on no one but herself. She created her own destiny and has become an expert at that. She's had to be. She has no one else."

Her letter is not easy for him to craft. He writes at length about her being one of the most talented artists Debbie Agrums has taught in eighteen years. He lauds her musical talent with piano, violin, guitar, and drums, and as a teacher of young pianists and violinists as well. But he also has to grapple with a difficult reality: Angela's parents are not letting her declare a major in art, which means to get into college, she is going to have to rely primarily not on her incredible portfolio, but on her academic record. That record does not rank among Whitney's best.

He decides the only plausible course of action is to confront the issue dead on, providing a reason for colleges to look beyond test scores and letter grades: He says plainly that Angela does not test well.

It's not a sin, he says. Some kids are not expert test takers, and Angela is one of them, he writes, even when she has mastered the material to the point that she tutors other students successfully, her test scores don't show it. It's been a lifelong problem for her—she freezes up. Even the SAT betrayed her: She self-tested on practice versions of the aptitude test several times, consistently scoring above 1300. But on the actual test, she scored two hundred points lower, an average score for an above-average student.

"Her scores and grades will never accurately reflect her knowledge," McHatton writes with uncharacteristic passion. "Angela deserves more than she's gotten out of life. She deserves to have an environment in which she is challenged, encouraged, and appreciated. She has overcome so much in her young life through her own efforts. Now is her time to shine. That time is way overdue. Angela is a treasure."

Angela appreciates McHatton's efforts on her behalf, but by the time of the interview she knows something her parents are still unwilling to accept: Their dream of sending her to Stanford University to become a doctor or lawyer is not going to happen. Which is an enormous relief to Angela.

A few weeks later, she gets an early acceptance letter from a small Christian college in Virginia. She comes to class more upbeat the next day than she has been all year, completely thrilled, even though the school offers nothing in her second-choice major, communications. "My parents don't want me to go, but I will prevail." She is unabashedly happy. She even looks healthier.

But a few weeks later, the dark circles are back under Angela's eyes and she is poring over a catalog from the Chicago Art Institute, where she has also been accepted, without her parents' knowledge. They have made it clear they won't pay for the Virginia school, and now Angela is trying to come up with an alternative. But her fears that they won't consider the art school are borne out, and they are not terribly impressed when three more schools say yes, including Cal Poly, San Luis Obispo, a lovely state university campus in the central part of coastal California, where the offerings mesh quite nicely with Angela's interests. "That can be a backup school," her father says. "But we want you to go to a University of California campus. No one's ever heard of any of those other schools. A UC has some prestige."

It is true that the University of California system is a Cadillac among public universities, with several of its campuses ranked among the best schools in the country, public or private, and where admissions are selective enough to be dominated by the top 4 percent of high school students in the state. But she feels certain she will be rejected by UCLA, where she would have happily gone but which is the toughest of the UC schools to get into, rejecting nine out of ten applicants. She has been praying that she gets turned down by the other UC campus she applied to, the University of California, Irvine. At her parents' insistence, she applied to Irvine, a large university with an excellent academic reputation (one notch below UCLA and Berkeley in exclusivity) but with a small and poorly regarded art department (with almost no class-room spaces for non-art majors). The sprawling and imper-sonal university in the heart of suburban Orange County south of L.A. is best known for being the most Asian of UC campuses, which is fine with many Whitney students, but which leads others to view it with a bit of disdain, as a kind of thirteenth-grade continuation of their high school environ-ment. Fair or not, Angela shares the latter view.

The irony for Angela is that she could easily gain admis-sion to the California State University system, which is far less exclusive but which, on its Long Beach campus, boasts one of the state's better arts programs. This is where Debbie Agrums was schooled and where the professors include Betty Edwards, author of *Drawing on the Right Side of the Brain.* But it is also a university system where a fourth of all enter-ing students must take remedial courses just to get up to speed. And so her parents would regard Cal State attendance as evidence of failure and an intolerable step down in pres-tige—an attitude fairly prevalent among Whitney parents and students. The president of Cal State, Long Beach, came to Whitney earlier in the year to make a personal appeal for applicants, offering all high school valedictorians a special scholarship that would cover full tuition, fees, books, and room and board, provide a stipend and a free computer, and give priority for getting into overbooked classes. Not only did he fail to attract any takers, none of the potentially eligible students at Whitney even expressed mild interest in an offer that would provide four years of cost-free and *debt*-free edu-cation, virtually unheard-of in this era of $30,000-a-year col-lege bills.

Angela begins checking her mailbox and e-mail with growing dread, as the admissions decision date for Irvine ap-proaches. "It is perverse to hope for rejection," she tells me, "but in this case, that's what I'm hoping for."

Then the notice arrives: Angela has been accepted to UC Irvine.

"Isn't it great, Angela?" her father exults, certain that he and his wife are doing what's best for their firstborn. "Your hard work on bringing up your grades in the last year really paid off."

That night, Angela stays up painting. She can't sleep.

21

"I was talking to my wife about her best friend, who's an older teacher, getting ready to retire soon. And she just *hates* technology. Doesn't want it. Doesn't see the point of it. Won't use it."

Terry Smithson shakes his head at this affront to twenty-first-century sensibilities. He is addressing a small gathering of teachers in the Whitney High School library, and this affable marketing manager of educational technology for the Intel Corporation sounds more like an evangelist than a salesman, preaching the power of computers, software, and Ethernets not merely to improve our public schools, but to reinvent, resuscitate, and resurrect them completely.

"So my wife says, 'Terry, please don't say anything to her about it, because you'll probably just end up saying she should be fired.' Well, she should be fired. *Any* teacher so resistant should be fired."

He says this with a small, resolute smile, then moves on to expound upon his happier vision of tech-savvy teachers with computer-enhanced white boards at the front of digitized classrooms across America. His vision is about to become reality, at least at Whitney, which Intel has anointed a "Technology School of the Future," a designation that brings with it millions in free computers, software, and tech support. The enthused computer exec does not seem to notice the mixture of appalled and shocked expressions his casually uttered hard line has evoked in his audience—teachers who do not, by and large, use any technology in their classrooms, and for the most part haven't missed it.

"Did he really say that?" Shirley Wold whispers, not quite trusting her ears. She can only imagine the backlash when word spreads to the rest of the faculty, a majority of whom conspicuously avoided attending this presentation. In the back of the library, Tom Brock's beaming smile assumes a queasy, frozen quality as he gauges his staff's reaction; he later stands up and performs damage control, assuring everyone that only teachers who really *want* new technology will get it in their classrooms.

It's no surprise, of course, that an executive from Intel, the inventor of the microprocessor, would consider lack of interest in technology a fireable offense. What shocks many of those present is that he would speak this thought aloud to teachers who work in a school not meaningfully updated since before "Microsoft" was a registered trademark, and where a significant number of the computers are older than the seventh graders using them. Where there are plenty of teachers who agree with Dave Bohannon's promise to accept computers in his classroom only after they pry the pencils and 3×5 index cards from his cold, dead fingers.

But Smithson, the driving force behind Intel's philan-thropic Model School Program, is a true believer. He thinks it's an unforgivable outrage that a doctor of 150 years ago would be hopelessly lost in a contemporary hospital, but that a teacher from that same Victorian era would feel quite at home in today's classrooms of blackboards, textbooks, number-two pencils, and desks in rows. At his recommenda-tion, Whitney has been chosen as one of two schools in the nation to be transformed into a school of the future by Intel's Model School Initiative, which Smithson unabashedly calls "the greatest force there is for educational innovation." (Miami Carol City Senior High School in Florida is the second recipient of Intel's largesse.) At least $3 million worth of technology will be donated by Intel and sixteen other companies to fuel this metamorphosis, though no one, as yet, is sure exactly what gadgets are coming or how they will fit into Whitney's curriculum—which is one source of the uneasiness among staff members. So Smithson has organized a two-day event, starting today, to resolve some of these concerns and to demonstrate some of the latest technologies. Two months later, there will follow a major press-and-politician event to publicly announce the project, with the governor's education secretary set to preside.

Now the future of education—at least as envisioned by the world's leading purveyor of smart silicon—is on display today in Whitney's cramped and humble library, a sample of what might be headed this way: intelligent, wall-mounted white boards that are really giant computer screens and Internet broadcasters. Interactive paperless textbooks. Software that takes attendance automatically when the kids flash their PDAs while walking in the door. (Sue Kessinger, the band teacher who blows ten minutes each morning taking attendance for 130 kids, is practically salivating over this one.) Purple keypads and a giant-screen TV that turn math problems or history lessons into classwide—or schoolwide or even nationwide—game show contests. (This one is so cool the teachers can't stop playing and trying to outscore one another.) Spreadsheet analyses of each student's strengths and weaknesses, computer-based testing (and grading), a hundred new laptops and a hundred new desktop computers with all the bells and whistles—the high-tech goodies are top of the line and cutting edge.

"With this, you are going to build a road map to the school of the twenty-first century," Smithson asserts. "This is really neat stuff. You guys are getting ready to make history in the next two months."

Smithson serves as master of ceremonies, head cheerleader, and air-traffic controller during the event. His laptop and cell phone are constantly buzzing and signaling as the representatives of companies from throughout the nation make their way to Cerritos. Corporate reps more accustomed to boardrooms, convention floors, and state capitols than Whitney's little library march in one at a time to make their demonstrations, pitches, and PowerPoint presentations.

It soon becomes clear that just what it means to be *The Technology School of the Future* depends on who's doing the talking. To Brock, whose unbridled enthusiasm lured Smithson to Whitney in the first place, it's about the free stuff—a chance to ignore his strained budget and rake in the sort of premium equipment Whitney has never been able to afford for its kids. The school's annual budget is about $5 million (almost all of it locked into salaries and other fixed costs), with only $54,000 of it reserved for technology (and that was a one-time grant)—which means the meager Internet pipeline is always backed up, the computer lab is a museum of pre-Pentium geezers, the kids are frustrated with the constant freezes and crashes. An influx of technology worth sixty times his annual budget for such things *has* to be good, no matter what it brings, Brock figures, especially when all the school has to do in return is make a few teachers and students available for interviews and press conferences, with the added bonus of raising the school's profile as well.

To Intel and the other companies involved, it's about marketing and enlightened self-interest—a chance to be altruistic while also building and publicizing a test bed for products they hope to sell by the thousands at other schools once the students at Whitney put them through their paces. One of the promises Whitney had to make in exchange for Intel's largesse was to make available to all interested educators, as well as Intel and the other companies on the project, any curriculum or instructional plans the school develops to put the new technology to use. That way, the companies will be able to sell not only a cool new machine, but a method for using the devices in the classroom, pioneered at one of the top schools in the country. What better marketing could there be? Ten years ago, Apple computers—which contain no Intel chips—were the most ubiquitous pieces of technology in America's classrooms, but now, as those machines slip into obsolescence and new technologies take their place, Intel is doing all it can to dominate this potentially enormous and lucrative market.

To teachers like Rod Ziolkowski and Mike Mustillo, who tinker under the hoods of their computers the way teenagers used to tear into their cars, this is a trip to the candy shop, a chance to run their science classes at a level as good as or even better than many colleges. And to some of the younger faculty members, who haven't got years or whole careers invested in a particular classroom approach, the new technology offers the *possibility* of more effective, more engaging, and more efficient teaching, a classroom environment where kids can work more independently and at different paces.

But to many of the other teachers here, the school of the twenty-first century seems as threatening as it is enticing. Though they feel (some) additional technology might make for fine classroom tools, they don't see anything revolutionary here. The heart of schooling to them will always be the interaction between teachers and students, a realm in which Whitney has proven itself adept for many years, and where they feel computers could just as easily impede as enhance. To them, the revolution arrived with Gutenberg. Everything else is just building a better mousetrap. And, bottom line, one teacher confides, "A lot of us don't really want to change the way we've run our classrooms for the last ten or twenty years and spend hundreds of unpaid hours changing our lesson plans and figuring out how to use this stuff, just so the kids can screw around on the Internet here instead of at home."

Even the enthusiastic Mr. Z, who has been quoted at length in a variety of Intel promotional materials and "advertorials" since the program first began taking shape a year earlier, expresses some reservations. "I'm worried that we're being told, *Here, take this stuff because it's cool. And because we're giving it to you free.* The technology—and what the companies are willing to donate—is driving the train, and we're being asked to find ways to use it. Which is all very nice and very generous. But if you really want to build the school of the future, you need to sit down and figure out what you need to accomplish that goal. We need to ask ourselves what do we need to make us more effective at educating our kids and make them more effective learners. That's what should come first, but we haven't really done that."

Still, it is impossible to sit in the library with this array of new technological toys spread out and not see some interesting possibilities. Even the skeptics are intrigued by some of it, particularly the computer white boards made by Calgary-based SMART Technologies, which has turned the age-old concept of slate and chalk into an instant multimedia showcase. The device is already used in Pentagon briefings and by some corporations, but it seems tailor-made for the classroom, and the company has had considerable success in the educational market already. It's basically an immense computer screen that can be drawn or written on (though the multicolored markers that come with it write with pixels, not ink). What makes the board so useful is its ability to instantly combine the teacher's markings with any sort of photo, file, or film that can be viewed on a computer or downloaded from the Web. As the teacher and class examine video of a chemistry experiment, or a page from a Shakespeare sonnet, or a life-size projection of a daVinci masterpiece, the teacher's annotations merge with the image—over, around, and inside it. The results can be beamed to other computers in the classroom or over the Internet for virtual classes located anywhere. The teacher's scrawl can even be transformed into typed text that can be printed out and used as worksheets or distributed via e-mail, and a whole presentation can be saved as a series of images that can be resurrected for a future class. No more writing the same stuff over and over on the blackboard.

Those present are so enamored of this product that Mike Mustillo begins immediately adding extra cabling, power supplies, and fixtures to the school's summer remodeling plans in hopes that enough of the devices will be donated for all thirty-five classrooms in the school. ("But we'd be happy to get half that number," Mustillo quickly adds, when the company reps blanch at the notion of donating that many of the devices during an economic downturn.)

The teachers are also entranced by a $40,000 product from the California company LearnStar, which allows students to compete with one another to answer questions on any subject or lesson plan. The questions are projected on a big-screen TV (or computer white board), and the students key in their answers with a wireless keypad; the faster they answer correctly, the more points they earn. A countdown clock shows the time left for each question, and clues are offered as time dwindles. When the quiz is done, the high scorers are automatically listed on the screen. Teachers can use off-the-shelf quizzes or their own questions. The program automatically assesses each student's strengths and weaknesses, generating a report for each and keeping track of progress over time, so that the teacher can work with each student individually and know when subjects have been mastered.

The company has cleverly positioned this program as a way for school districts to bump up performance on the all-important standardized tests, the one true growth market in education these days, but for Whitney's purposes, it's just a wildly fun way to review material covered in class. Civics classes can use them to take instant opinion polls, math classes to compete to solve equations. During the demonstration, teachers duke it out on a ninth-grade science competition (all but the science teachers are somewhat embarrassed by their inability to identify amphibian characteristics and volcano parts) and end up laughing and applauding, ready to sign up then and there to get them in their classrooms.

Less impressive are the Internet-based textbooks, at least one of which seems to be little more than a warmed-over on-line version of existing school texts with some hyperlinks thrown in. And some of the products seem out of place at Whitney, particularly an extensive suite of programs suitable for training kids for business careers right out of high school, a path no Whitney students are expected to take. Yet this is one of the most valuable items being donated in terms of dollar amount (the only seven-figure item in the room this day), and so it is presented with the expectation that the school will find a way to put it to use. The impressive claim that millions of dollars' worth of donations are being made may not hold up otherwise. Brock quickly comes up with a suggestion: The program could provide valuable training to some of the many Whitney students who work at family businesses part-time. But others worry that Rod Ziolkowski's cart-before-the-horse concerns might be on target.

And though there is a good deal of excitement generated at the meeting—at least among the half of the staff who dropped in—the event concludes on a somber note grounded in some dismal economic realities. This whole project was conceived during the boom end of the technology and Internet economy, when the sort of donations envisioned here could be made without a strain. Two years later, with the NASDAQ tanked, the new economy reduced to a Jay Leno routine, and government spending on education shrinking daily as tax revenues dwindle, the attraction for businesses to participate in this program is lessening by the minute. Building a road map for the future is all well and good, but if the school districts of America lack the money to buy the technologies being demonstrated here, there's not much of an upside for profit-making companies to give their very pricey stuff away. Several of the reps confide that they may have to cut back on what they can donate, and at least one fears his company may pull out because of California state budget cuts that are gutting purchases of its products. Most of the companies are sticking it out, however, as their officials genuinely wish to honor their promises and genuinely can't afford to invite the wrath of Intel, whose products and goodwill are essential to their businesses.

But Mustillo and Ziolkowski, who will share the tech-support and computer-training duties in the next school year when the new goodies are slated to come online, are uneasy. The new technology will only work if it is ubiquitous, they know. Fifteen or even ten SMART Boards permanently attached to classrooms have a good chance of being used every day, making the technology part of the way the school does business. Mr. Z, for one, says he would use his every day, for both his physics classes and his contemporary media class, where the ability to work on student films on one of these boards adds collaborative and learning opportunities just not possible with a desktop computer. But those opportunities will evaporate if the donations are cut to a handful of each type of device. If there are only three or four of the boards available, they'll have to be put on carts for portability so they can be shared by everyone, which is the way most schools use technology, from VCRs to slide projectors. And that would ruin the program. If a teacher has to go to the trouble to reserve, fetch, set up, and put to use a piece of equipment, nine times out of ten, it won't get used at all. If it's not right in the classroom, at the ready, available at the turn of a switch, most teachers, most of the time, will invest their time and effort elsewhere.

"We'll have a lot of expensive dust collectors," Mr. Z says. "I just would hate to see that happen. Because I really do believe there's the potential for something really special in all this."

At the other end of the spectrum of opinion are those teachers who are less concerned about Whitney getting too little new technology and more worried that there will be too much. Smithson's off-the-cuff comment about firing his wife's best friend makes the rounds quickly, and several teachers wonder if they will be mandated to use new gadgets whether they want to or not.

Debbie Agrums, who spends a great deal of time trying to stop her budding artists from thinking with their technologically adept, computer-game-playing, artless left brains, marches up to Brock and asks him point-blank, "Am I going to be fired if I refuse to use computers in my class?"

He assures her absolutely not and even seems amused by the whole question. This is a good thing for the school and everyone here, he says. But it's all voluntary, he promises. "We wouldn't dream of forcing anything on anyone."

Still, Agrums remains deeply suspicious. Keeping her art program together at Whitney has been a constant challenge, and though the state has just mandated at least one year of fine arts for high school students, after decades of making it optional, there is no additional money in the budget to cover the new requirements. She is going to be flooded next year with put-upon juniors and seniors in her beginning art classes, students who are enrolling only because they have to take her class in order to meet the new graduation requirement. The last thing she wants to have to do is wrestle with some new, complicated device. Yet even the notoriously computer-phobic art teacher is tempted (slightly) when she hears her ancient projector and prized, but deteriorating, collection of art slides could be preserved and jazzed up with a SMART Board and computer setup. In the end she recoils at the time and training involved in such a conversion, though Mr. Z keeps working on her. "What if I got some of my students to do the transfer for you, what then?" She agrees to think about it.

Beyond the nervousness of Agrums and some of the other teachers lies a deeper question. Without doubt, after many years of little change, schools are becoming increasingly immersed in new technologies. This transition is inevitable and it is already happening at Whitney. The change can be seen not just through the Intel program, but in a multitude of other, lower-profile ways, from the rise of text messaging as a more dominant form of communication for kids than talking on the telephone to some students' use of Web sites like CheatHouse.com for bootleg term papers (countered by anti-cheating teacher sites like TurnItIn.com). New programs for generating class rankings, student transcripts, report cards, and progress reports have been put into place at Whitney and in the rest of the school district this year (followed by several months of ongoing glitches, outages, and the sudden realization that there is no user manual for this complex new software). There are also new statewide computerized tests for gauging students' annual progress, their fitness for graduating, and their eligibility for state scholarships. The new digital filmmaking lab run by Rod Ziolkowski even has students under contract with the school district to write, direct, and produce a sexual harassment video to be viewed by new employees. So the question is not whether there will be more technology incorporated into schools. The question is what will be the results, anticipated and unintended, as more and more of it falls into place.

The notion Smithson put forth—that technology will have a revolutionary effect on education, rather than an evolutionary one—does not seem to be the majority view among the Whitney faculty. Many of the teachers seem more excited about getting their rooms painted, carpeted, and properly wired for telephones and electricity for the first time in a quarter century than they are about the computer stuff. Even the students are muted in their reactions; the kids in the Miami school chosen by Intel burst into a spontaneous ovation when the principal broke the news over the public-address system. At Whitney, the reaction was mild, more curious than bowled over. There was no clapping.

In Mr. Bohannon's honors history class, several of the students openly question why technology is being made a priority when some kids at the school are stuck with twelve-year-old textbooks; the cafeteria serves fattening, unhealthful meals that have provoked repeated petitions and boycotts; and teacher recruitment and salaries seem to the kids insufficient to attract enough qualified people into education careers.

"It just seems to me that when there are schools that can't even afford enough books, and we have teachers who can't afford to be teachers anymore, we should really be focusing on other things besides computers," says Jennifer, one of the more outspoken of Bohannon's juniors. "I just wonder if we have so many more computers, whether kids will just get distracted and go online all the time. Or find more ways to cheat."

These are exactly the sort of concerns many colleges now face as one after another embraces campuswide wireless network technology, which gives students with laptop computers access to the Internet almost anywhere on campus without plugging in, even in the middle of classrooms. The potential advantages of this technology are enormous: the ability to instantly network with other students and professors, to find documents and source material while sitting in the classroom or the dining commons instead of a research library, to fetch classroom handouts from the Web. But professors have also noticed the downside: kids computer gaming, e-mailing, and Instant Messaging in class whenever their attention wanders or they simply feel like screwing off. Students who try to pay attention in dense and difficult lectures are demoralized by others playing solitaire or online games. Professors can tell when they're losing their audiences when the sound of clicking keys and laptop screens flipping open accelerates. Some professors say this keeps them on their toes, forcing them to work harder to engage their classes, but others are rebelling, limiting computers in the classrooms or banning them outright as distractions for students who are already less serious and less prepared academically than previous, unwired generations.

The experience of Whitney students with their own computers and online access outside the classroom reveals a similar mixed bag of benefits and costs. There's no question that the ability to do research papers, to stay abreast of current events, and to produce high-quality, in-depth work has been improved by an order of magnitude through access to the Internet. Trying to do high school–level work without that resource is now unimaginable to most students at Whitney, who spend far less time in libraries than past generations of students, and who get most of their news from the Web, not television or radio. But the same distractions that crop up in university lecture halls are also afflicting Whitney students: Alluring games, Instant Messaging, music-sharing programs, and chat rooms occupy an enormous amount of the time parents believe is being devoted to homework and study— even the kids admit as much. There have been numerous cases of cheating linked to the ease of downloading and copying material on the Internet—a national problem. And Shirley Wold had to haul a group of five kids into her office because they were spending all their time in online game competitions and doing no homework or studying, unbe- knownst to their parents. It got so bad, one of the kids ulti- mately had to leave Whitney because of failing grades. Other kids arrange their social calendars via online chat and invest much of their emotional lives in the virtual realm as well. "All my closest relationships are online," says Hannah. "Hours will go by before I realize I haven't done my homework."

What few computers are available at Whitney at the mo- ment are regularly hijacked for nonacademic purposes. The desktop in back of Ms. Charmack's office is used to down- load Korean music videos. The rocket project computers in Mr. Z's class display video games and Britney Spears as often as they crunch momentum and trajectory data. While Terry Smithson and his corporate partners wax poetic on the future of wired, "active" learning through multimedia— which they say can be far more effective than traditional stand-and-lecture methods—the kids in Whitney's existing computer lab are cracking up over RateMyPoo.com, a Web site devoted to compiling popularity polls on photos of human excrement. Inevitably, Jennifer and other students at Whit- ney say, the possibilities for distraction multiply right along with the more positive gains new technology promises. "Somebody," Jennifer says, "has to factor that into the equa- tion, too."

———

It would be hard to imagine less-friendly terrain for technology than Mr. Bohannon's classroom.

He does not use an electronic organizer or PDA. When he needs to remember something, he scrawls short notes on little pieces of paper and shoves them in his pocket. The research papers he assigns must be written with references to real books with actual pages, not Internet addresses. Current-events presentations must be drawn from real newspapers, not pedigree-free Web sites (although he reluctantly agrees to let kids uses legitimate news media sites on the Internet rather than actual newsprint). He will not accept as excuses for late assignments any of the following: "My computer crashed"; "My computer ate my paper"; "My printer ran out of toner"; or any other variation on the terror-of-technology theme. ("There is always a way to get it done if you want to," he says simply.) There is an aging computer on his desk—the school insists on it—but only his teaching assistant, Kosha, ever actually turns it on.

"I had a student who tried every argument he could think of for three years to convince me to use that computer," Bohannon tells his class proudly. "He failed."

Bohannon's is one of those traditional classrooms that Terry Smithson so deplores, and that Ben Franklin (founder of the academy that became the University of Pennsylvania) would have easily recognized: The teacher lectures, assigns readings, leads discussions, encourages questions and debate, reviews the material covered, and tests. Every week, Bohannon repeats this pattern with a new period in American history.

This is teaching at its most basic, rudimentary, rigorous, or pure—the adjective depends on the point of view. There are no multimedia presentations. No streaming videos. Bohannon doesn't even use the blackboard, except to put down test dates and due dates for papers. He pointedly neglected to place his name on the list for a new computer white board, and he handled a district memorandum requiring teachers to incorporate more technology in their classrooms the way he handles every piece of paper from the administration that he doesn't like: He ignored it.

And yet, the old-fashioned Bohannon is one of the most beloved and favored teachers at the school; his students do well on their AP tests; he has been asked by numerous senior classes to speak at graduation ceremonies. There are as many reasons for this as there are students, but it seems to come down to Bohannon's approach to the subject: History to him is fascinating, a procession of stories and characters and high drama, and this carries through into his classes. Spend time in his classroom and it really is that simple: He knows his subject cold, he reads voraciously to keep up-to-date, and so continually surprises his students with telling details, insider moments, and refutations of conventional wisdom. Sure, he agrees with his students at one point, "Read *Uncle Tom's Cabin* today and it is horrible. You can't imagine what all the fuss is about. But read it through the eyes of the eighteen hundreds, when it was banned throughout the South, and it is revolutionary. To depict slaves with feelings, who have families, who act like people, that had simply never been done before. It was a revelation, and it was a bestseller."

He lets that sink in a moment. "Think about it: When you messed with people's belief that slaves were not people, then you threatened whole institutions, whole economies. One little book. Banning it didn't work—people wanted to read it even more. Even in Great Britain, where the slavery system came under fire as well, it was a bestseller. Lincoln met Harriet Beecher Stowe at a party, and he said to her, You are the lady who is responsible for all this."

The kids are delighted by this aside, which is typical of Bohannon: the big picture punctuated by a bit of pithy detail that is, in fact, a big picture in itself. From there the discussion ranges to contemporary problems with slave trading, to the differences between the forced immigration of slaves versus the voluntary immigration of other groups, such as Asian Americans, and how that difference may have helped set the pattern for each group's subsequent history and place in this country. (Whitney kids, for instance, know the voluntary South Korean immigrants to America tend to excel as a group in school, while Koreans in Japan, who have a history of being forcibly relocated, are viewed as poor students as a group.) In Bohannon's class, students seldom seem to find history irrelevant to their own lives, in part because they're bright kids who can make the connections, but also because their teacher makes it a point to find the parallels between the events of the day and the events of the past. There is also in Bohannon more than a bit of the contrarian, which the students especially eat up.

"In eighth grade, when you last studied this, history was more indoctrination," he says at one point. "Now you're in eleventh grade and we're looking at the way it really is.... Should we shatter the myths about Abraham Lincoln?" he asks the class.

"Yes," a chorus replies.

"Abraham Lincoln is known as the Great Emancipator. You all learned that in eighth grade, right? But he had no idea how to solve the slavery problem. Did you know he allowed the passage of laws preventing assemblages of blacks? That Mary Todd came from a prominent Kentucky slaveholding family? Her three brothers all died fighting for the Confederacy. She was accused of spying for the South. Lincoln had to testify before the House Judiciary Committee on her behalf."

Everyone in the class appears to be listening to this attentively. They have been told all their lives that Lincoln freed the slaves. It's just one of those givens. And there's Mr. Bohannon telling them, Just wait a minute: Lincoln was a great president, maybe the greatest wartime president the country has had, but not for the reasons he's now most celebrated.

"The Emancipation Proclamation freed exactly zero slaves," Bohannon tells them, something the textbooks and lessons in their earlier years never managed to mention. "It only affected areas the North controlled. But it served its main purpose: It kept Britain out of the war."

Then he passes out this week's terms—key topics they must study, such as King Cotton, poor white trash, the *Liberator,* Nat Turner—twenty-five in all, which encompass the main themes and events he feels are most important for this particular chapter of U.S. history. They will spend the week talking about each of them in class, and the students know in advance they'll be tested on a selection of them. The tests are only occasionally multiple-choice; often the students will be required to write a paragraph on each term instead. There are no surprises as far as testing goes in this class—pay attention, do the reading, and you'll get good grades. Get distracted, forget to read the textbook, ignore the terms, and you'll bomb. The certainty and the predictability of the method, combined with the lively presentation and discussion, works for most students. When they do poorly, they almost never blame the teacher. They know better.

Cecilia is one of those students who count Bohannon as one of their favorites at Whitney, one of many who find his "subversive" nature appealing.

"The first time I met him, he was loudly declaring the stupidity of females as a race," she recalls with affection. "So the next time he said something about how girls shouldn't be in the classroom, I said something like, 'Well, neither should old men, but you're still here.'...As class wore on, I found that he did this chauvinistic act to get people to speak up for themselves, to not let you get walked all over by these kind of people in the future. He isn't bound by the usual code of Don't get to know your students, always maintain a distance—he'll talk to you as if you were his equal. Which means you'll come under heavy fire from his sarcastic wit if you aren't equally as nimble with yours. He doesn't really give a Fig Newton for the rules and regs of the school, even though he knows them all. He abides by his own rules, but somehow, no one really has complained....Not that he would really care if they had."

Springtime brings to Whitney a visit from another believer in educational technology, Neil Bush, who arrives to a VIP's greeting and the honorary title of Principal for the Day.

He is here nominally to check on the progress of the eighth-grade social studies class testing out the interactive software made by his company, Ignite!, although most of his time is absorbed by a panel discussion he leads with several prominent educators from the area.

The event is surreal for a number of reasons, including Bush's opening remarks, which include a hearty recommendation of a book that decries the use of standardized tests in public schools, though such testing is the linchpin of his presidential brother's education policy (not to mention the basis of Whitney's reputation and top ranking among California schools). Odder still is the panel's use of microphones and amplifiers, as if addressing a large crowd. For there is no real audience in Whitney's Multi-Purpose Room—just the school principals, Aisha's crew of VIP escorts, a few stray staffers, the head of the PTA, and the Secret Service duo assigned to safeguard the president's younger brother since 9/11.

But Bush delivers his remarks (which sound the same themes he brought up on his last visit) as if he were before a packed convention hall, explaining how his new company's mission and his own interest in improving education stem from his personal—and negative—experiences in school. "I was doing enough to get through elementary school, but by middle school, where the rubber meets the road, they realized I wasn't doing well because I couldn't read. I couldn't keep up. I was bored."

His struggles, eventually found to be the result of dyslexia, led to a lifelong distaste for traditional schooling, although this didn't translate into a passion to reform education until he had three kids of his own, and he feared history would repeat. "My girls did well in the prisonlike environment we create, and got As and Bs," he says. "But my son is more of a hunter and warrior type. He is talented...but making him sit in a traditional classroom all day went against every grain of the way he thinks and works."

His son, Bush says, began having the same experience in school that he had weathered. "We create these prisonlike environments, then we take our hunter-warrior types and label them attention-deficit disordered and put them on drugs," he complains. "Instead, we should be asking how do we alter the learning environment to get the kids we want—and not do it like we have done for the last one hundred fifty years."

Bush recalls how he began to search for an educational approach that would allow his son to succeed by putting his natural gifts to work instead of trying to suppress them. He found what he was looking for in the theory of "multiple intelligences"—the intriguing, potentially useful but unproven (and probably unprovable in the strictest scientific sense) notion that people possess different forms of intelligence, from tactile and kinesthetic to visual, musical, and interpersonal, that are involved in learning. The theory, developed by Harvard cognition expert Howard Gardner, holds that only some of these intelligences are engaged by traditional schooling methods. People who are strong in these areas respond well to traditional schooling. Others, like Bush's son and Bush himself, can find school frustrating, boring, and defeating.

Bolstered by this theory, Bush seems to believe that if a child is inattentive, unwilling to do schoolwork, and reluctant to sit still in class, the classroom, curriculum, and teacher are the likeliest places to look for fault. Schools should not try to subdue this "hunter-warrior" nature, but instead should replace "boring" and "useless" material with lessons that are more appealing to such children and that capitalize on Gardner's theoretical construct of how the human mind learns.

This is the theoretical basis for Ignite!'s interactive software, and Bush believes this multiple-intelligences approach can work for all students, not just troubled ones, by giving them more control over how they learn. If putting math equations to music helps a kid learn, that's what the program will do, customizing lessons for each student's individual "intelligence."

Bush's presentation gives no hint of the objections many researchers have to multiple-intelligences theory, namely that it confuses *talents* with intelligence, and that by wildly expanding the definition of intelligence beyond traditional IQ tests, the theory has created an alluring, feel-good alternative to accepting an unpleasant reality: Some people are just smarter than others.

Nevertheless, Bush is successfully marketing Ignite!'s products in several states, particularly Florida, where his older brother Jeb is governor, and Neil is not shy about using the Bush family name elsewhere. He fits his visits to Whitney into a busy globe-trotting schedule that has him first meeting Ignite! investors in Japan, Egypt, and Saudi Arabia, then joining forces with an education company chaired by former junk-bond-king-turned-convict-turned-philanthropist Michael Milken, followed by private dinners with the crown prince of Dubai and the president of China.

Although the other panelists appearing with Bush—all but one of them local educators—speak to the opportunities offered by new technology to transform schools, they do not endorse Bush's specific theories, nor do they embrace his comparison of their schools to the penitentiary. The one non-educator on the panel, Frank Chao, president of the school's fund-raising Whitney Foundation, mildly contradicts Bush, saying a change in technology is less important to improving schools than a change in attitudes. He poignantly tells the story of his initial resistance to his son's desire to parlay excellent grades into an appointment to one of the nation's military academies rather than attendance at an Ivy League school, as Chao had hoped. Their conflict over this, and Chao's eventual realization that a fine education and a life-changing, life-forming experience can be found at more than ten or fifteen elite universities, has been a bit of a watershed at Whitney. Sometimes parents need to let their kids make these decisions, Chao says—a revelation for an influential figure at Whitney, where parental ambitions are keen and often unrelenting. Brock has recruited Chao to spread the word about his change in attitude, to try to convince parents to look beyond HYP—a slow process, to be sure, but one that Chao believes could have a much greater impact than technology in the classroom.

Bush seems befuddled by this, and he quickly closes off discussion of the concerns of high-achieving students and their collegiate choices and returns to his theme of schools as prisons. Like his presidential brother, Bush projects a pleasant, plainspoken manner, and the resemblance between the two men is striking at times. But Neil Bush's apparent distaste for schools and the standard measures used to gauge their effectiveness begins to assert itself, arousing a marked testiness in him when he says, "I'm looking for some agreement here." He asserts that real reform will occur only when educators shift focus from the many boring and useless subjects now taught in so many classrooms—the ones the hunter-warrior types despise—to a core of essential knowledge and cultural literacy that students really will need in life. When that core is mastered, probably at the end of middle school or soon after, students should be given greater power to decide their own courses of study, Bush says.

"We are sentencing our kids to a joyless environment," he says. "But for what? . . . We have fifty-eight engineers at Ignite! Not one was hired because of their SAT scores. We look for core competencies, communication skills. . . . There's a lot more to a person, to the ability to succeed, than their performance on a test."

It is a notion with undeniable appeal—both for over-stressed, high-achieving students who might want a break, and for people like Bush, whose advantages in life and access to power have little to do with their academic accomplishments or merit. Bush is right: The crown prince of Dubai does not take a meeting with Neil Bush because of his college boards. Even so, it strikes many present as a strange point to emphasize when you're Principal for the Day at a high school known for its high SAT scores and pursuit of advanced academic studies. While the remark provokes no response from the adults present, several students in the VIP entourage, who had been whispering to one another and growing increasingly restive for the past ten minutes, can no longer restrain themselves.

"There is value in 'boring' material, because there is some knowledge we need to obtain, even when it's unpleasant," says Adam, a junior seriously considering one of the military academies for his undergraduate education. "Active learning programs are great, they're fun, but there are limitations. Take an AP Biology course. There is a massive amount of information you must assimilate in order to pass the test and get college credit. You can't do that with active learning. There's no time. So there has to be a balance."

Ricky, a middle school student who immigrated from Taiwan while in sixth grade, seems bewildered by Bush's position. "In Taiwan, they put discipline over discipline over discipline. You do the work and have no choice. In the U.S., it's more lenient. It feels like nothing is restricted. I'm worried that learning might just slip away by making pleasure more important in school."

Bush, who had listened silently to the students' feedback until this point, is clearly stunned by this comment. He blurts in astonishment, "And you think school is a pleasure?"

"In some areas, yes. Gaining knowledge is a pleasure."

Aisha steps in to support the now-flummoxed Bush, who appears genuinely surprised that any thirteen-year-old would claim to find school pleasant. She feels an obligation as his head escort, and also harbors great affection for the Bush family because of the president's post–9/11 efforts to quell hate crimes by visiting a mosque and meeting with Muslim leaders. So Aisha suggests that Bush has a point about joylessness: She argues that schools like Whitney can become so focused on academic achievement that kids may be shortchanged on learning social and communication skills or experiencing the simple pleasures of life. Aisha considers herself blessed: Her parents have always urged her to strike a balance, and they are critical of the pressures so many of her fellow students must endure. She describes an eighth grader whose mother takes him to after-school academies until seven in the evening every day and makes him do extra schoolwork on weekends. One day he started refusing to do his homework, and his teacher sent him to Aisha for tutoring. "I sent him outside to play," she says. "Because he needed that, not tutoring."

But, in the end, not even Aisha can embrace Bush's basic premise that schools are prisons that must be torn down. She says she still favors—and enjoys—high standards and rigorous, traditional studies. She just would like to see more balance and more attention paid to the "whole student," without so much "overschooling."

And then it's Kosha's turn. She came in late, invited by Brock, who slipped out to find someone to liven things up. He got his wish.

"I don't think we're overschooled. I went to a tutoring academy. I went to Indian School—I wanted to embrace my culture. It wasn't a burden, it was a gift....I hear students say, 'Oh, math is boring, this or that subject is boring, so I don't want to do it.' I say, that's an excuse, a crutch. A student should want to learn about *everything*. That's what we're here for."

Bush is again taken by surprise. Kosha is a strong speaker with definite opinions; she has the poise one would expect of a young woman who just won California's statewide Junior Miss contest, and though she is unfailingly polite, she pulls no punches. Few students are as busy as Kosha, even at Whitney, and few seem to balance so effortlessly academic rigor and outside interests, so she knows what she's talking about when it comes to the state and the potential of public education. Only when she mentions the study of calculus does Bush sense an opening, and he interrupts, seizing on what he perceives to be a flaw in her argument. No one really wants to study calculus, he says triumphantly, calling it a prime example of being "forced to study something a kid thinks is terribly useless and obscure."

"I like calculus," Kosha answers, looking him in the eye. "It instills critical thinking....It's definitely a challenge, but it forces you to think in creative ways. Some students may think school should be a cakewalk, that it shouldn't be hard, that you should play all day. But that's not the way to excellence."

"That's an interesting defense of what I consider to be a broken system," Bush says dismissively. But several other students jump in to support Kosha's point. One after another, they decry the notion they sense is lurking behind Bush's criticisms—the idea that school should be made easier, more entertaining. The problem, as they see it, isn't that school is too boring or too hard, but that too many young people are unwilling to work and extend themselves to master difficult subjects. Too many kids—and parents and teachers—have low expectations, they say. They should be urged to reach higher, not settle for less, Kosha and the other Whitney students argue.

"But I truly believe there is a boundary to teaching kids core knowledge, critical skills," Bush argues. His tone is almost pleading now, as he finds himself alone, pitted against six kids with near perfect SATs and a love for higher math, and no support from his fellow panelists. "Once you get to high school, you have special interests evolving. I don't see what's wrong in allowing kids to pursue their interests.... Why must we continue to cram this other stuff down their throats?"

"Well, you would just have apprenticeships then, instead of high school," Kosha says.

"So what's wrong with that?" Bush responds.

"Because it abandons the whole notion of building a whole person!"

Before Bush can answer that, two more seniors, Tara and Angela R., jump up. "We don't have the life experiences to make those decisions," Tara says.

"We're not ready to decide what we're interested in," Angela R. adds. "We need to learn more. That's why we go to college."

Patty Hager leans over and whispers, "He's losing the argument because the system works for these kids. Really, it works for most kids, not just at Whitney. But he's focused on the failure." In a few crisp words, the coprincipal has crystallized not just Bush's philosophy, but the whole national debate on the future of public education—and the unbridgeable chasm that separates those who are interested in what's working, and those who are fixated on what's not. Bush has built a computer program, along with an entire worldview, around the notion that the whole educational system is broken, and he appears confounded by a school that succeeds and students who excel.

In the end, even Aisha has to abandon Bush, albeit gently. She, too, believes high school students need to be given as broad an education as possible, whether they want it or not. As an example, she describes the experience of her older sister, who entered the workplace right after high school and some community college, only to find she wanted different opportunities than those that were open to her. Even as a high school graduate, Aisha says, her sister hadn't been ready to decide her entire future, and she ended up going back to a four-year college to get the experience and knowledge she needed to chart her course in life.

"You don't get that going back to school," Bush says bluntly, closing off further debate and leaving his chief defender looking wounded. "You get that from life, from working in a business."

In Jenny Shellhamer's eighth-grade class, Bush's belief that traditional schoolroom approaches are "broken" and classrooms like Dave Bohannon's are prisons is clearly embodied in his company's interactive social studies program. One of Shellhamer's classes has been putting it through its paces this year.

It is not going well.

First there were the technical problems. The program is accessed over the Internet with a secure password for each student, a setup that is the current rage in educational technology because it means the school doesn't need huge amounts of computing power and memory, while the company gets to keep control and custody of its software. But there is a downside: glitches can occur at either end of the digital pipeline, and they have, both at Ignite!'s Texas headquarters and at Whitney's end. The problems have kept the program from running properly much of the year; it crashed regularly for months, forcing Shellhamer to use standard texts and lessons, just like her regular classes.

More than halfway through the school year, the bugs are fixed and Shellhamer is finally able to put the program to work. As promised, it makes for a very different classroom environment: Her students work individually, staring at their computers instead of her, running through interactive lessons tailored to each of their learning styles—their "intelligences." Some are studying early American conflicts with Indian tribes through music, others through games, still others through a variety of audiovisual presentations. The content covered is all basically the same for each, and the lessons seem far less challenging than the textbook Shellhamer uses with her other classes, with only the presentation style varying.

The kids quickly master the very simple, often cartoonish lessons, then figure out how to access presentations for other learning styles to see which one is most enjoyable; no one worries about whether these match up with their type of intelligence or not. Once those possibilities are exhausted— often well before the period ends—Shellhamer finds herself returning to the more in-depth traditional lessons she uses with her other classes.

In its quest to make history more lively and entertaining, the program makes some startling leaps and sometimes seems to be reaching for the lowest common denominator. The Seminole Wars are presented at one point as an imaginary football game, with players crashing helmets together in a game dubbed "The Jacksons *vs.* the Seminoles."

"I was appalled by that," Shellhamer says afterward. "It was not a football game. People get up when they get knocked down in a football game. This was a war. People died."

Even the tests at the end of each session seem too easy, she finds: A mere eight questions for an amount of material she would normally cover in fifty. More often than not, Shellhamer finds herself breaking up the computer sessions with discussions and readings, and she ends up using the program more as a supplement to traditional texts and lectures, though it was intended to be the primary mode of study.

As the end of the school year nears, Shellhamer and her students decide that the program is not right for Whitney and probably not the best choice for most eighth graders. The teacher has decided she will not use it again. It might have some utility for failing students who can't or won't respond to traditional classes, one boy suggests (and, in fact, Brock pushed Bush to provide the program to a nearby middle school with a high number of such students). But for most kids, at least at Whitney, Ignite! seems to have achieved exactly the opposite of what Bush intended, as far as making school more interesting and engaging.

"It makes social studies too easy, really," the boy says. "It's boring."

22

There are a few important things to remember about Christine. She began shopping for books at age three at the Harvard University bookstore, when she still spoke only Chinese. The first title she selected on her own was a book about bugs. She loved that book. She still has that book.

Later that same year, her father, a radiologist, bought her *Webster's Collegiate Dictionary*: the real one, not a child's version, almost too heavy for her to carry. She read it. She still has that one, too.

She is known to rise at two in the morning to study for AP bio. She took calculus eight hours a day all summer so she could step up to advanced calc when school started. Christine learned ballroom dancing for an article she wrote for a Taiwanese teen magazine, assigned herself the task of reading forty of the world's literary masterpieces, and is addicted to the Amelia Peabody mysteries set in Edwardian Egypt. She wants to be everything: a marine biologist (ever since her scientist mom bought her fish at age five), a chef, a journalist, an archaeologist, maybe a lawyer, maybe even a doctor, despite the fact that her parents desperately wish it to be so. Everything. And regardless of which path she chooses, there will be the writing. She writes so incessantly and so well, her prose and the mind behind it so thoughtful, observant, and wry, that Whitney's part-time journalism teacher just knew Christine had to be a plagiarist when she first submitted her work a few years back. The poem she wrote at age fourteen about her grandfather began:

> *Most of all I remember textures:*
> *his jacket of nubby brown tweed,*
> *scented with toothpaste and soap—*
> *the stubborn scratch of five o'clock shadow—*
> *the geography of skin worn by age.*
> *From his pockets sprang odd treasures:*
> *Candied orange peel, yellow checkers,*
> *Japanese toffees with skins of gold...*

Fourteen-year-old kids don't write like this, the teacher said, do they?

"Yes," Christine's English teachers assured him. "That's how she writes. That's how she's *always* written."

Christine's nickname is Bunny, for her love of rabbits. She speaks French. She has a surprisingly deep laugh, all diaphragm and delight, though she lets it out of its cage all too rarely for her friends' taste. She keeps secrets well, others' and her own. She scored a near perfect 1550 on her SATs (and perfect 800s on the SAT II math, writing, French, and world history tests). She has picked a few gray hairs out of her head, but nothing like some of her classmates. She's seventeen.

Spring brings a growing tension among the seniors, as college acceptance—and rejection—notices intermittently arrive in the mail and via the Internet. Christine should have been spared this anxiety because of her early-admissions acceptance to Yale University, her future for the next four years settled all the way back in December. But she finds herself just as tense as her friends, as she and her parents manage to maintain a long disagreement about her course of study next year and the career choice it will imply.

Her mother and father have always indulged her interests—her passion for gourmet cooking, her instinct for journalism, her writing—but they always knew these things were just pursuits "on the side," rather than a main direction in life. But when she announced that she wanted to be an archaeologist a year ago, and she presented them with a very complete dossier on a very serious summer program through which she could participate in a research dig, her parents, in her words, "went bonkers."

"Why did your father work so hard for all these years, if this is what you are going to do with your life? Digging in dirt!" her horrified mother exclaimed. The three of them had one of their worst fights ever, sending Christine retreating to her room to stew—and then to write.

Later, long after her parents' bedtime, in the hours when she does all her best writing, Christine slipped a letter under their door. She hasn't been able to look at it since, but she knows it was laden with emotion, a passionate but systematic argument about how she had simply sought to make summer plans, not plans for a career, that she did not live in their world but her own, that there is beauty in history. It was quite long, but her parents read every word. When next they spoke, Christine's parents rejected her proposal to participate on digs in Italy and at a Roman fort in England, but they capitulated to her fallback position, a dig at a fourteenth-century site in New Mexico on an old Spanish land grant ranch, thirty minutes outside of Albuquerque. The letter earned her a dusty and hard two weeks helping to unearth a sprawling fourteenth-century pueblo, but she loved the toil and the camaraderie of archaeology, the intimacy of uncovering and holding in her hands the remnants of a lost civilization. "I could do it for the rest of my life," she says now, though not to her parents. "But it's not the *only* thing I could do for the rest of my life."

She's thinking now archaeology may be a hobby she pursues intermittently, seizing opportunities to participate in digs while she makes a career in another field. She looked into it enough to know that it's a life of sacrifices, of dropping everything and moving to difficult places, a field in which there are few openings, ten at any one time at the major universities, controlled by a good ol' boys' network that probably doesn't include a whole lot of brilliant, young Taiwanese American women—which, perversely, adds to the allure and challenge of breaking in. These issues she did discuss with her parents (except for the allure part), and they were relieved, another wild notion their daughter has outgrown, or so she lets them think.

Christine has not ruled out a medical career, but she has spent years—since seventh or eighth grade—preparing her parents for the possibility that she will not go that route. Yet even now, after she's settled on Yale and not a premed program, and the suspense over her future plans is resolved for the next four years, they hold out hope that she will come to her senses and announce to them her intentions of going into medicine. She does not understand this until she mentions she is seriously considering law school after college. She would like to at least partially satisfy her passion for archaeology by exploring a specialty in art and antiquities law—a typical Christine move, looking for the compromise that lets her have everything she wants. But her mother reacts in shock, which in turn shocks Christine. Her dad's disappointment, though silent, lingers for days.

Her anxiety only grows when she attends a talk by a young Taiwanese American writer whose own experiences seem to mirror Christine's exactly: Her parents supported all her extracurricular interests wholeheartedly, but under the assumption that their daughter was doing them solely to enhance her chances of getting into Yale. When it became clear that she actually wanted to make a career of writing, they were mystified and crushed.

Christine still has time to work this out, to sort through her expectations and her parents', and to make peace between them both—years of time. Yet it weighs on her; the months before college are such a nervous, touchy time, every concern seems magnified. Late the next night, after her parents are in bed, she sits down at her computer and begins to write, trying to find some sense in all this, a daughter whose accomplishments are many and fine, and whose kind and loving parents are justifiably proud, yet also, in one way at least, disappointed in her.

"At the very least," she writes, "I thought being a lawyer was a compromise of sorts between the extremes of passion and respectability. To discover that they consider law—along with even engineering, business, and computer science—to be somewhat 'lesser' careers is disappointing to *me*.

"I've told myself that I'm not going to worry about this matter yet. But it still irks me, a little thorn in my brain. I started writing this in a very good, calm, refreshed mood, and now I just feel lost again."

Each week during March and early April, a different University of California campus sends out e-mails to its waiting applicants, notifying them all, simultaneously, whether they are in or out. This is supposed to make the whole acceptance thing easier on everyone—quick, easy, no worrying about the post office.

In practice, however, something very much like mass hysteria grips Whitney on the day UCLA sends its notifications. This top public university is immensely popular with Whitney students; more graduates will go there than any other school, and over half Whitney's senior class will land at one of the UC system's nine campuses. The culmination of everything these kids have worked for over the last six years will be summed up in an automated e-mail. They don't even get the fat or thin envelope to fret about.

Concentrating on classes is difficult on this day, particularly when seniors keep slinking off to log on in the computer lab or at a teacher's desktop. Then, shortly after ten in the morning on the appointed day, the school begins buzzing. Kids can be seen high-fiving and cheering. Whoops can be heard across the school. They're in.

Others can be seen consoling one another, weeping or walking arm in arm, faces downcast. One girl, Angela R., is doubly devastated, turned down by UCLA and the University of Southern California, where she was eager for a place in the school's entertainment-business program. "They just have a way of reducing you to a form letter and making you feel worthless," she complains to a friend, her eyes red. "It's going to be a terrible day."

In civics class, Cecilia sits stiff-lipped in disappointment, not even sketching, as she almost always does while waiting for the teacher to get started. She did not get into UCLA, a serious blow—not devastating, but still a big disappointment.

"It's okay. It doesn't matter," she says. A single tear slips down her cheek and she wipes it away, furious at herself. "Stupid university."

The blow is not cushioned by already having been accepted to UC Irvine's honors program, which is open to only 5 percent of incoming freshmen and which allows students to work in small classes and seminars directly with professors, not teaching assistants or grad students. But she does not want to go to Irvine, for the same reason Angela doesn't want to go there: If art is your passion, Irvine is not going to be your first or second or even third choice.

Cecilia is consoled, however, when word arrives the following week that she has been accepted to UC Berkeley, another popular choice with Whitney students. The art program isn't quite as good as UCLA's, in Cecilia's opinion, but it is an excellent school, and has the distinct advantage of being much farther from home. "That part is good," she says. "The umbilical cord shall be cut, even if it is with a butter knife."

The stress of this time of year shows itself in innumerable ways, much of it burned off in healthy, harmless activities— loud music outside during lunch breaks, kids playing minor pranks on one another, more Homer Simpson "*Whoo-hoo*" added to Shirley Wold's computer (the hackers also managed to bust the Windows code and change the "Start" button to the "Mold" button—"Short for Ms. Wold," David proudly announces). But there are also some occasionally disturbing moments.

One of the worst comes during a major test in Wold's biology class. One of her seniors abruptly bursts into tears. In itself, this is not so unusual—Wold has seen plenty of students tear up when they take a look at a test for which they are not fully prepared. But the teacher gets worried a few minutes later, when the girl's tears are replaced by laughter. It is not a good laugh. It is a hysterical laugh, quiet and persistent and completely mirthless.

Then the girl begins muttering to herself and wandering around the room, staring at the wall, at pictures, at a cereal bowl that, for some reason, she finds howlingly funny. One by one, the other students look up from their tests and begin to stare. When Wold asks her to calm down and stop disrupting the class, the girl grows furious and hurls her test paper at the teacher. She had been working on it for half an hour. It's blank. A moment later, so is the expression on the girl's face, anger replaced by apathy.

Her parents are called, the school nurse talks with her, then the district psychologist. The girl is hospitalized later that day with a nervous breakdown. Her mother calls from the hospital to say she may not be back for months, if at all, her graduation on hold, her college plans ruined. She had been an A student but had grown increasingly insecure all year, insisting the school provide her tutors, which it did, recruiting two very patient seniors to work with her. Wold later learned she had been calling them at home at all hours, berating them for not doing enough, though they had worked with her every day. The pressure, real and imagined, just became too much for her.

Then there is the puzzle of Henry,* a junior who has been in and out of Shirley Wold's office all year. His test scores show him to be extremely capable, but he has simply refused for months to do his homework.

When Brock and Wold meet with him, they ask Henry to explain his refusal to do schoolwork. But he sits there stonily on Brock's office couch, unable or unwilling to provide any real reason. Was it rebellion, problems at home, was he depressed? No, no, no, he says, nothing like that. The conversation goes nowhere. Still, despite his failing grades for classes in which he had previously excelled, Brock and Wold decide to give him more time. Wold even talks him out of a plan to drop out of Whitney so he can get a general equivalency diploma and go to community college immediately. "You're capable of so much more," Wold tells him. "Don't sell yourself short."

A few weeks later, however, after he is repeatedly spotted in the hallways between classes, a teacher nails him with an after-school detention. A few minutes later, in front of witnesses in the main office, he threatens to kill her.

He is gone within hours.

At first defiant, saying he wanted to leave Whitney anyway, his air of ambivalence crumbles when his parents are called and told to pick him up. He swears he was joking, that he would never harm a soul. He begs to be given one more chance.

"I'm sorry, but this is the one area where we have zero tolerance, and no choice," Wold says. "It wouldn't have mattered who said it, you or anyone else. By law, we have to protect a teacher. This is an era when kids are coming in with guns and opening fire."

"But I didn't mean it." `

"Then don't say it! You know this is not the climate to say that kind of thing. Be glad we don't call the police. They call it terrorist threats these days, and lock people up."

He leaves, but tries to sneak back into the school, and begs Wold again to be allowed to stay. She looks stricken at his abject begging, but she says no. It's clear to her that he's been trying to bail out on Whitney all year, that's he's been doing everything possible to be kicked out.

"Everyone on this staff was willing to throw you a life-saver," she tells Henry. "But your hand was not out. And now you fixed it so you can't stay. You got what you wanted, and now it's too late to say you didn't want it after all."

Then Henry is escorted off campus, a kid with potential who a great school could not reach or even figure out. But a few months later, he is back—working as an aide in the Whitney college center, though he attends another high school. He apologized for the threat and works quite hard as an aide. When he turns eighteen, he leaves to join the army, hoping to serve overseas and to use the G.I. Bill benefits for college.

Angela is in a particularly bad state this same day, her eyes deeply shadowed. She hasn't been sleeping since getting into Irvine.

Now that her college is chosen, she is finding the remainder of the school year unbearable. She is supposed to take an AP Statistics exam in a few days, she has been studying hard, yet it now seems so pointless to her. She does not need it to get into college, she will not get credit for it at her new school, yet she cannot bring herself to skip it. Her classes are excruciating, except for art. She has even lost interest in the senior prom, though she had been working on a dress for weeks.

This weekend, everything is coming to a head: She is supposed to stay overnight at the university, a kind of get-acquainted experience at her school-to-be. But she doesn't want to go. And so she spends much of the afternoon in the art room, hunched over a canvas, her brush strokes so forceful they sound like a saw blade.

When she goes home and tells her parents she would rather not do the overnight visit, they grow impatient with her. They are genuinely bewildered by Angela's intransigence. You should be happy, they say. Do you know how many kids would kill for such opportunity? "You're going," her father says simply, closing off further debate.

"I don't approve of your lifestyle," her mother adds, concerned about her daughter's lack of sleep. "If you keep going like this, I don't know how you'll ever make it through college."

"C'mon, Mom, I'm not even there yet," Angela protests.

The next afternoon, her father drives her to the university. She pretends to be asleep in the car on the way there, expecting the visit to be a disaster.

The first thing Angela learns on reporting to the campus housing office is that her host has canceled at the last minute. This is the person who is supposed to share a dorm room with her, show Angela around the campus, and take her to classes. Don't worry, though, Angela is told. Someone named Diane has agreed to take over as host. The only problem is, she can't make it until five P.M. Angela has arrived, as scheduled, at two o'clock.

Angela would like to leave then and there, but there is

nothing she can do. Protesting will not help. She can't go home—her dad has left. So she sits and waits in the office for three hours. She has nothing to do and no one to talk to, so she grabs some scratch paper and starts doodling and writing. She ends up covering several papers with the words *I hate UCI* written over and over.

Diane finally shows up at half past five and proves to be, in every way imaginable, Angela's complete opposite in life. There Angela is in some nice khaki pants and a conservative collared shirt. Diane shows up in a tight miniskirt, a tank top with bare midriff, and a pierced tongue. *And Mom's worried about my lifestyle now,* Angela can't help thinking.

They go to Diane's dorm room. Angela tries to keep a neutral expression, but she is horrified, and it probably shows. The room is a complete mess, which isn't so bad in itself. Angela's room gets a little scary sometimes, too. But as Angela remembers it, everyone in the vicinity of Diane's room is dressed in tight, revealing clothes, with bellies exposed and multiple body piercings in evidence—navels, eyebrows, tongues, noses. There are nude pictures up on the walls. People are running in and out of each other's dorm rooms, partying, looking at porn on the Internet, exchanging racy Instant Messages. Angela likes to think of herself as open-minded, but she is an intensely modest, socially conservative kid who is just not used to this sort of thing. She ends up being left alone in Diane's room, sitting on the bed, thinking, *Oh god, why am I here?*

Then Diane returns with her friends and tells Angela about a frat party that night. "It'll be great," Diane says repeatedly. But Angela doesn't want to go. She mumbles something about having to study for an AP test, but all through dinner at the dining commons (where, she grudgingly admits, the food is pretty good) they keep trying to talk her into the frat party. Back at the dorm, another girl starts throwing clothes at her for the party, but she is clearly size zero, way too petite for Angela. In desperation, Angela sits down at Diane's computer and Instant Messages a girl she spotted at dinner, an old friend from Whitney. "Save me!" she writes, praying the other girl is online.

"I'll be there in ten minutes," comes the reply.

Things get better after that, a little at least. Her friend, Wendy, lives in the honors dorm, much calmer, much more in keeping with Angela's more buttoned-down personality. Angela calls Diane and lets her know she'll be staying with Wendy for the night, and her host does not hide her relief. The party girls end up staying out until three in the morning, while Wendy and Angela stay up late talking, with the older girl passing on some valuable tips about life at Irvine.

A weary-looking Diane picks up Angela for breakfast. She doesn't bring her to any classes or do anything else, just wishes her good luck and leaves. Angela's first day at her new college is over, and it would be hard to imagine a worse first impression. Her father arrives to drive her home a short time later.

She cries for a while, refusing to talk. "Why are you sending me here? I hate it," she says finally. Then, exhausted, she falls asleep.

When she wakes up, she discovers her father has not driven to their house but to the campus of Chapman University, a small, private liberal arts school in Orange that Angela has applied to and loves. For a wild moment, her hopes soar: Could her father have finally been moved to a change of heart by her unhappiness? But no, he has a specific destination in mind. Somehow, he has found a former Chapman student and arranged a meeting. The young man proceeds to explain all the things he dislikes about the school and the many reasons why Angela would be better off elsewhere.

Angela is mortified. "Dad, you don't have to do this," she exclaims. "I'm going to UCI, you don't have to worry."

He says he just wanted to help her see that she'll be happy and better off at UCI. They drive home and she drifts back to sleep. But she has a plan now, one she'll keep to herself. She learned from Wendy that there is a community college five minutes from the UCI campus. It has an excellent art program, serving all the students at the university who can't get the courses they want from their own school. If she must attend Irvine, then she will take extra courses down the road and continue her art training. Then, in two years, she'll apply to the fabled Art Center in Pasadena, one of the top art schools in the country.

She doesn't know if she can get in, but she has to hold on to that hope, she says. It's all that will make going to this school bearable for her.

23

During the last days of April and the first days of May, just as the angst is fading from the college admissions rite of passage, another springtime ritual long dreaded in California schools kicks off: the annual STAR week.

The Standardized Testing and Reporting program—STAR—is a three-day testing hell, a series of multiple-choice exams in reading, math, and a selection of other subjects given to every student in the state (except for high school seniors) in order to calculate the academic performance of each and every student, racial group, and school in California. And when the testing is done, each of the schools are ranked by their scores, all 8,757 of them. The rankings are made in groupings that lump similar schools together rather than providing an absolute top and bottom, the idea being it would be unfair to compare the test scores of an impoverished inner-city school with a place like Whitney. Nevertheless, newspapers, Web sites, enterprising parents, and proud principals routinely unravel this oblique presentation to give a straight up and down numerical ranking for various schools. The school rankings produced through the STAR exams are referred to as the Academic Performance Index,[17] a high-stakes sorting of the successful from the failing and everything in between, with budgets, bonuses, reputations, and even local real estate values keyed to the results, out of all rational proportion with what's being measured. The index is, like the class-size reduction program, a creation of politicians rather than educators. It measures a number of things. What kids are learning every day in their classrooms is not one of them.

In California, as in most other states, STAR time is marked by a frenzy of drilling and preparation at many schools, as anguish over what might happen if scores decline grips principals and teachers who know that each budget year grows more precarious than the next. Just a few percentage points difference up or down from last year's test scores can mean the difference between a school getting thousands of extra dollars for books, teaching aides, or new equipment, and being placed on the dreaded list of failing schools, where there are no extra dollars, where recruiting new teachers becomes doubly hard, and where parents demand to know why those scores in the newspaper aren't as good as the school's down the road.

Teachers loathe the STAR program, and not just because of the pressures it creates in the name of holding schools accountable and providing incentives to improve. Much of the test is based on a nationally standardized, off-the-shelf test, the Stanford 9 (a test first created in 1923 by the *World Book Encyclopedia* folks, revised many times, and now run out of San Antonio by Harcourt Educational Measurement), which does not necessarily match up with what's being taught that year inside California classrooms. Ninth graders will be asked social studies questions covered in the tenth-grade curriculum; eleventh graders are tested on material covered four years earlier. And so, in schools across the state, teachers interrupt their lessons to review material covered in the tests rather than their actual curriculum, using the sorts of quick and dirty drilling methods that can create a short-term up-swing in test scores but which have little to do with real learning or comprehension. The kids despise it because the tests have nothing to do with their own report cards, graduation requirements, or promotion to the next grade. The process of education grinds to a standstill during the tests.

Persistent questions and press reports challenging the reliability of the tests and index add to the perception that this can be a capricious means of holding schools accountable—especially because the failure label may be attached if any one demographic group within a student body declines in its scores, even if the rest of the students at a school excel. This sort of bizarre contradiction worries Shirley Wold; she fears something like that could happen at Whitney if they're not careful. This is just one reason why she is questioning her sanity this spring for agreeing to be this year's "STAR Czar" at Whitney. The test has put the school at the top of the Academic Performance Index, but this high scoring has the perverse effect of making it impossible to get bonus funding because there is virtually no room left for improvement. "There's only room to go down," Wold says, "and I'm afraid these kids might not put in the effort this year. They're just too overloaded."

Wold is not having a good week. She is in her second day of testing, a Tuesday. Her face is flushed, her hair is flying, she has worked the entire weekend getting things ready. Her prep work should have meant everything would go smoothly, but the tests are a mess. The district botched the order for math exams for the juniors and sophomores: there are over two hundred missing and none to be found anywhere. They are being ordered from San Antonio, but no one can say if they'll get to Whitney on time. Wold worries that customer service might be a bit dicey with the testing company at the moment, because the state of California chose to announce, just before testing was to begin, that a new company would get the STAR contract in the future.

Meanwhile, the eleventh graders are in a snit. First a group of them panicked when a substitute teacher started the timer for their reading test while he was reciting the exam instructions. He hadn't administered this test before and so it took awhile; a fourth of the allotted time had gone by before he was done. The kids were outraged, but he ignored their entreaties to reset the clock. One student finally ran out of the room and dashed to Wold's office. "Ms. Wold, Ms. Wold, the sub is doing the test all wrong and he won't believe us." Wold had to race over and instruct him to give the students more time.

After a break, the juniors who are supposed to take the math test have nothing else to do for the rest of the day. Kids who can reach their parents by cell phone are allowed to leave if the parents call the office and authorize an outside pass. But most of the students are stuck, unable to leave, with nothing to do. And the teachers are stuck, too, because they have to watch the kids, a wasted day all around.

The missing tests finally arrive on the last day of testing, trundled in on a dolly by a United Parcel Services deliveryman, then parceled out to the waiting students. After an assortment of other near catastrophes—incorrectly filled-out forms, the wrong bar code on a critical test sheet—the ordeal is over at last, most of a school week wasted, with Wold looking ready to collapse. A teacher actually stops by, looks in her office, and says, "So, things seem to be going pretty smoothly this year, eh?" Wold nearly chokes on the latte a kindly student had brought her. She wishes Homer had spoken for her by bellowing, *"D'oh!"* but he rarely speaks on cue. "If I wasn't so strung out, I'd tell you how smooth things were going," she finally manages to say. The other teacher scurries away without a word.

"It's not accountability that I'm against—I'm all for it," Wold says later. "But this test is not doing it. It's a sop to the public, a way for politicians to say, 'Hey, we're improving the schools, we're holding their feet to the fire.' And now it's not just California, it's the whole country."

Wold is referring to a new federal law on the books this school year—the No Child Left Behind Act—that mandates this sort of testing nationwide and gives, in theory at least, parents the right to leave underperforming schools that fail to improve for two consecutive years. The idea stems from a program pioneered in Texas, one of George W. Bush's signature campaign issues: the so-called "Texas Miracle," a system of school accountability through testing that, Bush argued, raised the pass rate for state tests from just over half the students in 1995 to 80 percent in 2000. Testing drives reform, Bush declared, by rewarding the good and weeding out the failing schools. Now California and the rest of the country are headed down a similar path.

But a closer look at the Texas experience suggests it might be as much mirage as miracle: While Texas students have performed better in successive years on the state's homegrown tests, their scores on the federally administered National Assessment of Educational Progress have shown no such gains. Since Bush was elected president, researchers have pointed to explanations for rising scores in Texas that have nothing to do with rising academic achievement: a lowering of the official score needed to pass; an abrupt doubling of the number of kids in special education classes, where students are exempt from taking the test; and an acceleration of high school dropout rates in the state, which weeds out the students likely to score the lowest. A twenty-eight state study by researchers at Arizona State University, meanwhile, found no evidence that high-stakes testing had improved student achievement in Texas or anywhere else.[18]

For all the testing and accountability-driven reforms aimed at bolstering student achievement around the country, the 2002 National Assessment of Educational Progress revealed these depressing facts: Eight out of ten American high school seniors cannot pass a basic science test. Sixty-three percent of seniors cannot perform the simple fourth-grade multiplication necessary to determine how much postage is needed on a package of a given weight. Nine out of ten cannot say how much money they would earn in interest from their savings accounts—even with a calculator. This is why hundreds of thousands of college students must take remedial math classes (often taught at the middle school level), why there are ever-fewer American-born math, science, and engineering majors, and why Whitney is so keen to have all its students take one, if not two, years of calculus: because if they do, the colleges treat them like gods. And it illustrates why twenty years of national testing for accountability is great at showing what's wrong. But as an engine for fixing schools, it has yet to be proven; the basic math scores on the national assessment, in fact, have declined for most grade levels since 1980.

But the testing machine shows no sign of slowing; testing is a politically popular and potent symbol of accountability, whether it improves student achievement or not. The irony for Whitney is that the school benefits from the tests it hates. And though Wold's prediction that scores might decline is later borne out—there's a retreat of nine points compared to the previous year—the drop is statistically insignificant and does nothing to alter the school's top ranking. Whitney's score is 956 out of a possible 1,000; the next nearest high school is Whitney's old role model, Lowell High in San Francisco, with a score of 928; only three other high schools in the entire state score at 900 or above this same year. That's rarefied territory, considering only 6 percent of California's high schools boast a score of 800 or more—the official performance goal for *all* schools in the state. The average school score is several hundred points lower than this target. This does not bode well for the state's ambitious, high-pressure goal of having, by the year 2014, every student in the state graduate with academic skills sufficient for entering a four-year college. A huge majority of the students now fall short of that standard, which Whitney has routinely met for years.

"We hate the tests," Wold says, "but we love to talk about the scores. It's what the parents want to see, it's what the district wants to see, it's what people think makes us special. And if we ever stop getting those high scores, look out. All the people who have always wanted to shut us down will finally have the ammunition they need to do it."

A very different sort of test is under way in Rod Ziolkowski's honors physics class, where the ill-fated Group 5 has tried, once again, to assemble a credible presentation.

But if they were chastened by their last meeting with Mr. Z, they have also been consumed by other concerns that have blunted their efforts to bear down in physics. Irene is fretting about which of her second-choice colleges she should attend (Johns Hopkins University appears to be winning), having missed out on her first choices. Cher and Brian are swamped with other classwork. Albert is still cramming to retake his SATs in hopes of boosting his chances of getting into a primo undergraduate business program next year, and he worries, "My extracurriculars suck: basketball, Red Cross, student council—they're just not enough." He's an excellent tennis player, and he has considered going for a scholarship as one of his cousins has done, but Albert wants to be a regular teenager. He doesn't want to make tennis his life the way his cousin has had to do.

The upshot of all this is that Group 5's new presentation on their rocket experiment is shaky at best. They have assembled a better model from their launch tests, but the part of the PowerPoint presentation reserved for the mathematical model, the one that uses the laws of physics to predict where the film canister/rocket will land, is a cobbled-together nightmare whose shortcomings cannot be disguised by a slick computer graphic. But that's all they've got.

"That's the way this group is," Cher says. "Last night, we stayed up late working on it, but we spent all our time getting chicken from Pollo Loco and looking at lights in the sky."

Mr. Z is more weary than angry this time as he picks out one flaw after another in their latest attempt to explain the motion and pressures affecting their experimental rocket. They have answered the most basic question that eluded them last time: they realize that the water is the "fuel" for this rocket, shooting out of the bottom of the canister because of the Alka-Seltzer-induced pressure inside. The canister reacts by moving in the opposite direction. Yet their equations do not reflect this simple fact, Mr. Z says, pointing to their chart on the computer screen that depicts the weight of the rocket as it leaves the launchpad—a critical number in figuring out how far it will travel.

"Look here. You added the mass of the water and the mass of the container together, like they were one solid thing. They have to be separate equations. What you have here is impossible: the water never leaves the canister in this model."

It is as if they had told Mr. Z that they had a car that can run indefinitely, yet never use up any gas. The four students shift uncomfortably. Brian says, "Oops."

They look at him fearfully, but there is no yelling from Mr. Z this time. He just looks sad, which, Cher says later, is even worse, "like disappointing your dad." He points out a number of other problems in their work—areas that the rest of the class waded through and solved weeks earlier. "We've made progress," he says, "but we're still a long way from where everyone else is. Right now, I'd be hard-pressed to say this is C work."

C work. Nothing strikes terror in the average Whitney student more than the prospect of a C, which, in the minds of these students and their parents, is not much different from an F. One C on their transcripts, they fear, will become a neon sign flashing to HYP and all the other top schools, saying: *Pass Me By.* Albert says afterward, "I can't get a C in this class, no way. My parents would kill me."

In the end, Mr. Z takes pity on them. He provides them a road map for completing the project, a number of broad hints about what to do next. He had vowed not to do this at the beginning of the project—this was supposed to be about not getting spoon-fed for a change—but he's unwilling to let them continue to flail with time running out. The kids are relieved. Out of earshot, Albert says, "Once he lays it out for us, we can do it. This unstructured stuff is really not our thing."

As he speaks, several of the other groups are busily modifying the designs of the canisters, making them ever more sleek and aerodynamic. Group 5's remains unchanged, a simple film container that never seems to land in the same place twice.

A week later, Mr. Z stands before the class. They will work on their project two more days, he announces, then later in the month, they will present to the visiting engineers, and have their test shots in the gym.

"Many of you have been working hard in here every day. Something, even if it was something small, gets done every day. Some of you have wasted the last six weeks. You come in and nothing gets done. . . . But I'm proud of most of you."

Mr. Z isn't looking at anyone in particular as he speaks, but there is no doubt about whom he's referring to. Irene peers around the computer on her lab table and frowns at the others. Albert and Brian, looking sheepish, stare down at their notebooks.

"He's talking about us," Cher whispers unnecessarily, unable to help herself.

The physics teacher continues, his voice wistful. "It's like that story about pearls. Some of you pick them up and say, 'Oh, that's cool.' And others have not picked them up because you won't take the trouble to bend your knees to see what's down on the ground. So you get what you put into it. Like anything else in life. Some of you found out a lot about physics. Some of you learned something about yourselves. And that's yours forever. And some of you learned very little. And that's yours, too. That's life, my friends. The pearls are out there, if you want to find them."

Then he straightens up, dusts his hands off, and says, "Okay, let's move on."

Before class, Mr. Z had pulled Group 5 aside, ascertained that they had made no real progress during the last week of work, and told them there was no point in continuing. They would only embarrass themselves before the professional engineers if he allowed them to present. Better if they pulled out now, and he'd give them some reading assignments and a conventional test as a means of eking out a decent grade.

Somehow, they seemed both surprised and hurt by this, although their teacher had given them ample warning. Cher is silent, but Irene and Albert, stung by Mr. Z's mild yet pointed remarks, gripe that he's being too tough on them. "I mean, he cursed us out," Albert says.

They look around at their rival groups. In each, it seems, at least one student, often more than one, put in extra time and effort to keep their groups on track. "If we had David, we'd be ahead of everyone else, too," Albert says, referring to the student in the class generally acknowledged to be a physics and math genius. "Every group has one person in it who does all the work, and then tells the others. They're here all the time. But we have too much other stuff to do."

The excuses are flying fast now. They know they're gobbling sour grapes, several admit, but they can't seem to help themselves. Irene says, "It's unfair that this project required us to work so much on our own time. At lunch, after school."

"Well," Cher disagrees in a very sad, quiet voice, "it *required* us to do that.... We just didn't *do* it."

"One of us could have assumed that leadership role, too," Brian says. "But we didn't." That ends the complaints, because everyone knows he and Cher are right. Any one of them could have stepped up to the plate and changed the course of the project, and they seem as mystified as their teacher as to why none of them did.

Mr. Z doesn't hear any of this. Group 5's table is in the back of the lab, and they are speaking softly. But he can see them and guesses how they feel. He feels the same way: He's not sure he can count this project a success, with only 80 percent of his students finding it a worthwhile experience. Will Group 5 learn something useful from this? Will they do better next time they are confronted with independence, the unexpected, a chance to snatch some pearls? Mr. Z wishes he could say yes, but the truth is, he just doesn't know, and that leaves him feeling disappointed long after the school day ends.

The engineers arrive in ties and jackets, looking so businesslike and serious that a visible wave of nerves passes through the lab room, a clattering of books and stools and dry throats. Coffee, doughnuts, and juice have been set out, but the kids, uncharacteristically, don't touch them. Mr. Z gives his engineer volunteers a rousing introduction, which only heightens everyone's nervousness.

"They're here because they are genuinely interested in what you're doing, because they love being engineers, and they hope some of you might take that path," Mr. Z tells his class, smiling broadly. "We're really lucky to have these gentlemen. You can't underestimate that kind of volunteering."

He turns to his panel of experts next, telling them the students are in their hands, that they should be as tough on them as they would be with colleagues making a presentation. He wants his students to experience what they'll find in the real world of engineering.

"I haven't seen the final products," he tells them. "What I can tell you is, I'm very proud of them. These are exceptional young men and women. I wouldn't waste your time, I wouldn't bring you here, unless I thought it would be worth your while."

The Group 5 kids sit through this with their expressions frozen, enduring it in silence. The other students divide up into their groups and go to different locations around the school to make their presentations in a quiet place without distractions, one engineer per group. Irene, Cher, Brian, and Albert remain behind, then move to another classroom to take Mr. Z's written test on the chapter of their physics book that deals with momentum.

Mr. Z gets them settled in and then drifts through the school, looking in on each of the presentations. He ends up lingering in the conference room, where he watches the three girls he had worried about so much, Group 4, Stacy, Remie, and Jennifer, run through their findings. They are making their PowerPoint presentation to John Takas, an engineer from Boeing who volunteers regularly in Mr. Z's Wednesday after-school robotics class, a man known for his patience— and for pulling no punches when there's a mistake.

Mr. Z is mildly surprised to see Stacy, so quiet in class and a regular fixture at his lunchtime catch-up sessions, at the front of the conference room, chosen by the group as the principal speaker, explaining each step of their experimentation. She is dressed in conservative business clothes instead of her customary jeans and platform shoes, and she suddenly looks much older and less waifish than usual. Her poise and command of the material stun Mr. Z—she's really quite a good public speaker, something he would never have guessed without this project. She might never have known it, either: She barely said a word in class before.

As Stacy runs through an account of their attempts to create a mathematical simulation, Takas interrupts. "How often did you meet outside class?"

Remie speaks up: "*Very* often." The engineer smiles approvingly.

Later, he interrupts a presentation on the data they collected during test launches of the canister. "Exactly what did you measure?" he asks.

Jennifer begins to list the items—mass, dimensions of the container...then loses her way, flustered for a moment. But it's almost unnoticeable, because Stacy smoothly steps in and says, "Why don't we just show you." She clicks the computer mouse and the next slide slips into view with the answer to Takas's question. In the back, Mr. Z is nodding.

The girls take turns explaining the graphs and charts, making it clear that they all fully grasp the underlying physics behind their experiments, culminating with the complex equation they developed that allows them to accurately predict the distance a canister will travel with each launch. They show off the extremely small margin of error with pride; the three are confident and well prepared—professional in their presentation in a way that Ziolkowski never would have expected at the start of the school year. The students who started out struggling most with physics have outperformed some of his strongest students, and he feels certain there will be no going back for them. Later, when he mentions this to Takas, the engineer is surprised. "I just assumed they were among your top students. They were just too good."

When all the groups are finished with their presentations, everyone assembles in the gym to fire their rockets and test the accuracy of their equations. The engineers have given each of the groups high marks on their presentations, and now As—and the champion group—will be determined by the test launches.

Mr. Z shows them a hula hoop, about one meter in diameter. They may position that hoop anywhere they like, flat on the ground, and all they have to do is get the rocket to land inside it. They will get three chances, and they must hit it at least once to get the highest marks.

The distance traveled in a launch varies greatly with the amount of water inside the canister; with the right amount, some of the little rockets climb to rooftop levels and travel over thirty feet from the launcher. Mr. Z randomly chooses eleven milliliters as the amount of water for each group to mix with the Alka-Seltzer. The first group works out their equation, comes up with a distance just under twenty-three feet, positions the hoop, and hits it two out of three tries, setting a high bar for everyone else right from the start.

The next group misses badly on all their tries. The kids are crushed and only later discover that a pinhole leak in their canister bled off enough pressure to ruin their accuracy. "We've all been there," one of the engineers consoles the despondent group members. "That's what it feels like when you push that button and the rocket takes off—and what it feels like when it doesn't hit the target and *everyone* knows. That's real-world engineering."

David's group comes up with a distance of nineteen feet for its canister. Their first shot misses by about a foot. The second goes wide by a matter of inches. The kids are so nervous as they set up their third and final try that they spill the

water and have to start over. The third shot arcs high and just
barely falls inside the target. The whole gym cheers, including
numerous basketball players who dropped what they were
doing to check out this odd display of whooping kids shooting off little plastic containers.

When Stacy, Remie, and Jennifer come up to bat, they
hover over their calculators and run the equation over and
over, making certain of their answer: just over sixteen feet.
When Stacy snaps the lid shut and slides it into the launcher,
the rocket seems to take much longer to launch than the others. For a long moment, it just sits there. Then the high-
pitched pop accompanying liftoff startles the crowd, even
though they knew it was coming.

Two seconds later, the canister lands in the hoop to a
round of applause. A second launch gets the same result. A
third and final try, for the championship, arcs across the gym,
and lands dead center in the hoop, a bull's-eye. Even the engineers are clapping at this point.

"Well," a beaming Ziolkowski says, "there's really no
question who won the accuracy contest. Good job Stacy,
Remie, and Jennifer."

Back in the lab, the snacks and drinks finally start disap-
pearing as everyone relaxes—except for the group that
missed the mark. They had put in some of the longest hours
of any of the groups, and their failure was due to a malfunc-
tion in the equipment, not a problem with their calculations.
One of the kids' girlfriends stops by to console him with a
hug, he is so crestfallen. Finally, they ask Mr. Z how their
flubbed launches will affect their grades—even on this project, they can't forget the bottom line. He tells them not to
worry too much. "Fortunately, I have other measures of your
performance to rely on. I know the effort you put into it."

Then the kids move on to their next class, relieved to be
through with the project but also sorry to see it end. Except
for Group 5, and a few other kids who coasted while others

did the work, Mr. Z's students say the project was one of their best experiences at school all year; some say the best ever. "I never imagined we would win—we just worried about keeping up," Stacy says. "But as each week went by, it seemed like we were not only doing it, but that other kids were following *us*."

Mr. Z, meanwhile, is jubilant, his doubts about the value of this project erased. He can't wait to share the outcome with his colleagues, his wife, his friends. "That was a home run," he says.

The only down moment is when he hands out the exam results to Group 5. As usual, they tested well: high Bs for two of them, As for the other two. Mr. Z still doesn't know what to make of their performance, but it is time to move on to the next area of study, and he treats them just the same as always for the remainder of the school year. But he knows, and they know it, too, that he will never look at them in quite the same way.

Still, he loved everything else about the project, even that the David group had to sweat it out until their third launch before they hit the target, while the Stacy, Remie, Jennifer group cruised with a perfect three for three.

"The award went to the hardest workers, not the most gifted," Mr. Z says, pumping his fist as if he had just coached a winning Olympic team. "The great scales of justice balanced out."

As he stows the gear from the experiment for a final time, he's already thinking about the project he'll undertake next year. He can't do this one again: He knows the solution now, and that would spoil the teacher-student role reversal. But he has this idea that each member of the class could build their own primitive computer, then use it throughout the year for experiments. Wouldn't that, he asks, be totally cool?

24

Attendance in the essay-writing workshop has dwindled, which is only natural. The days grow longer and the outer classroom doors are propped open to admit the newly balmy air and the faint rattle of palm fronds. Working on essays that won't be due for another eight months—and that require the writers to admit there will soon be an end to life inside Whitney's pressurized, comforting cocoon—just can't compete with other distractions and demands.

There are semester projects to complete, parties to plan, final exams, final courses at the local SAT academy, a final exhausted push to get through a year of sleep deprivation and AP exams. There is the decision making for those students who have too many college acceptances to consider—and for those students who have too few. And then there are the kids who fill up empty cartons with takeout from In-N-Out burgers and the boba tea place and the local noodle house, reselling their purchases at impromptu food stands set up in the school yard, the profits going to Red Cross or the yearbook or some other campus club or cause. The delicious smells and greasy food wrappers draw six-deep crowds of kids, which pleases everyone except the district department that runs the overpriced official lunch counter, where the manager threatens

to go to the district administration if the school doesn't eliminate the food competition. The students, of course, are outraged and plot a boycott of the Hutch. How can essays match
that?

The most enthused juniors signed up for the workshop
months earlier and have long since completed the two-week,
four-class session. By May, those anxious to participate have
finished, and now those least eager to launch the college
application process are finding themselves in the stuffy conference room, attending mostly out of a sense of obligation
or dread, or even worse, because a parent heard about those
workshops with a "real" writer and told them to sign up, it'll
look good on your college applications (as long as you're just
doing it to get into college, of course, not to actually become
a writer, God forbid).

The subject of parents comes up often in the essay workshop, particularly in these later sessions. Parents are one of the
most common essay topics—which surprises me. My Asian
American students seem especially fond of writing about the
trials and tribulations they face on the home front, and I've
lost count of the number of essays I've read in which the author claims to reveal the true nature of the typical Chinese
Parent or Korean Parent, an exercise of breathtaking stereotyping. This is not a theme that white, black, or brown kids
commonly explore in the workshop, probably because they
do not believe there is such a thing as a typical white, black,
or brown parent—and to suggest otherwise undoubtedly
would offend them. Many of my Asian American writers
don't seem to see it that way: In their essays, mothers and fa-
thers routinely are cast as types, as Jeffrey does in his essay,
choosing the pushy, demanding Auntie Lindo of *The Joy
Luck Club* as his archetype. This is by no means universal, of
course; several of my students and most (though not all) of
the parents I've met openly scoff at this bit of mythologizing.
But the writers who choose this topic insist they are not en-

gaging in unfair stereotypes. The same teenagers who hate being typed as Asian whiz kids, who point out that not all are gifted or excel at math and science or want to go to Harvard, Yale, or Princeton—the same sort of kids who were outraged at being typecast in the ill-fated *Anthem* exercise—have no compunction about reducing the Asian Parent to a monolithic stereotype. When I call them on this inconsistency, they offer a simple explanation: In this case, they answer, their stereotypical portraits happen to be accurate.

I am a sixteen-year-old Chinese teenager. I have the great fortune and misfortune of having two Chinese parents. What truly defines a Chinese parent? It is extremely difficult not to stereotype for I have yet to encounter one with no regard for his or her child's education or acceptance among other parents. Chinese parents come in two kinds: competitive and even more competitive. They seem to constantly live vicariously through their children's accomplishments. . . .

The first questions I am greeted with after school are, "How was your day at school?" and "How did you do on your tests?" (regardless of whether I had a test that day or not). My parents can't help but compare me with more intelligent students and their parents' constant bragging. I am constantly pounded with stories of the amazing boy from Beijing, who came to America in his high school years with limited English-speaking abilities and got a full-ride scholarship to Cal-Tech university. . . .

When gathered around the dinner table with other Chinese parents, Chinese parents talk about life back in China, discuss the deliciousness of certain dishes, and endlessly compare their children in terms of grades, sports, music, and physical appearance. "What did your child get on the SATs?" is one of the common questions asked during these gatherings.

I assumed at first that the parent-as-essay topic was just another way of avoiding the subject of self. But one day when I make an offhanded remark, the kids' response to it is a bit of a revelation. I happen to mention that I've encountered only one other identifiable group given to such chronic, gross generalizations about their parents as ethnic "types": the kids I knew growing up who similarly complained about their Jewish mothers.

The students' reaction to this bit of cultural slander surprises me once again. They are fascinated, even startled, by the notion of an earlier generation of kids experiencing the same problems with overly ambitious and bossy parents with immigrant roots—and non-Asian roots at that. The notion that they might not be alone in this long-suffering role is a new and comforting one to a number of the students. One seeks to drive home the point with the story of a recent Whitney graduate who visited a few months earlier while home from one of the HYP schools. The alum explained what a revelation it was for him to find himself, an Asian American, in the minority on a campus after six years of being in the ethnic majority at Whitney. Then my student delivers the alum's punch line: "He said he was surprised to find that there really *are* a lot of smart white people out there!"

Now, as awful and arrogant and ethnocentric as that sounds, it was clear that my young writer didn't mean it that way. He's a nice kid without a racist bone in his body—it was just his way of making fun of both the visitor's parochial outlook and the sheltered life most of the kids at Whitney lead, where the smart white kids (and the smart African American and smart Latino kids, for that matter) are the clear minorities, and where many tend to think their particular lot in life is unique and unknown outside the Whitney cocoon.

And that, I realize, is probably the real reason why so many of my workshop kids write about The Asian Parent. They think no one outside their rarefied world knows what they go through, no one else experiences their pressures and desires to please. They do not yet grasp that hyperambitious parents are a cross-cultural phenomenon. They don't see that the ever-growing stress over grades and tests scores they grapple with is a national obsession gripping every school, not just theirs. They even seem to forget that America's colleges have enormous ethnic-Asian populations, which means admissions offices are inundated with these kinds of essays—their battles with their parents are old news.

These essays speak to a naïveté and lack of awareness that is both endearing and a bit scary, and I begin to understand better why Shirley Wold and the other counselors worry about what will happen to these kids when they enter the whirlwind chaos of a typical college campus.

The seniors finally realize that the school year's end is near, and that they really are going to have to leave Whitney High School, when Gary McHatton starts appearing in their classes with instructions on how to obtain extra tickets to the graduation ceremony—and a warning not to try to bootleg tickets on eBay.

The graduation ceremony for Whitney is a hot event, with people flying in from all over the world to see their nieces, nephews, and grandchildren "make the walk." There are only 165 graduates this year, but the school will fill most of an entire concert hall. Each student is entitled to eight tickets, with additional seats available by lottery—and it is here that the spirit of entrepreneurship collides with school policies.

Several enterprising students earned a few hundred dollars last year selling coveted "front-center" tickets through the online auction house eBay, catering to the Whitney parents who wanted to impress family members visiting from abroad. A few of the current crop of seniors have been not-too-quietly plotting to attempt a similar sale, something McHatton informs them would be "unethical."

"There are plenty of tickets and there are no bad seats, so there's no reason to go crazy," McHatton says.

He's right. The Cerritos Center for the Performing Arts, a sparkling new theater and concert venue, has transformed Whitney's traditional heat-stroke-and-mud-clod ceremony on the soccer field into a classy, pleasant event, and even the upper-deck seats offer a great view. But human nature and greed are intractable, and the kids are quick to note that McHatton said eBay sales would be unethical, not *illegal*. The schemes and trading over the front-most seats continue, inadvertently stoked by something else McHatton has said: This year there will be a crackdown on parents mobbing the area in front of the stage to snap pictures.

"They won't be allowed to do that this year," McHatton says. "It was like a media frenzy last time."

One young entrepreneur leans over and whispers to a friend, "The price just went up on the tickets for the front rows."

As he makes the rounds with his graduation announcements, McHatton has also been plugging a planned senior retreat to the mountains. The idea is to have several days away from school, homework, the Internet, and parents for a series of discussions and seminars to help ready students for the world beyond Whitney. As a sop to parents, who are unlikely to go for the idea without an academic component, McHatton says they have included AP exam study sessions on the agenda, although these are not expected to actually draw many students. But to the counselors' surprise, few students or parents seem interested in the idea of a retreat no matter what's on the agenda.

"The only reason this retreat idea came up at all," McHatton tells the seniors, "was because we've had graduates come back and tell us they were academically prepared for college, but not socially. They told us they could have used more information about drug abuse, alcohol abuse, sex abuse—

about girls being lured to fraternity parties and taken advantage of.... We're not going to sugarcoat this stuff.... We want to give you some tools to deal with these social issues when you're on your own at college, so you know what to do when your roommate comes in drunk three out of five nights.... We really think this is important for you."

Tom Brock is also very eager to get this retreat going and institutionalized as an annual ritual. The complaint that Whitney graduates get blindsided by the nonacademic side of college has been a recurring theme for years. It was made all the more poignant by the suicide a year earlier of a gifted Whitney alum in his fourth year at Harvard, where he had become increasingly depressed and isolated with each passing year, unable to cope.

But the seniors are less concerned with such weighty matters and more worried about the accommodations at the old YMCA camp in the mountains that the school has chosen. The creature comforts are few, there are no private bathrooms, the subject matter is just too serious at a time of year when seniors are ready to cut loose. Several student leaders openly mock the whole idea, and in the end, so few kids sign up that the retreat is canceled. The counselors can't hide their disappointment at their weekly leadership meeting. They decide to start talking up the idea of next year's retreat with the juniors now, planting the seed for a more successful attempt in twelve months.

"Every year, it's the same; the seniors think they know everything there is to know," Wold says. "And then they get to college, and they're punk freshmen again, and they find out they have a lot to learn."

The possibility of another kind of retreat—one for incoming seventh graders—is also being discussed; under consideration is a summer session to help bring newcomers up to speed. A record number of seventh graders are on the "at risk" list of low academic performers this year—nearly two dozen—and the school administration is getting worried. The incoming class of twelve- and thirteen-year-olds often struggles, but this year is the worst in a long time.

Part of this may be due to a simple slipping through the cracks. While the new system of grade-level advisors has gotten good reviews from many of the students and faculty members, seventh graders have been a low priority. McHatton has been so consumed with dealing with his seniors, writing college letters, and planning for awards and graduation rehearsals, he has had scant time for the other half of his charges, Whitney's youngest kids. Many do not even know who their counselor is.

"I really feel invisible here," Nisreen complains under her breath as she works on a portrait of a fellow student in art class. She is struggling with the intricate, shell-like contours of the boy's ear. "It's really hard going from the top of the food chain to the very bottom. The only class I'm doing well in is art. And P.E."

It has been a tough year for Nizzy. She is exaggerating a bit; she has brought her grades up in math and social studies since the first quarter, but she is still in the bottom half of her class in terms of grade point average—way below the expectations her parents have for her. Nisreen isn't in too much trouble yet; her struggles are not due to a lack of ability so much as horrendously bad time-management skills, a matter of attitude, of preferring soccer and girl talk and thirteen-year-old crushes to hard-core academics. And she is still rebelling against having her mother so close by all the time. She just can't get over the fact that her teachers end up talking about her to her mother regularly over lunch and at faculty meetings. "I can't even sass a teacher without hearing about it that same night," she says sorrowfully. "I guess I'm not so invisible, after all."

Nisreen figures she'll bounce back in eighth grade, ninth at the latest—there's plenty of time to get serious, as she sees it. But there are some others among the seventh-grade class whose poor performance is rooted in lack of preparation in the lower grades, and teachers worry that Whitney is not doing as much as it once did to help them catch up. Starting college preparation at this early age has always been Whitney's strength, but some of the school's original efforts to help the youngest kids get started—the assignment of older mentors to incoming seventh graders, for one—have fallen by the wayside over the years.

"I may not come back next year," says one of Nisreen's classmates, who is failing several subjects yet has not been required to take advantage of Whitney's program of student tutors. "It's too hard here. I wasn't ready for this. I think I'd be happier at a regular middle school. But my mom wants me to stay. We fight about it all the time."

The plight of this minority of seventh graders at Whitney reflects a larger national struggle. When Whitney had to eliminate its affirmative action quotas in favor of the current system of geographic percentages, it inherited a new problem: what to do with students who would not, in previous years, have qualified for admission. Particularly in math, some of the seventh graders who attended schools in the poorer neighborhoods of the district have not been as academically prepared as their classmates from more affluent schools. This is the very issue that plagues college admissions programs in California and Texas, where the same system of non-race-based preferences has helped maintain diversity in the student body, but has, in some cases, created opportunities for students to attend elite programs for which they are unprepared.

Brock has decided that the school's mission must include helping these kids keep pace, and the best way to do that, he and his staff agree, would be to catch them *before* seventh grade. And so he has spent much of the school year trying to set up programs with some of the elementary and middle schools that have sent Whitney struggling seventh graders in the past, looking for ways to bolster their math and reading skills before they arrive. So far, the results have been mixed; an ambitious plan that moved Whitney's college counselor, Betty Zavala, to an elementary school so she could start a college-prep program there has just been canceled after a few months because of a lack of interest. And the old antipathy around the district about Whitney is still a factor; some school officials are sensitive and even indignant about having someone from Whitney tell them how to teach their kids. So, for the time being, the school will have to deal with the problem on its own, which is why they are talking about a summer program or retreat for seventh graders—much like the one Brock organized so many years ago at his old middle school in Lennox.

"Seventh graders will be our next big push," promises Wold, who will be taking them over next year as the counseling duties rotate. "We can't afford to cast them adrift."

The last part of May and first weeks of June are a prolonged good-bye at Whitney, where the usual high school partings are intensified by the fact that everyone knows everyone.

"Most of the people I know are going to stay eighteen forever for me," Aisha says as she assembles her crew of ambassadors for one final VIP visit. "For six years, we all changed together, grew up together. Now it's all going to be about catching up. I never had to catch up with anyone here before."

While the kids say good-bye, with their long and labored notes to one another in letters and yearbooks, the teachers are frantically boxing up and labeling their papers, tapes, books, and teaching materials. There is no sentimentality here: Everything has to be removed from the school and loaded into metal storage containers the size of trucks; anything left behind will be hauled to the trash. The bulldozers, construction crews, carpenters, and painters will arrive the day after school ends, and it's anybody's guess whether the place will be ready by the start of the next school year, which is why the pressure is on to start renovations at the soonest possible moment.

Mike Mustillo is everywhere, taking measurements, urging teachers to label things clearly (unmarked boxes may never be found again, he warns), and creating a small panic when he tells teachers who have already begun loading boxes into the storage containers not to pack anything that can melt—old record albums, cassettes, computer disks—because the metal containers turn into pizza ovens in the sun.

In art class, where the boxing has been going on for months and has filled more than one giant storage container so far, Cecilia and Angela present Ms. Agrums with some of their favorite pieces. Her desk is already piled high with gifts. Ms. Palmieri, meanwhile, is treated to a hilarious parody of John Donne and other classics covered in AP English, in which a male student dresses as the teacher, mimicking her mannerisms to perfection as she runs off for an affair with the dead poet she so ardently admires. In Mr. Z's digital media workshop, where the final project is a short biographical film of each student, the normally taciturn and withdrawn Sharleen pulls her teacher aside and thanks him for believing in her and urging her to take on greater amounts of responsibility.

Her biographical video is searing in its honest and raw emotion, completely unexpected from the sphinxlike Sharleen, who day after day works hard to reveal nothing of herself while at a school. She is pleasant, quiet, competent—but utterly uninvolved. She explains why in her piece: "School is just part of my day. It's something to do. If I just dedicated one hundred percent effort to it, what could I do? I don't know.... But in six years there, I've made no connection."

The film attempts to explain this flaw in its author's character by focusing on her family, depicting them over the course of an ordinary day, while a quietly powerful voice-over from Sharleen describes her feelings for the father who deserted her and her worries about the mother he continually hurts. A completely different side of Sharleen is revealed later in the film in scenes with her two girlfriends; they have formed a band, and play and dance for the camera, showing a talent and vivaciousness Sharleen gives no hint of at school. Mr. Z can't help but compare the grim scenes with Sharleen's family with the exuberant piece from another student, Sheila, who performs a sweet karaoke duet with her father, then says of her parents: "I can talk to them about anything. There's nothing I won't tell them, about love, about school, about life. They are my best friends." The contrast between the two films is heartbreaking.

When Sharleen's film is through, he tells her it is beautifully done, A-plus work, haunting and honest in a way few of the other kids could manage. But what he's thinking is, he wishes he had seen it earlier in the year, or six years ago. Sharleen has done well at Whitney, her grades are good, she's going to college, but she could have been a star, Mr. Z realizes, if only someone had been able to make the connection he suddenly has with her—one week before graduation. How many of the other silent, stressed kids, he wonders, are passing through the school in the same boat?

"I look at this," he tells Sharleen, "and I know that nobody at this school knows you. And that is a shame. You have to let people know you. Not everyone will abandon you. Some will want what you have to share."

"I know," she says after a long silence. "And I think I

made a lot of progress this year.... I could never have shown you this last year."

Two weeks before graduation, the school district management association has its annual scholarship and awards reception in the Skyline Room at the new Cerritos Public Library. One student from each school in the district is to be recognized for outstanding achievement and contributions in school.

This year, Angela is Whitney's winner, one of five high school students to be so honored. She receives a plaque and three hundred dollars. It is not a huge amount, but it's still welcome, enough for books and some spending money next year at college. Angela was chosen by the faculty and principals at Whitney for her artistic skills, her tutoring of other students, and her extensive volunteer work, including many hours spent hanging other students' artwork throughout the school in a rotating series of displays.

Angela had never heard of this particular award before, and her parents seemed unimpressed when she mentioned it to them. She's been so busy and stressed, and she still has a project to do for statistics—she invented a music holder for the marching-band drummers and is using statistical measures to validate its usefulness. She has one last all-nighter left in her before it will be finished. The project is due on the day after the awards ceremony, so she had decided to skip the event. But her teachers and counselor urge her to attend, assuring her that it's a bigger deal than she realizes, that the district superintendent will be there, and that she shouldn't miss it. She finally agrees to go, and at the last minute, her parents decide to come as well.

The Skyline Room is an opulent conference and banquet hall with panoramic views, not at all typical of a public library.

Angela's parents are duly impressed by the surroundings, as well as by the guests—all the senior officials of the school district. "We never realized what a big honor this is," her mother whispers proudly. "Only one student from Whitney gets it!" Her father, meanwhile, whips out a camera and starts snapping pictures.

This award is unique in the district because it is not based on such tangible accomplishments as having the highest grades or test scores or being a top athlete or musician or even an artist. This award is completely subjective. The counselors and the principals and the department heads at Whitney were sitting in a meeting talking about which student deserved recognition simply because having that person there made the school a better place; they were looking for someone with heart and dedication, someone whose efforts rarely fell short, even if his or her grades didn't show it. As they discussed possible recipients, each of them glanced at the wall facing the head of the conference table, where a dozen works of student art had been lovingly displayed for all to admire—Angela's handiwork. Debbie Agrums had suggested her for the award, and everyone agreed there could be no better choice.

"We are very proud of Angela," Patty Hager says at the ceremony, as she presents Angela to the gathering. "She is the epitome of what we hope to produce at Whitney." Angela feels like hugging her—having her parents hear that she is the epitome of a Whitney student is worth a dozen three-hundred-dollar checks, she says later.

The high school recipients are invited to say a few words and, surprisingly, Angela accepts the invitation. She is normally uncomfortable as a public speaker, but today she stands tall and speaks in a loud, clear voice—not confident, exactly, but determined.

"I want to say something to the young people," she says, gazing at the line of elementary and middle school students who have come for their awards. "High school is not easy. But try hard." Then she shifts her eyes to her mother and father, smiling and proud. "And don't let other people's expectations get you down. If you do your best, you'll do fine."

Afterward, she and her parents linger a few minutes to sample the snacks and chat, then they separate. Angela is headed over to a friend's house for that all-nighter, and she is looking forward to a night of hanging out and eating pizza and getting a little work done, too, just one more time before high school ends.

"I almost said, don't let your *parents'* expectations get you down," she says as she walks to her car. "But I bit my tongue. I didn't want to make my parents feel bad." She thinks a bit, then says, "Maybe they knew who I was talking about anyway. But I doubt it. No, probably not. Definitely not."

But it's okay, she says. Angela is resigned to going to Irvine now. It is not her dream school, but she says she will make it work, with the community college art courses on the side, and some classes in communications and psychology, her other two interests. She has this idea that she can perhaps combine her interests by exploring some of the ways art has been used to diagnose and provide therapy for children with mental and emotional disturbances.

"That would be really cool, a way of using my art and also doing something more practical. Because my mom and dad are right about one thing when they say it's hard to make a living at art. So this might be a good compromise. We'll see."

Angela seems more upbeat than she has in months. Perhaps it's the end of uncertainty, or the fact that she has nothing much left to battle over with her parents. Maybe it was hearing her mom and dad telling her they were proud. She can't say why, exactly, but she feels hopeful about the fall.

"It's always going to be a battle with my parents, but I know they really just want what's best for me, at least I keep telling myself that," she says. "Someday, though, it will be my life entirely, and I'll get to decide. That'll be scary. But it'll be good.... I think."

After a brief and anticlimactic rehearsal the day before, in which mass confusion reigns and kids keep forgetting they're supposed to shake hands with their right and grab the diploma with their left, graduation day arrives.

The ceremony, like most other graduation ceremonies, is too long and too slow and no one present would miss it for the world. There are the gowns and the medals, the songs and the student speeches, a seemingly endless number of them, before the long procession to accept the diplomas finally begins. In a constant stream, moms defy Gary McHatton's edict and race up to the stage to snap a picture of their daughters and sons completing their rites of passage. If any of them got their tickets on eBay, they're not talking about it.

The real fun comes afterward, of course, out in the teeming courtyard, crammed with kids and parents and teachers and aunts, uncles, and grandparents, all in their finest clothes, balloons and flowers and banners everywhere, a babble of languages from every continent, everyone lingering, hugging, giddy at finally being done, and sad, too, not quite ready for it to end. School will go on several more weeks for everyone else, but for the seniors, it's over. Summer has begun—their last before college.

And so the farewells begin. There's Anna, smiling broadly as always, one of the many Whitney grads headed to UCLA, her mother next to her, Anna's thoughts on her dad as she hugs her way through the crowd, missing him. There's an art student presenting a beautiful Korean sculpture to Ms. Agrums. There's Charles standing tall and handsome in a gray suit, healthy and sober, his arms draped over friends' shoulders. There are Dennis and Tony laughing uproariously at absolutely nothing. There's Christine in her father's arms. And there's Stella escaping her parents and telling Christine she can't believe what her mother just said ("Why don't you have medals around your neck like the valedictorians?"). There's Irene looking stunned, saying, "It hasn't sunk in yet," and Cecilia standing on a bench shouting, "It's over! It's over!"

There will be fancy restaurants and parties later in the evening, a chance to stay out late with no consequences, nothing to study, no need to chug Starbucks to stay awake, except if you want to. Some kids are just planning to go home and go to bed and sleep in late, as late as they want, something they haven't done in a long time.

As the gathering finally begins to break up, Cecilia looks like she is crying. I ask her about it, but she says she's fine, it's nothing, she's just overcome with excitement and emotion. There was no fight about her future, as I initially suspected. In fact, she says, her parents have given in to her at last in the face of her determined, reasoned argument—and in the wake of her earning honorable mention in a prestigious national graphic arts contest sponsored by Coca-Cola, blunting arguments that her art is impractical as a career choice. The year started with no art, ever, no way, her portfolio tossed in the street. And it has ended with her parents agreeing to a compromise: a double major, in art and English, with a minor in business when she starts Berkeley in the fall. "My mom still figures I'll come to my senses," Cecilia says with a smile, the tears gone, seemingly forgotten. "She should know better."

Only much later does Cecilia share something her father said to her, which I suspect was the real reason for her tears. For the first time that she can remember, on the night of her graduation from Whitney High School, her father told her he loved her.

Epilogue

"Well," Nizzy says tactfully, "it looks...cleaner. But it's still the same old Whitney."

Summer brought Whitney High School its long-awaited face-lift—new paint, new carpeting, a new music wing, an improved college center, and walls that don't move. Band uniforms no longer have to be hung in back of the Hutch to be permeated with the smells of hamburgers and cooking grease. The wiring is no longer a cruel joke. The new technology promised by Intel has arrived—state-of-the-art computers, fifteen SMART Boards, numerous other tech toys—although it is a painstaking process to actually get it up and running (by spring, only Mr. Z is using his computerized white board regularly). In many ways, Whitney is still the same old, homely square of a building, with its fitful air-conditioning and abysmal cafeteria and sturdy orange lockers (the budget ran dry before they could be electroplated blue). Whitney's attraction will never be its looks, and Nisreen and her friends perhaps can be forgiven for being a bit more blasé about the remodel than the school administration. Their own metamorphosis over the summer has been so much more dramatic.

Nisreen and the other members of the Class of 2007 walked through the doors of their freshly painted school as newly minted eighth graders, no longer the little kids on campus but actual teenagers, taller, more confident, beginning the slow and difficult process of establishing separate lives from their parents—increasingly adult lives. It is an amazing and rewarding and horrible and secretive time, Nisreen says—and that's just socially. The schoolwork has stepped up, too, with her homework running as long as four hours a night now, although the march of all-nighters has not yet begun in earnest—just one a month or so for her. But with soccer and volleyball eating into her time—and time management still not her strong suit—Nizzy, like many of her friends, has found herself scrambling to finish her homework on the day it is due, all too often scribbling it out at the last moment while sitting in other classes. In the new school year, like the last, she is throwing herself into art, still suffering through math, still figuring she is destined for great things, even if she has no idea what they will be. Which is as it should be; too many of her fellow students, she says, have their days, summers, and futures already programmed with academies and dream schools and vacation "enrichments."

"My parents are pretty good about not doing that," she says. "Of course, my mom expected me to do exceptionally well because she works here.... And my teachers still talk to her if anything happens, good or bad. Kind of uncomfortable sometimes.... Just a little more stress. That's life at Whitney, I guess."

So even Nisreen, still only thirteen at the start of the school year, is beginning to feel the heat: She loves Whitney, believes in its program, can't imagine being anywhere else... yet she recognizes that, sometimes, there is a price for all the extra academic firepower and gold-plated test results. There is the periodic stress, the sleepless nights, and the ever-present danger that grades and scores will be elevated above the learning they are intended to measure. Whitney kids, even eighth graders like Nisreen, know that the nation's top universities will take a long and careful look at their applications, considering all of their abilities and qualities, the whole person. But first that whole person must get his or her foot in the door. To make that cut, the kids know, they have to have the scores and the grades.

And the higher they reach, the more they sweat, which is why Albert, a senior now, signed up to retake the SAT the day after he received his score of 1470—a score that already put him in the top 4 percent of students nationally. He didn't even hesitate. And after a thousand-dollar pass through a local academy, Albert brought his score up to a near-perfect 1560 (only 2 percent of SAT test takers can equal that). Even then, he wasn't satisfied. "I just hope it's enough," he said afterward. "You can never have too high a score."

There is good reason for such insecurities in these test-obsessed times, a point hit home particularly hard in the spring, when Whitney sent a delegation to the East Coast to meet with admissions officers from the Ivy League and several other prestigious universities Whitney grads favor. This was something new for the school, paid for by the parent-run fund-raising foundation, in an attempt to forge the sorts of personal connections that top private schools have trafficked in for years. Promoting students in person offers the possibility of earning not just a first look, but a second and third for promising applicants.

At Yale University, the Whitney visitors asked about one of their top students who had been rejected. The admissions officer pulled out a page from the thick application packet, a multiple-choice form filled out by the young man's counselor. He pointed to one question concerning the student's leadership ability. It had been checked "good."

"That put him out of the running right there," the admissions officer said. "You didn't mark 'excellent.'"

A single multiple-choice question had led to rejection, simply because it suggested an otherwise stellar student with soaring grades and high SATs still had some room to grow as a leader. Other high schools might have simply checked "excellent," knowing that was what the college wanted to hear, knowing that inflating that assessment of the student's abilities would be rewarded while candor could be penalized. Gary McHatton, who had filled out the form, felt terrible about it—though he and his colleagues say they have to answer the questions honestly, or risk losing all credibility. "Isn't college supposed to be a place where you learn to be a leader?" McHatton mused afterward. "Why should that be negative?"

The young man took the matter in stride; he was not one of those students who felt his life would be over if he did not get into a certain college. It didn't hurt, of course, that he was accepted by several other excellent schools. But the fact that a teenager's future could turn on one multiple-choice question on a form filled out by a counselor was a sobering reminder of the high-stress tightrope the school and its students must walk every day, searching for a balance between learning and the grade, between cultivating high achievement and satisfying the growing national fixation on multiple-choice tests and scores.

High-stakes testing continues to drive public education at every level, preeminent not only in the classroom and as the gateway to college, but as the prime force for public school reform, particularly as envisioned in President George W. Bush's No Child Left Behind Act. This law requires all states and school systems in the nation to set measurable standards and to show—through standardized testing—that they are making progress in raising achievement, with a goal of having 100 percent of students proficient and at grade level by the year 2014.

Schools that fail to show progress for two years in a row risk being closed, taken over, or replaced through vouchers, privatization, or other alternatives. This outcome seems to be the unstated goal of the law, which mandates so much that failure is all but assured, while providing little in the way of federal money to bolster shaky schools (for all this new federal control over local schools, the feds are providing only 7 percent of public school funding). At least one in five schools were in the "failing" category when the law took effect, and as many as eight in ten schools could end up in the failing column over the next few years. The states with the highest standards will suffer the most, such as California, which has set the wildly unrealistic goal of having *all* graduates prepared to enter college within the next fourteen years; at present, half the kids in the state are bombing out on the new high school exit exam, which sets a far lower bar. Other states with more lax standards get off easier under the federal law, creating an incentive for the entire nation to reach low rather than high in terms of setting educational goals.

The intended purpose of all this is just the opposite: accountability and the creation of incentives for teachers, schools, and districts to raise achievement. The problem is that the tests in current use measure the *floor* of student achievement, not the ceiling—they are designed to guarantee a minimum level of proficiency, not to set expectations high. As such, the tests can identify failure, but they are not very good at telling us about success—how to duplicate it, nurture it, reward it. There is no attempt anywhere in the No Child Left Behind law to study and duplicate a Whitney High School, or to foster a culture of high expectations in our schools. The law rewards poor schools that show at least some improvement, while ignoring (or even punishing) good schools that hold their ground.

Under the law's provisions, Whitney High School could drop a bit in its test scores for a year or two and be labeled a "failing school"—even while remaining the top school in the state of California. This sort of schizophrenia has already hit nineteen schools around the nation, which were simultaneously lauded as schools of excellence by the federal education department, while also making the list of failing schools.[19] States are actually given incentives to *lower* their standards so more schools can be called improving and more students labeled proficient, thereby preserving the flow of federal dollars and avoiding the draconian penalties of No Child Left Behind. That's the real magic behind the "Texas Miracle" now being used as a model for the nation—it's not hard to show increased test scores and graduation rates when the high school exit exam questions hover at the elementary school level.

As the new school year began at Whitney, the testing pendulum has swung even further: The prestigious Blue Ribbon Schools program, which relied for more than twenty years on a comprehensive review and site visit by teams of educators (such as Tom Brock) in its annual awards to the nation's top schools, has been transformed into the No Child Left Behind Blue Ribbons Schools program. Detailed reviews of programs and philosophies—and actual visits to the schools—are out of favor. Only test scores will count from now on.

"It's really a shame, the direction they're taking," says Bart Teal, head of the nonprofit National Blue Ribbon Institute, which advocates using the original Blue Ribbon application process as a tool for evaluating and improving schools. Whitney's applications—it has won the Blue Ribbon three times—were models for any school that would like to succeed, Teal says. "Test scores do not tell the whole story, not even close. And the tests are now being written to please politicians, not to serve any useful educational purpose. The results come in five, six, even nine months later—that's an eternity for kids. They are useless documents the day they arrive."

On a typical school day, while Whitney High seniors grapple with calculus and Shakespeare soliloquies, twelfth graders a half hour's drive away struggle through long-division problems and short stories written at a sixth-grade level. Both sets of teenagers rank among the better scholars at their respective schools. Under current standards enforced by No Child Left Behind, each group will be deemed sufficiently educated at the end of the year to graduate and enter college, adulthood, the march of American life. And if either of these schools garners media attention or public accolades, it will most likely be the second of them—for improving student test scores (irrespective of how low those scores were to begin with).

Such is life inside the two separate and unequal school systems American children enter, live in, and survive each day, success and failure separated by a chasm so profound that many of us no longer see it clearly, much less imagine navigable roads to bring the two together. This much seems clear: No amount of testing will close that divide, although the gamesmanship surrounding standardized tests may mask it for a time, at least until the kids who are said to be proficient attempt to make it in college and find themselves unprepared.

With testing and minimum proficiency driving the education debate, there is a tendency to write off as inapplicable the lessons of highly successful schools such as Whitney High. Whitney, after all, enjoys two major advantages many other schools do not share: a largely middle-class student population the majority of whom are Asian American, and an admissions process that limits students to those on the college track. Occasional attempts at identifying top high

schools in the nation—*Newsweek, U.S. News, Fortune* magazine, and the *Washington Post* all have made stabs at creating a
rating system—routinely omit Whitney and similar schools
from consideration because they have achievement-based
admissions systems and so are considered "special cases." Yet
there is much about Whitney's path to success that could
serve as model for schools of all sorts, including more typical
neighborhood campuses with different demographics and no
admissions criteria.

On the admissions front, while there can be no doubt
that selectivity helps the school immensely, it turns out to be
only a part of the equation. When compared to the achievement of students with similar aptitude from across the nation, Whitney students seem to outperform their peers by as
much as two to one. This differential shows up in College
Board analyses that link the PSAT (Preliminary Scholastic
Aptitude Test), which most college-bound students take in
tenth grade, and the rigorous Advanced Placement tests. Nationally, for example, a student who scores 41–45 in the PSAT
verbal test has (based on historical performance) a 35 percent chance of passing an Advanced Placement U.S. History
test. Students with a score of 51–55 have a 60 percent chance
of passing, and those with PSATs in the 66–70 range pass the
AP 88 percent of the time. Whitney students with those same
PSAT scores, however, pass the AP U.S. History exam at a 75
percent, 94 percent, and 100 percent rate, respectively. The
same performance gap favors Whitney in the AP English
Language exam, too.[20] Whitney, it appears, is not simply a
collection of top students who would do just as well at any
other school, as critics have long suggested. On the contrary,
the College Board stats suggest that the school is doing something extra to spur academic achievement.

As for the second Whitney advantage, economic stability
and the education levels of parents certainly have an obvious

positive effect on academic achievement, and nowhere is this more pronounced than among the Asian American families with sons and daughters at the school. For a variety of cultural and familial reasons, students of Asian heritage, particularly first- and second-generation immigrants, have long been the most academically successful group in the nation. Survey after survey reveals that Asian American kids spend more time on homework than any other group. Their parents spend more time helping them with schoolwork. Asian American families are more likely to pay for tutors (even if it requires financial help from extended family), the kids' self-esteem is more closely tied to school success than in any other ethnic group, and tradition emphasizes hard work over innate talent as the key to academic prowess—in contrast to whites and other ethnic groups, who tend to believe ability trumps all. And these trends, in varying degrees, cut across income levels as well as the many different ethnicities that make up the diverse group commonly called Asian—families of modest means embrace these values and sacrifice a great deal to invest in education, significantly more than the average American household.[21]

The combination of a school built upon high expectations and a student population whose dominant culture elevates learning to a high priority—and hard work in school to an absolute necessity—makes for a kind of education echo chamber at Whitney. The expectations of the school and the families reinforce one another, with family expectations informing the ethos of the school and helping to raise achievement for all students, regardless of ethnicity.

This echo effect, in varying degrees, is being repeated at a number of schools around the country where principals and teachers have identified the qualities that help schools and their students succeed. The Bronx Preparatory Charter School in New York boosted achievement for its fifth and sixth graders with a two-hundred-day school year, a school day that runs from 7:15 A.M. to 5:15 P.M., and a Whitney-like mission that states that 100 percent of the students will go to a top college. The Black River Public School in Holland, Michigan, with grades four through twelve, has achieved high test scores with a program that emphasizes college-prep and AP courses, longer class periods (eighty-five minutes each), small class size, and a school-without-walls independent study component called the "capstone experience." The Accelerated School of South Central Los Angeles, an impoverished area of the city best known as the epicenter of L.A.'s 1992 riots, estimates it has increased standardized test scores by nearly 300 percent compared to other schools in the area. Its kindergarten through eighth-grade classes have achieved a 98 percent attendance rate (about the same as Whitney's) with a rigorous program that expects top performance from its students, introducing the same material to supposedly "slow" learners as to gifted students. This approach is coupled with large amounts of parental involvement—parents have to sign a contract agreeing to work thirty hours a year at the school in order to enroll their children. There is a clear mission: to close the achievement gap between kids in South Central and kids in the suburbs, and ready inner-city kids for college with a prep-school-style education. Like Whitney, Accelerated's accomplishments have come in a primitive, low-tech physical facility—a group of prefab buildings on an asphalt yard. The 360-student school has a waiting list five times that number, and it was named in 2001 by *Time* magazine as the "Elementary School of the Year."

Examples of public schools succeeding just as dramatically can be found scattered throughout the country, and to spend time in such places is to see the potential within America's vast system of public education to build true schools of the twenty-first century. What often stands out on these campuses is not the technology or how gleaming and new the buildings are, or how relentlessly the kids are drilled in advance of standardized tests. What stands out among these varied programs in diverse communities is the embrace of fundamental qualities common among Whitney's families and integral to the school's philosophy. These are small, intimate, attentive schools that are marked by high expectations put to work in tangible ways (as opposed to the boilerplate policy statements every school hands out to parents); rigorous traditional studies (as opposed to rigorous drilling for annual high-stakes tests); longer hours of study and work; strong parental involvement (in terms of time, money, and political support); low absenteeism and few discipline problems; and leadership with a vision.

These are the qualities that transformed Whitney two decades ago from a school for failures to a school of successes. This same formula, in small but meaningful ways, is renewing troubled schools and leading to new and better ones nationwide. This is a worthy model for improving public education in ways that the latest laws and current national reform campaigns rarely consider.[22]

Whitney's Class of 2002 is gradually adjusting to college life. Kosha is settled in at Stanford University and doing well, as is Aisha, who got over her disappointment at not getting into Princeton. Tony is settled in at Berkeley, Irene at Johns Hopkins, Cher at the University of Southern California. Anna is reveling in several film classes at UCLA, where her biggest concern so far seems to be a difficult roommate. Christine is at Yale, the California girl trying to cope with the Connecticut winter, her parents trying to adjust to the wild red hair color she sported at spring break. The university and her first year there are nothing like she dreamed they would be; Christine describes her experience as "different in infinite ways and ultimately better than my expectations." The Yale newspaper wasn't for her, but she has thrown herself into the Intercollegiate Taiwanese-American Students Association, and is cochairing its annual East Coast conference, pretty heady stuff for a freshman. She is swamped with work, up all hours, but finally free of a yearlong bout of writer's block. She has decided she will probably major in English, then go on to law school—ruling out, finally, the career in medicine her parents covet for her.

Members of the Class of 2003, meanwhile, are beginning their good-byes. Albert's high SAT scores and excellent work at Whitney (he decided not to mention in his college essay his ill-fated passage through Mr. Z's rocket experiment) earned a full scholarship at USC. His partner in the physics experiment, Brian, is headed to Cornell University. Both are grappling with a mix of senioritis, the frenzy that marks the end of their long years at Whitney, and worry over what the future will hold. Unlike their predecessors, this crop of seniors opted to go with the school counselors on a retreat to the mountains, dividing their time between playing in the snow and getting some frank advice on how to cope with college life.

The larger universities seem to pose the toughest adjustment after six years in the small and intimate confines of Whitney, it seems: Among the seniors, Stella is conflicted about staying at University of California's Santa Barbara campus, one of the most scenic in the state, a jewel overlooking the frothing Pacific shoreline. She likes the setting, but Santa Barbara is often pigeonholed as a party school, and Stella doesn't care for that atmosphere, taking the two-hour drive home most weekends. She arrived thinking she'd transfer as soon as possible to another UC campus, though she has begun rethinking that move. Santa Barbara's classes are not as packed as those at the more popular Berkeley and UCLA, giving her the opportunity to pursue a double major in Asian studies and business or biology (she's not sure which as yet). "Staying here means I can pursue that dream," she says. "I couldn't do that at the other schools. But my parents keep complaining that I'm not in a more prestigious school....I'm not sure what to do."

Cecilia, meanwhile, finally got into her first art class at Berkeley in the spring, just an intro course, hectic and disorganized, but a huge milestone for her nevertheless. She is relishing the freedom of being away from home, but nervous about it, too; freed from the cocoon, she is now confronted by the daily realities of balancing a checkbook, paying bills, dealing with laundry, and doing schoolwork without any parental reminders.

At Irvine, Angela has tried to find the positives in her reluctant choice of universities, and by the new year, she had found that she was enjoying her new school more than she expected. Her grades have been excellent and the Whitney work ethic has served her well—the demands on her time, as many of her fellow grads have discovered, often seem less than during high school. There are fewer all-nighters and marathon study sessions for Angela. "I'm sleeping more than I have in years," she says.

There have been some bitter pills to swallow, though: She has not been able to take any outside art classes so far, and is not sure when—or if—that will change. Perhaps over summer break, she hopes. But she still paints and draws and does crafts in her spare time, and she returned to Whitney in the spring for several weekends to work on a new mosaic countertop in Debbie Agrums's renovated art room. The social milieu of the university is not really to her liking: She was unprepared, like many other Whitney kids, for the level of partying, drinking, and coupling going on in the dorms, and has ended up spending most weekends at home. For better or worse, this will change after her first year: The school only guarantees housing to freshmen. Next year, she and her room-mates will have to find an apartment, an extra expense that worries Angela, who has given up junk food in order to save every penny.

She has had trouble getting into the classes she wants—demand is too high, a chronic problem at the school—al-though she has found several coveted spots (one in particular, a biology class, left her so passionate about the AIDS epi-demic that she has become a campus activist for prevention of the disease).

But then a computer glitch at the school incorrectly showed she had not paid her tuition, causing her to be dropped from every one of her spring semester classes. Here, the contrast between the hands-on, everybody-knows-your-name high school and the impersonal university with 23,000 students could not be more clear: Her complaints went nowhere, and she had to scramble to beg professors to let her back in. Two said no, their classes were full up, and the uni-versity would not intervene.

She spent a week crying every day, railing at the school, hating it all over again, wishing she were anywhere else—until something unexpected happened. Her father arrived. They marched into the registrar's office side by side, his de-termination to make things right for his daughter clear in the set of his jaw and the tone of his voice. She wasn't sure how much good it would do, at least in terms of her classes that semester. But for the first time in a long time, Angela found, she and her father were on the same side in a crisis. And that, she is later surprised to realize, made her class enrollment disaster almost worth the trouble.

In the spring of 2003, Whitney was cited once again by the state of California as a "Distinguished School," an honor be-stowed on about 5 percent of public schools in the state deemed to be the most exemplary and inspiring. Whitney also continued to lead the state in its standardized test scores, topping California's Academic Performance Index once again, even as kids piled on their Advanced Placement courses, extracurricular activities, and after-school academies, searching for that magic formula that would take them to the next school of their dreams.

Notes

1. It is extremely difficult to compare achievement at high schools in different states because of the different testing systems in use. One of the few raw measures that is consistent between states, as well as between public and private schools, are SAT scores, and some rough comparisons can be drawn between college-prep schools, where most of the student body can be expected to sit for the SATs.

On the private side, Whitney's SAT scores differed by one point from the combined verbal and math scores for Phillips Andover Academy (1344 for Phillips, 1343 for Whitney, in 2001) while the Groton School in Massachusetts had a combined SAT that year of 1380.

On the public school side, the two oldest continuously operated public high schools in the nation, Boston Latin High School and Philadelphia's Central High School, are comparable college-prep high schools with admissions requirements (the former, also with a grades seven through twelve program, counts Cotton Mather, Benjamin Franklin, Ralph Waldo Emerson, George Santayana, and Sumner Redstone among many of its luminary alumni, while the latter helped produce such figures as Thomas Eakins, Langston Hughes, and Bill Cosby). Other comparable schools include Stuyvesant High School in New York

City, New Trier High School outside Chicago, and the North Carolina School of Mathematics and Science in Durham—all public schools with admissions restrictions, and all routinely listed by education experts, the College Board, and the popular press as among the best public high schools in the nation. With the exception of Stuyvesant, New York's top-ranked public school, SAT scores at Whitney exceeded these other high-achieving public high schools in 2001.

2. The joint public-private National Commission on the High School Senior Year, in its January 17, 2001, final report, found that the graduation year in many public high schools increasingly is marked by a refusal to do homework, excessive absenteeism, cuts, tardiness, and low expectations. The commission, chaired by Governor Paul E. Patton of Kentucky and Jacquelyn M. Belcher, president of Georgia Perimeter College, noted in a press release accompanying the final report: "Even the most highly motivated seniors...turn their backs on school, treating the senior year as a prolonged farewell to adolescence." The commission report suggested that, in an age in which many high school graduates arrive at college ill-prepared, wasting senior year on anything less than rigorous classes was unforgivable.

3. The Advanced Placement tests measure a student's mastery of a nationally standardized course of study in a variety of subjects—a foreign language, a science, history, literature. There are thirty-five AP classes in all, taken by nearly one million students each year. The program has been growing by a phenomenal 10 percent annually as more students sign up for more tests than ever before, a constant escalation in academic competition as college admissions offices reward students for pursuing the most demanding courses of study, thus favoring private schools and well-financed public schools, where there is a greater likelihood of finding the money to add AP courses to the curriculum and retaining well-qualified instructors to teach them.

The tests are scored on a scale from one to five; a score of three is considered passing. Some colleges will allow course credit for any passing score; others will accept only a four or above. Some colleges offer no credit for AP courses.

The AP program has been criticized in recent years because of the heavy workload that multiple AP courses create for students and because the courses can be taught with such a strong emphasis on passing the AP tests that in-depth learning is sacrificed in favor of a broad and shallow survey approach to the subject.

4.   A variety of studies seem to suggest Tony's attitude has a marked effect and that the AP program may have become too much of a good thing. A 2002 National Research Council report, "Learning and Understanding," expressed concern about Advanced Placement's growing importance in the academic pantheon, criticizing the program for covering too much material with insufficient depth. Meanwhile, the owner of the program, the College Board, concluded in a recent study that AP may contribute to weaker, not stronger, overall academic backgrounds for some students. In recognition of this, some colleges and universities are refusing to accept AP credits, while others are raising the bar before allowing credit—only a top score of five (rather than a passing grade of three or four) will suffice at Harvard University, where an in-house study found that students allowed to skip introductory courses in economics and chemistry because of their AP credits lagged behind in more advanced classes in those same subjects.

5.   Based on a College Board survey of 212 colleges offering early-decision admissions—about half the schools in the country that offer some form of advance admissions decisions. The system has become so controversial because of the pressure it adds to the college application process that Yale University and Stanford University in 2002 each decided to remove the binding nature of the program; students will now be free to

apply to other schools even after being admitted under the early-decision process at Stanford and Yale. Most colleges with early-admissions programs seek to bind applicants to their school alone. Other schools with open-ended early-admissions programs, sometimes called early-action admissions, include Harvard University, Massachusetts Institute of Technology, Fordham University, Beloit University, and the University of North Carolina.

6.   Dissatisfaction with school quality stretches back to the founding of the nation; Americans have always had a love-hate relationship with whatever school system existed at the time. The concerns date at least to the Founders, who advocated (but could never achieve) universal public education as the surest method of preserving the then-fledgling Republic and its democratic guarantees. Thomas Jefferson, fearing democracy could not survive if literacy and knowledge were reserved for the elite, championed a failed law that would have created a state-run system of public schools in Virginia. Adam Smith and Thomas Paine both proposed without success government grants (a precursor to today's voucher proposals) to enable parents of modest means to finance their children's education rather than rely on the notoriously sporadic and voluntary community common schools of the era.

7.   Diane Ravitch, author, professor, and former U.S. Department of Education official, has provided a definitive history of the progressive reforms of the early twentieth century (and the resurgence of a similar anti-intellectualism she perceives in sixties-era reforms) in her book, *Left Back: A Century of Failed School Reforms*, New York: Simon & Schuster, 2000.

8.   The self-schooled "father" of American public education, Horace Mann, used his post as Massachusetts's original secretary of education in 1852 to hammer through the country's first compulsory school attendance law after years of campaigning.

He convinced the Massachusetts legislature and business leaders that it was the state's duty to build a system of tax-supported elementary and high schools; these developments were soon mirrored nationwide. Mann's belief that schools would become engines of civil and economic equality still influence modern public schools.

9.   Small schools, compared to large schools of more than 1,000 students with similar demographics, tend to have higher grade point averages and raise student achievement, tend to be less violent and have fewer behavioral problems, have higher attendance and graduation rates, and have greater parental involvement. From Barbara Kent Lawrence, Ed.D. et al., "Dollars & Sense: The Cost Effectiveness of Small Schools," Cincinnati, Ohio: KnowledgeWorks Foundations, 2002, and William Ayers et al., "The Ultimate Education Reform? Make Schools Smaller," Center for Education Research, Analysis, and Innovation, University of Wisconsin–Milwaukee, 2000. Both of these reports contain compilations of numerous university and government studies to support the argument in favor of small schools.

10. *A Nation at Risk* was released by the Reagan administration in 1983, the culmination of a decade of increasing alarm about the state of public schools in America. Later criticized—even by the same U.S. Department of Education that produced it— as being long on conclusions and short on evidence, the report was nothing if not scathing in its indictment of American public schools of the 1970s as factories of scientific, literary, and mathematical illiteracy. The report warned that the "educational foundations of our society are presently being eroded by a rising tide of mediocrity that threatens our very future." The report fell into the familiar pattern of decrying the poor quality of public education as compared to some past golden age that never actually existed. There was a case to be made that test scores such as the SAT had declined overall, but the report's proponents rarely considered explanations other than the

wholesale decline of public schools as the cause, thus ignoring such factors as the expanding and increasingly diverse population of young people taking the SAT and seeking college educations. The report's principal contention—that America's global competitiveness and national security would be threatened and decline without wholesale public education reform—remains unproven, although the economic downturn of the 1980s seemed to buttress the claim. When the economy boomed in the 1990s, *A Nation at Risk* sounded rather dated. As the report's thirty-year anniversary approached, however, the economy had been faltering, and the report was once again being cited as visionary and valid by critics of public education. There is no doubt that the report has had enormous impact, its flaws notwithstanding, and the concerns about education quality that it raised helped create a climate in which schools such as Whitney could thrive.

11. There were two principal arguments in favor of closing Whitney High: First, it was alleged the school was too costly and that closing it would save money, and, second, it was said to be elitist and undemocratic compared to other high schools in the district, and therefore should be closed. Both arguments were flawed.

The argument that Whitney High was a budgetary albatross ignored the fact that it spent less per pupil than other schools in the district. Originally an unpopular vocational and alternative school that was costing the district additional funds, Whitney became an academic powerhouse without any additional funding for the conversion. It has always operated on the bare minimum yearly allotment per student, in 2002 about six thousand dollars—a fraction of what a comparable education at a private school would cost. All the other schools in the district receive "categorical" funds—the federal and state dollars earmarked for specific programs, everything from services for at-risk youth, to special education instruction, to gifted and talented magnet programs. Whitney receives none of those dollars; indeed, what little it received was lost when the school switched from a vocational to an academic program. Far from being a drain on the budget, the school ran more economically than any other in the district.

The second argument, that it is somehow morally wrong to set up public academies with restricted admissions, is, of course, a matter of philosophical debate, but the practice was a common and longstanding one among the nation's public school districts long before Whitney came along. Many districts around the country have elite high school campuses reserved for the area's top students, with entrance requirements based wholly or in part on achievement. It is also true that *every* high school is an aggregation of elites. The teachers most vociferous in pursuing Whitney's closure ran Advanced Placement and honors classes at their own high schools, the same sort of high-level and exclusive courses taught at Whitney, accessible only to the top, college-bound students—an academic elite, separate from the other students within the larger high school population. The only difference is that Whitney puts such students on a separate campus, rather than in the separate classrooms comprehensive schools use, although the underlying "elitism" is essentially the same. Furthermore, some of the junior and senior high schools in the district where teachers petitioned against Whitney also have federally funded magnet programs with intensive instruction in law, communications, the arts, engineering, and other fields, all equipped with state-of-the-art labs and facilities (long denied Whitney) and open to only a limited number of students, by application only.

Magnet programs, now touted primarily as academic enhancements, were originally conceived and funded in the seventies throughout the nation as a means of voluntary desegregation of neighborhood schools; their unique course offerings were supposed to draw students of all races and build diversity, but they have never contributed significantly to integration and are now another means of conferring special privileges on a select group of students. The same schools so hostile to Whitney also had other sorts of favored groups from which most students were excluded, in particular the top athletes, who could receive academic preferences and social accolades denied others for throwing a football or shooting free throws. These schools used tests, grades, tryouts, and other means to group students by ability, just as Whitney used its admissions test.

12. Whitney's ethnic breakdown in the 2001–2002 school year was 69.6 percent Asian American, 12.4 percent white, 8.7 percent Filipino, 6.1 percent Latino, and 2.1 percent African American (percentages exceed 100 because of category overlap). The school district population overall—encompassing the cities of Cerritos, Artesia, Hawaiian Gardens, and parts of Long Beach, Norwalk, and Lakewood—was 32.2 percent Asian American, 13 percent white, 9.2 percent Filipino, 36.8 percent Latino, and 9.9 percent African American.

13. Whitney's geographic formula works by offering seventh-grade spots to the top students from each of the district's middle and elementary school attendance areas, rather than ranking students districtwide. Many of the attendance areas tend to be ethnically and racially homogenous, so the geographic selection system ensures at least some measure of diversity. The irony of such approaches is that they rely upon segregation at one level to promote diversity at another. Diversity still remains a major concern for the school—black and Latino enrollment continues to lag far behind the district population. Whitney has made extensive efforts to offer tutoring, mentoring, and prep courses for students enrolling from the poorer areas of the district, where preparation for the rigors of Whitney may be more spotty even among the top students. Retaining some of these students past the eighth grade has been a challenge for Whitney; transfers to other high schools are common for many of these students.

14. Beall went on to a short stint as principal at an elementary school, where many parents lauded him for his hands-on, high-

standards approach, but where he soon generated controversy by attempting to reserve one kindergarten class for the most gifted and advanced students. Because of some ethnic imbalances in the classes, Beall was accused of racism by a small group of parents and teachers. He was relegated to a district desk job with an empty desk and no duties, then retired. He is now a consultant.

15. The Class Size Reduction Research Consortium reported in 2002 that evidence linking California's class-size reduction program to test-score gains was "inconclusive." Some grades showed modest improvements; others performed identically independent of class size; in a few cases, larger classes outscored the reduced ones. There is no doubt that classes of fifteen or less with well-trained teachers in the classroom have a measurable and positive effect on achievement, the consortium reported. Despite the lack of return on the enormous investment in class-size reduction, the program is hugely popular and politically untouchable, even during the state's 2003 budget crisis, which threatened to gut many other educational programs.

16. The annual U.S. Department of Health's survey of adolescent drug use—*Monitoring the Future*—has shown small declines in drug use in recent years, although reported use is still considerably higher for most drugs in 2002 compared to 1992. In 2002, the drug of choice, as in years past, was marijuana: 19.2 percent of eighth graders, 38.7 percent of tenth graders, and 47.8 percent of twelfth graders had used it. Among seniors, 12 percent report using LSD or other hallucinogens; 4.1 percent of eighth graders and 10.5 percent of seniors report using the popular club and rave drug ecstasy. Even higher percentages took methamphetamines or other amphetamine drugs: 16.8 percent of seniors, 14.9 percent of tenth graders, and 8.7 percent of eighth graders. And nearly a quarter of all eighth graders, half of all tenth graders, and 62 percent of high school

seniors report drinking enough alcohol to get drunk, the survey found.

The accuracy of such voluntary surveys is always open to question (Do kids underreport or overreport or just lie for the hell of it?), but taken over a period of decades and parsed with other sources of information—emergency room admissions, juvenile arrests, statistics from drug-treatment programs—they undeniably point to significant and intractable trends that cut across all demographics, income groups, and ethnicities, and that suggest antidrug efforts in recent years have had little discernible effect on teenage drug and alcohol use.

17. The Academic Performance Index was created by California state law in 1999, supplanting previous schemes for rating and ranking public schools, after widespread alarm that student achievement in the state was in decline and that existing tests were insufficient to hold schools accountable. The API uses a scale of 200 to 1,000 to measure the performance and growth of every school in the state, then compares the performance of each school to that of a group of demographically similar schools in order to determine which are academically improving, declining, or treading water. Initially based on the Stanford 9 nationally normed standardized tests in reading and math, the index has expanded to include additional tests more closely matched to the actual curriculum of California schools. In 2002, the Stanford 9 test was dropped in favor of another national standardized test, the California Achievement Test. The index was introduced with great fanfare as a tool for awarding extra funds as incentives to improving schools, as well as rewarding teachers by giving bonuses of up to $25,000 to teachers at schools showing great improvement from one year to the next. Many of the promised bonuses were reduced or never delivered at all when the state's tax revenues declined as the economy slowed, and the incentives were canceled completely a year later, eliminating one of the main rationales for the plan. The

state's goal is to have every school reach a score of 800; in 2002, only 6 percent of California's schools met that goal. Whitney High School has had the highest score on the index since its inception.

18. "The Impact of High-Stakes Tests on Student Academic Performance," Audrey L. Amrein and David C. Berliner, Tempe, Ariz.: Education Policy Research Unit, Arizona State University, December 2002, found no evidence of improved achievement after states implemented high-stakes testing programs. In a companion report, the authors found unintended negative consequences of the nationwide push to pin educational reform, funding, and even high school graduation to standardized tests: In sixteen states, they report finding increased dropout rates, decreased graduation rates, and higher rates of younger people taking the GED exams in lieu of earning high school diplomas.

The report contradicts claims made by some states that their testing programs have led to measurable advances in achievement and graduation rates. These claims have been challenged in recent years, particularly the "Texas Miracle" (touted by Governor Bush in his run to become President Bush), which is the model for current federal policy. The achievement claims in Texas have been placed in doubt because of widely reported evidence of test-taking manipulation and the fact that fourth- or fifth-grade-level questions pepper the state's high-school-level graduation exams. An example of a typical test question on the spring 2002 Texas High School exit exam, which students must pass to graduate:

At a candy store, chocolate costs $0.35 per ounce. Hector bought 8.25 ounces, Jeanette bought 8.7 ounces, James bought 8.05 ounces, and Shanika bought 8.42 ounces. Which list shows these weights in order from least to greatest?

A. 8.05 oz, 8.25 oz, 8.42 oz, 8.7 oz

B. 8.42 oz, 8.05 oz, 8.25 oz, 8.7 oz

C. 8.05 oz, 8.7 oz, 8.25 oz, 8.42 oz

D. 8.7 oz, 8.05 oz, 8.25 oz, 8.42 oz

The rudimentary decimal number skills this question tests are typically covered in fourth and fifth grade.

Another question, this one among the "hardest"—one of twenty-five intended to separate average students achieving at grade level from those on the college track—is also surprisingly simple:

If postage for parcels costs 34 cents for the first ounce and 23 cents for each additional ounce, what is the cost to mail an 8-ounce parcel?

A. $1.84

B. $1.87

C. $1.95

D. $2.38

E. Not Here

This question is indistinguishable from problems expected to be mastered in the fifth-grade math curriculum in the state of California. Yet in Texas, it and others of similar difficulty are being used to identify college readiness.

Writer George Scott has analyzed the Texas test and what it says about the state of American education, which can be found at www.educationnews.org as of spring 2003.

19. This curious duality can occur because a school can have overall excellent test results but can still be labeled failing under the No Child Left Behind law whenever any one demographic subgroup (low-income students, special education students, minorities, or limited-English speakers) at the school fails to make academic progress for two years in a row. The failing school label is attached regardless of whether the subgroup represents a large or small portion of the entire student body. USA Today found nineteen schools awarded Blue Ribbon excellence awards from the U.S. Department of Education had also been simultaneously declared failing under No Child

Left Behind. ("School Excellence Thrown a Grading Curve," Karen Thomas and Anthony DeBarros, *USA Today*, August 4, 2002.)

20. These were the only AP tests for which Whitney-specific test data was available. The complete comparisons are shown in the charts at the bottom of this page and the top of the following page.

21. For an excellent summary of research on Asian Americans' educational values and experience, see "The Differential Effects of Family Processes and SES on Academic Self-Concepts and Achievement of Gifted Asian American and Gifted Caucasian High School Students," Marilyn Ann Verna and James Reed Campbell, St. John's University. This paper and other related

AP UNITED STATES HISTORY Spring 2002 Class of 2003 (based on their 2000 PSAT results)				
	% of students scoring 3+		% of students scoring 4+	
PSAT Verbal Score Range	Whitney	Nation	Whitney	Nation
76–80	100	95	100	83
71–75	100	94	100	78
66–70	100	88	88	67
61–65	80	80	80	54
56–60	83	68	56	40
51–55	94	60	50	31
46–50	78	47	56	21
41–45	75	35		13
36–40		24		8
31–35		15		5
26–30		10		3
20–25		8		2

AP ENGLISH LANGUAGE Spring 2002 Class of 2003 (based on their 2000 PSAT results)				
	% of students scoring 3+		% of students scoring 4+	
PSAT Verbal Score Range	Whitney	Nation	Whitney	Nation
76–80	100	99	100	92
71–75	100	98	100	85
66–70	100	96	100	73
61–65	95	90	81	59
56–60	100	78	69	39
51–55	91	67	45	24
46–50	85	48	46	11
41–45	50	28		4
36–40		13		1
31–35		5		1
26–30		3		1
20–25		2		1

The charts and Whitney-specific data were provided by Whitney High School and are based upon test results for a sample of 106 students. PSAT scores can be converted to the SAT scale by multiplying scores by ten, with a perfect 80 being comparable to a perfect 800 on the SAT. Advanced Placement tests are scored from one to five, with three considered passing and a four or five often required for college credit.

research materials can be found on the U.S. Department of Education's ERIC Internet site (Educational Resources Information Center) at *http://eric-web.tc.columbia.edu/pathways/asian_pacific/ default.asp*. It should be noted, however, that the image of Asian Americans as academic stars has created a great deal of concern among educators and in the Asian American community, contributing to a stereotype of all ethnic Asian students as "whiz kids" or a "model minority." While the academic achievements of Asian Americans overall do exceed other groups', some sub-groups within the Asian American community, notably some immigrants from Southeast Asia, have struggled academically and show high dropout rates. This aspect of Asian Americans' educational experience is explored in "Asian-American Children: What Teachers Should Know," Jinhua Feng, the ERIC Clearinghouse on Elementary and Early Childhood Education, *http://ericps.ed.uiuc. edu/eece/pubs/digests/1994/feng94.html* and in "Asia-Nation: The Model Minority Image," *http://www.asian-nation.org/issues2.html.*

22. Americans seemingly long for the best possible schools for their children, and polls routinely reveal education to be a top concern for the public. But opining about education is one thing; making the actual day-to-day, down-in-the-trenches commitment to realize that goal is another. And in an array of measurable ways, that commitment in America clearly lags behind other nations.

Our average 180-day school year is the shortest in the developed world. Our test scores in math and science trail behind the leading nations of Europe and Asia. Our per-pupil spending is ninth out of sixteen developed nations. And, compared to most other developed nations, American teachers are held in far lower esteem, professionally and financially, and are subject to fewer years of training in order to obtain their credentials. A majority of Americans say they find little or no time to get involved with their children's schools and would do so only in the event of a major crisis. Yet few make a connection between this lack of involvement and poor student achievement.

Personal spending by American families is also illuminating when it comes to school: The U.S. Department of Commerce reports that the average American household spends $2,137 a year on restaurant meals, $3,418 in car payments, and $2,066 on entertainment (television sets, videos, movie tickets, and the like). Education spending comes in at $632 a year on average, even after factoring in the hefty sums many families pay for college tuition.

Spending on reading materials (including magazines and newspapers) is even more paltry: $146 a year in the average American household (where the average American adult reads one book a year, and reads it with the skills and comprehension of a seventh grader). Spending on books and other reading is less than half the amount the average household spends on to-bacco products and a third of spending on such personal care services as hair styling. The average American child spends 78 minutes a week reading, 102 minutes a week on homework and study, and 12 *hours* a week watching television. An industrywide initiative is under way in the pharmaceutical business to sim-plify labels and instructions because American adults, it turns out, cannot understand medical instructions written for adults. Mousse, Marlboros, and *Who Wants to Be a Millionaire* are, in terms of money and time, more important to Americans than reading and learning, and it shows.

Asking schools, where children spend only 10 percent of their time, to compensate for this set of priorities is asking a great deal. If households simply reversed the status quo, reducing kids' television watching to 78 minutes and boosting their read-ing to 12 hours a week, it would do more to improve academic achievement in America than a thousand high-stakes tests and a century of No Child Left Behind measures. With such a switch in priorities, nearly every school could be a Whitney High. But achieving such a sea change would take a consciousness-shifting campaign of almost unprecedented magnitude, more powerful than the "Keep America Beautiful" anti-litter campaign of the six-ties or the successful anti-drunk-driving campaign of the eight-ies, both of which literally changed the way Americans looked at the world and their own behavior.

The No Child Left Behind law contains many nonacademic extras tucked into its recesses, including a stealthily added re-quirement that schools conduct voluntary prayer in class, but it makes no attempt to persuade Americans to shift their priori-ties and make more of a commitment to learning.

Index